Stories from the Bog

On Madness, Philosophy, and Psychoanalysis

Patrick B. Kavanaugh

Rodopi

Amsterdam - New York, NY 2012

Cover illustration: www.morgueFile.com

Cover Design: Studio Pollmann

The paper on which this book is printed meets the requirements of "ISO 9706:1994, Information and documentation - Paper for documents - Requirements for permanence".

ISBN: 978-90-420-3487-7
E-Book ISBN: 978-94-012-0764-5

Printed in the Netherlands

Stories from the Bog

Contemporary Psychoanalytic Studies
14

Contemporary Psychoanalytic Studies (*CPS*) is an international scholarly book series devoted to all aspects of psychoanalytic inquiry in theoretical, philosophical, applied, and clinical psychoanalysis. Its aims are broadly academic, interdisciplinary, and pluralistic, emphasizing secularism and tolerance across the psychoanalytic domain. CPS aims to promote open and inclusive dialogue among the humanities and the social-behavioral sciences including such disciplines as philosophy, anthropology, history, literature, religion, cultural studies, sociology, feminism, gender studies, political thought, moral psychology, art, drama, and film, biography, law, economics, biology, and cognitive-neuroscience.

Brigid

These words will never carve
your image out of bog oak
but that is what they want to do
to dig down into the moist wetness
to touch the layers of centuries
that have made you
woman, goddess, saint
to see your shape emerge intact
from the dark earth.

My instruments are crude for such a work
the bog resistant to intruders
as an ancient tribal memory
in its dark and secret places.

But I must search out these roots
this memory as vital as breath.
I must drag this ancient oak
from the centre of the bog.

I will wait as I must
for the time of dryness where I can see
the shape of what you were and what you are…

From the Collection,
Singing From the
Belly of the Whale (Dublin, 2009)
by Anne F. O'Reilly

Contents

Acknowledgements

I would like to acknowledge some of the different people, life-experiences, and groups that have influenced my thinking over the years about philosophy, madness and psychoanalysis.

First and foremost, I feel privileged and deeply indebted to those people who shared their stories with me over the years at various residential treatment facilities, day treatment programs and in private practice. Not only did these storytelling and institutional experiences allow me to learn something about institutional life and the profundity of the human spirit, they enabled me to learn something more about the analytic discourse, myself, and the notion that, indeed, we are all more alike than otherwise.

While certain identifying information and circumstances have been altered in the following stories in the interests of confidentiality, the mystery, magic and muscle of the analytic discourse as a unique storytelling process remains. The selection, organization, understanding and recounting of the following stories are functions of my own perceptions and constructions of reality.

Having come from a blue-collar background and ethic, my first introduction to the method and madness of institutions and their discourses of power, knowledge(s) and ethics -outside the institution of the family, that is- came from significant experiences gathered from my "misspent youth," involvement in the military, and membership in the Teamsters union while working as a truck driver. Although not fully appreciated at the time, these early experiences proved to be quite valuable in my later involvements with institutions in professional life whether they were residential-treatment, academic-educational, or professional-political.

The rationality of an institution's seemingly irrational discourse(s) follows its own discursive rules. The awareness and understanding of these rules, I came to realize, is absolutely crucial so as to function effectively and ethically within its discourse(s) -and, often times, to do so in spite of them. Collectively, these institutional experiences played a major role in shaping my views on the inseparability of culture and psychoanalysis, the significant and dynamic interplay of context and meaning, and the necessity of appreciating and respecting the relativity of reality in attempting to understand the complex and often times contradictory meanings of a person's life-story.

I would like to acknowledge Dr. La Maurice Gardner for his generous support, advisements, and sharing of knowledge(s) in helping me navigate the institutional power, discourses and madness I encountered early on in my professional life.

Attending the University of Windsor for my doctoral studies involved crossing the border between Detroit and Windsor on a daily basis. These border crossings paralleled those occurring in my classroom and internship experiences at university where a multi-cultural worldview combined with an interdisciplinary approach in the context of a student-centered learning philosophy and format. My educational experiences in the doctoral program set in motion a long-standing interest in the importance of psychoanalytical educational experiences and philosophy matching with the defining concept of psychoanalysis that, for me, is the Freudian unconscious.

I would like to acknowledge and thank Drs. Frank Auld, Marvin Hyman, Paul Lerner, Ray Daly and Mel Weinberg for their respective influences and contributions to my thinking during these early years of my formation. I feel fortunate that the educational philosophy and atmosphere was one in which I was able to seek what they had sought, not what they had found.

Of course, I would be remiss if I did not acknowledge the frequent and thorough searches by the customs agents I encountered in my daily border crossings from Windsor to Detroit. They had a profound and lasting influence in shaping my thinking about the exercise of power evoked by differences in appearance, thinking or knowledge(s): The search for contraband ideas, concepts and notions that run counter to the customs, values, and sanctioned ways of thinking of the community, psychoanalytic or otherwise, can take many different and, at times, insidious forms.

In the early 70's, I took an experimental position on the residential inpatient unit of the Detroit Psychiatric Institute (DPI), an inner-city state hospital that was terribly underfunded and understaffed in serving those known as the underprivileged and underserved. As a teaching hospital in the psychoanalytic tradition, however, there was a rich and varied menu of ongoing seminars and study groups offered on topics ranging from the theory of diagnostics and psychotherapy to continuous case conferences and individual supervisory experiences: Freud's systems of thinking, notions of the unconscious, and theory of dream interpretation provided the backdrop for many of the seminars. The teaching and supervising faculty at DPI was comprised mostly of psychoanalysts from the local institute who provided these educational opportunities for both staff and those in training.

It was at DPI that I experienced a more formal introduction to various psychoanalytic thinkers and their respective theories of madness and psychoanalysis. It was during this time that I immersed myself in the writings and thinking of practitioners in the Chestnut Lodge tradition, the spirit, philosophy and voices of whom might be heard in-between the lines of the following stories. The thinking of such psychoanalytic practitioners as Harry Stack Sullivan, Frieda Fromm-Reichmann, Harold Searles, and Otto Will was, for me, inspirational. Many of their writings on working with madness were experienced as running into "old friends" who wrapped some words and ways of understanding around my experiences of madness and institutions, and the madness of institutions.

It was also at this time that I became more formally immersed in my own analytical education and experiences. My previous experiences with the power and influence of an institutional discourse premised on a medical-scientific way of thinking, however, led me to seek an alternative to the more traditional Institute-based faculty-centered program. I chose to pursue a student-centered program of study that was more in the Vienna tradition: a self-initiated, self-designed and self-implemented program of education and training. Thus, I sought out and collaboratively planned a program of study and analytical experiences with those in the analytic community whom I respected and from whom I believed I could learn more about the Freudian unconscious as process and dynamic. And so, I bootlegged my psychoanalytic education, as they use to say, so that I could speakeasy in my psychoanalytical experiences.

And, it was at DPI that I began working with people on the in-patient unit in an intensive analytical discourse. I would like to acknowledge the influences of Drs. Marty Mayman and, especially, Marvin Hyman who has been a mentor, colleague and friend throughout my professional life. It was Marv who first introduced me to a skeptical form of phenomenalism, a solipsistic philosophy and worldview, and the associative-interpretive process as the primary mode of communication in the analytical discourse. Eventually, my newly kindled interests led to the thinking of such others as Anton Kris, Barnaby Barratt, Jonathan Lear, John Dorsey, and Christopher Bollas. Their philosophical thinking and reflections on the nature of human nature, psychoanalysis, and the associative-interpretive process can be heard in the stories and essays that follow. And of course, there were significant others who were influential in both my ongoing formation and synthesis and practice of psychoanalysis: Joyce McDougall, L. Bryce-Boyer, Peter Giovaccini, Bertram Karon, Thomas Szasz, Julia Kristeva, Helene Cixous, Michael Eigen, and James Grottstein - to name a few.

While I was at DPI, I met with people on the in-patient unit for about seven years, the last five of which included serving as the Co-Clinical Director of the unit. During these years, I was deeply immersed in the study and understanding of the milieu's structure, dynamic and process. And my previous experiences with the complexities of the institutional discourse somehow came together with the day to day experiences of working with the ward staff and residents at DPI eventuating in a milieu treatment program in which human contact and connectedness was most highly valued and a talking therapy was the treatment of choice. Indeed, a process understanding of the milieu's administrative-clinical policies and its dynamic movements and inexplicable happenings was foundational in working-playing in its madness. And in the crazy-making matrix of the ward, the mystery, magic and muscle of the human spirit were integral aspects of this understanding.

I would like to respectfully acknowledge both the residents and ward staff with whom I was privileged to work with at DPI. It was quite an amazing experience: During those years, there was a significant and dramatic reduction in the residents' average length of stay and the ward's daily census, and in the use of and reliance on medications and restraint belts. Correspondingly, staff morale was consistently high and absenteeism was significantly lower than on the other wards in the hospital. One of the personal meanings I took from my analytical experiences at DPI is that when two or more people mutually agree to work together for the purpose of attempting to understand and word the inexplicable, the possibilities of possibilities are really quite endless.

After about seven years on the ward, there was a severe budget crisis, a significant loss of funding and staff, and a rapid transformation of the ward back into a chemical cocoon where the chemistry of human interactions was replaced by the chemicals of medications and intramuscular injections. For twenty years after I left the ward, I continued my involvement at DPI as a member of the teaching and supervisory faculty in the pre- and postdoctoral training programs in psychology, transmitting knowledge(s) through seminars, study groups, case conferences and supervisory experiences. I am grateful to the other members of the teaching and supervisory faculties, the post-doctoral candidates, and the psychiatric residents with whom I worked during these years at DPI (1971-1997).

In addition to the people and experiences at DPI, there were significant others I would like to acknowledge: The participants in the seminars and study groups on Dream Interpretation and the Freudian Unconscious (1988-2002), the faculty and graduate students at the University of Detroit (1980-1997), and the faculty and students in the Program for Advanced Psychoanalytic Studies at the Wyandotte General Hospital (1988-1992). The thoughtful and searching discussions of these different groups helped to refine many of the concepts and ideas contained in the following stories and essays.

Also, I am grateful to the board of directors and members of the International Federation for Psychoanalytic Education (1995-2008), the Michigan Society for Psychoanalytic Psychology, and the Academy for the Study of the Psychoanalytic Arts at whose respective forums many of the ideas and stories in the following chapters were initially presented and discussed. In many respects, these groups have provided me with a conceptual home over the past thirty years.

I would like to acknowledge and thank Jon Mills, editor of Contemporary Psychoanlytic Studies. It has been a pleasure working with him: His encouragement and enthusiasm for the project has been greatly appreciated. And, I would like to acknowledge and thank Dan Waltz for permission to use his creative illustrations that, at once, introduce each of the following chapters and add to the novella quality and nature of the analytic discourse.

I acknowledge with gratitude permission to use all or portions of earlier versions of the previously published stories and articles. 'Stories from the bog: On the underworld, the underconsciousness, and the undertaking' was published in The Psychoanalytic Review, 94(5), 791-815. It is reprinted by permission of Guilford Publications, Inc.. 'Frankenstein's genie-ology: The magical visionary experience and the associative method' was published in The Psychoanalytic Review, 91(5),

643-661. It is reprinted by permission of Guilford Publications, Inc.. 'The dead poets society ventures into a radioactive psychoanalytic space' was published in The Psychoanalytic Review, 90(3), 341-361. It is reprinted by permission of Guilford Publications, Inc.. 'An ethic of free association: Questioning a uniform and coercive code of ethics' was published in The Psychoanalytic Review, 86(4), 643-662. It is reprinted by permission of Guilford Publications, Inc.. 'Wang Fo and an ethic of free association: Poetic imagination, mythical stories, and moral philosophy' was published in The Psychoanalytic Review, 92(4), 487-511. It is reprinted by permission of Guilford Publications, Inc.. 'The dramatic meaning of madness in psycho(analy)sis: The ear-rationality of treating illusion as reality' was published in The Psychoanalytic Review, 96(6), 983-1005. It is reprinted by permission of Guilford Publications, Inc.. "Escaping the phantom's ghostly grasp: On psychoanalysis as a performance art in the spirit world" was published in The Psychoanalytic Review, 97(5), 733-756. It is reprinted by permission of Guilford Publications, Inc.. An earlier version of "Developing competencies in the destruction of psychoanalysis: Political, pedagogical, and practice philosophies" was first published in Otherwise (2010), an e-journal of the International Forum for Psychoanalytic Education. It is reprinted by permission of the editors.

Lastly, I would like to acknowledge the invaluable contributions and valued presence of Linda, my partner in life and to whom this book is dedicated.

Introduction

> We see men haying far in the meadow, their heads waving like the grass they cut. In the distance, the wind seemed to bend all alike.
>
> -Thoreau-

It was an early November morning some forty years ago. I was on my way to the county psychiatric hospital located far out in the country, conveniently distanced from the city and the everyday lives of most people. I could tell I was approaching the institutional grounds as I found myself riding alongside the black iron-spiked fence that encircled the main buildings of this massive residential treatment facility built in the mid 1800's. After about a mile or so, there was a break in the iron-spikes and I slowed, turned in at the main entrance, and entered the grounds. With a sense of nervous excitement, I slowly began the long, winding drive up to the Victorian-styled Admissions Building where I was to report for the final processing of my paperwork and begin orientation for my first professional position.

I still remember seeing about 15 to 20 men cutting the grass with push-mowers as I drove up the long, winding drive. They were lined-up behind each other in staggered, overlapping rows so that as they walked in their stiff and lurching kind of unison, they cut a swath about 20 to 25 feet wide. It was one of those very late fall, early winter Michigan mornings when the sky is painted a blackish-gray, streaked with deep purples and rich bluish-reds. A foggy mist was hanging heavily in a kind of suspended state just above the ground. I pulled over to the side of the road and watched. It was quite an eerie sight to see the men walking stiffly, pushing their mowers, and cutting the grass that no longer needed cutting. Completing their rows, they would then turn, once again line-up, and begin walking in staggered precision down the next row until, one by one, each disappeared back into the thick, foggy mist. Several minutes later, each would re-emerge from the thick fog about twenty feet further over. After sitting and watching for awhile, I restarted the car and continued on my way to the steeple-tipped Admissions Building where I filled out the final paperwork authorizing my admission into the institutional community behind the iron-spiked fence. And, so I began the introduction in the story of my professional life.

In this massive edifice complex, many of the 75 buildings were alphabetized from A through Z; "A-Building" was, of course, the admissions building, "B-Building" was the staff residence, "C-Building" was the patient-run store, "D" through "G" signified and housed the back wards people, and so on through 26 buildings. And these were the ABC's of institutional life and the alphabetized structures that held its 5,000 people. It should be mentioned that those buildings housing people *not* signified by alphabetical letters were located at the back of the institution's grounds. Professionals rarely went to these buildings as, perhaps, they were not part of the alphabetized system and, thus, did not exist: I really don't know. I wanted, however, to reference in words those people who lived outside the institution's alphabetical system so that they might now exist – even in their anonymity- in this written text and space. Such is the power of the letters of the alphabet and institutional systems of signification.

As I gradually came to learn during the years of my stay, this institution was a community unto itself. Situated on about 900 acres, it had its own farm and the equipment necessary to raise crops and animals, a patient-run laundry and store, a printing press and newsletter, a police and fire station, a community center and hospital, living quarters for patients and many of the staff, and a cemetery where over 7,000 former patients were buried. In the place of the person's name, however, each tombstone was marked with a four-digit number corresponding to his or her medical chart. Upon admission, a chart number such as, for example, #3296 was assigned to each person. This chart number, at once, constituted his or her identity in the community and shepherded him or her through the complexities of the community's sociocratic maze from the time of his or her admission to, most often, his or her final resting place.

Inside the perimeter of its black iron-spiked fence, this community had its own distinct culture in which its institutionalized systems of thinking, sets of beliefs, and core values structured, signified, and legitimized certain ways of thinking about the world and each of the people who passed through A-Building. Its alphabetized system of signification and medical chart numbers constituted a kind of communal language: They were emblematic of the technocratic practices that established the discursive rationality, constructed the social reality, and provided a sense of social coherence for the residents and staff alike. The institutional discourse defined the natural order of things in the community in which power and prestige flowed from the hierarchically ordered relationships between the staff and patients, and privilege and prerogative derived from the dichotomized distinctions between the sane and the insane. In so doing, the institutional discourse made the world(s) behind the iron-spiked fence more understandable, comprehensible, and coherent.

These same systems of signification also provided a context in which something of the historical text of the community was written. I eventually came to learn, for example, that those who pushed the lawn mowers in their predetermined rows were affectionately known in the community as "The Lobo Brigade," an abbreviated reference to "The Brigade of the Lobotomized." Back in the 1940's and '50s, the institution's treatment of choice had been to routinely perform prefrontal lobotomies on those signified as mentally ill. In the history of psychiatric treatments, lobotomies were at that time in the forefront of the more sophisticated and scientific of psychiatric interventions to alter mood and behavior. Those people who silently greeted me at the entrance to the grounds were living and breathing monuments to the ways of thinking and forms of treatment of that earlier time that had long since faded into the foggy mist of days past. The Lobo Brigade constituted an iconic chapter in the historical text of the community. They were part of the A, B, C's that structured the everyday institutional life of the staff (the *sane*) and the residents (the *insane*) alike.

In time, I moved on. This institution has long since been downsized through the demolition of its alphabetized buildings and the deinstitutionalization of its patient population. The demolition of its alphabetized structures - and those structures existing outside the alphabet - could be understood as a quite literalized form of deconstructing a particular residential treatment philosophy, influenced in no small measure, no doubt, by its increasing property value as the suburbs slowly and inexorably enveloped the countryside. Those few buildings that remained were updated, renamed, and continue to this day to provide services to the surrounding communities as a regional psychiatric hospital. Where there was once the patient-run store, there now sits a MacDonald's restaurant serving the local community under its golden arches. The black iron-spiked fence has long since been removed. And only questions remain such as, for example, "Did de-fence of the institutionalized Truth and ways of thinking really separate the rational (the *sane*) from the irrational (the *insane*)?"

INSIDE THE IRON-SPIKED FENCE: MODERNISTIC SYSTEMS OF THINKING

Since leaving the grounds of this institution, I have been at several other residential treatment facilities, day treatment programs, and various educational institutions, the majority of which, interestingly, were enclosed by an iron-spiked fence. During these early years of my formation, I increasingly became interested in their institutional systems of thinking and the underlying assumptions they shared about people, life and madness. Namely, a worldview premised on the assumptions of classical epistemology, a core medical ideology grounded in biology, medicine and the natural sciences, and a dominating rationality that rested on the organizing conceptual framework of symptomatology, etiology and psychopathology. And there was something else...

More than simply reflecting a science and pathology paradigm, these institutional systems of thinking rested on certain underlying assumptions- philosophic in nature- that come together to unite in a nineteenth-century worldview: *linear time*, *determinism*, *naturalism*, *atomistic thinking*, *nomothetic principles*, *laws*, and *explanations*, and an *amorality in science*. These assumptions constitute the epistemological and intellectual foundations of our modernistic systems of thinking (Slife, 1997). Infused with a medical ideology, they unite in the medical model of psychoanalysis, considered in some detail in chapter ten. In so doing, these assumptions form a paradigmatic way of thinking, knowing and perceiving that made the management of madness behind the iron-spiked fence more coherent and comprehensible while, at the same time, excluded the voice of madness from its psychology and discourse. And over the years, I found myself thinking more and more frequently of the Lobo Brigade as they appeared and disappeared into the thick foggy mist, cutting grass that no longer needed cutting and signifying a time from a much different era.

A central thesis of this book is that our understandings of madness and psychoanalysis are inseparable from the cultural and historical context in which they make their appearance. In the history of madness and its institutions, that strange state of being known as *madness* has been understood as, for example, a religious or philosophical phenomenon such as an experience of inspiration or the loss of one's mind. During the eighteenth century, certain cultural, legal, political, philosophical, and sociological discourses came together to perceive madness as a medical disease and the object of scientific inquiry (Foucault, 2009). And madness fell under the medical-scientific gaze where it has remained during the eighteenth, nineteenth, and most of the twentieth centuries.

As the understanding of madness moved from an artistic or religious phenomenon to an objective medical condition, the irrational (the *insane*) were excluded from society by the rational (the *sane*) and placed in asylums or psychiatric hospitals for their scientific study, treatment and cure. Indeed, the latter part of the eighteenth century witnessed the creation of special institutions similar to where the Lobo Brigade methodically cut the grass that no longer needed cutting. These psychiatric institutions were dedicated to the care and study of those signified by society as mad. And the scientific bodies of knowledge(s) discovered at these institutions understood and spoke the analytic practitioner as a dispassionate scientist-observer, as a healthcare professional coming from a medical-scientific tradition, and as a scientific-researcher discovering various forms of psychosis and specifying them in our diagnostic and statistical manuals.

Is it not time to call into question the analytic practitioner's identity as a healthcare professional lest our bodies of knowledge(s) continue to speak him or her into the 21st century as written on the pages of a 19th century historical text? To do otherwise, it seems to me, is to continue recycling psychoanalytic orthodoxies that rest on a Cartesian-Newtonian worldview, housing people in the numerical designations and symptom structures of our diagnostic and statistical manuals, and promulgating professional standards consistent with those of the physical healthcare professions. In so doing, do we not unwittingly form our own communal version of the Lobo Brigade and monumentalize an historical time and ways of thinking that have long since passed?

Contrary to the medical-scientific narrative, the passage of madness from a religious phenomenon to an objective medical essence does not represent an inevitable evolutionary progression of understanding moving from the more primitive and superstitious to the more advanced and scientifically discovered medical truth of the modern era. Indeed, our contemporary times are changing profoundly and irreversibly: A literary experience of madness seems to be ushering in a literary construction of madness that, in turn, enables a more inclusive relationship and dialogue between madness, literature, and psychoanalysis. This more contemporary narrative speaks madness as a literary, spiritual, and mystical phenomenon and suggests a very different way of thinking about psychoanalysis as both theory and discourse, and about the theory of its discourse with madness.

PSYCHOANALYSIS AND MADNESS IN THE 21ST CENTURY: MADNESS AS A LITERARY, SPIRITUAL AND MYSTICAL PHENOMENON

Contemporary psychoanalysis is moving away from a medical-scientific view of madness with its foundations rooted in evolutionary biology, westernized medicine and the natural sciences to a literary, spiritual and mystical view with its conceptual foundations situated in philosophy, the humanities and the arts. This paradigmatic shift produces bodies of knowledge(s) that, as considered in each of the following chapters, speak the analytic practitioner as the contemporary shaman of the twenty-first century: The One Who Remembers as a mind-poet and philosopher-historian, who sees the world through a magical –as opposed to a scientific- visionary experience, and whose purpose is to translate the ideothetic story told in the analytic space. As considered in chapters nine and ten, the mind-poet's epistemology, bodies of knowledge(s), and learning philosophy match more closely with Freud's initial and intuitive grasp of the unconscious, understood as *representation's other*.

Currently, many different versions of psychoanalysis exist in the analytic culture, each having a different philosophical premise, set of theoretical assumptions, and purpose and objective of the analytic discourse. In the United States, however, the medical model of psychoanalysis continues to dominate in the psychoanalytic community: Its medical-scientific paradigm continues to provide the assumptions underlying its epistemology and concept and measures of competency (chapter nine). Its values and traditions continue to provide the foundations for its professional standards in psychoanalytic education, theory, practice, and ethics. And organized psychology and psychoanalysis continue to represent psychoanalysis to the analytic community, the public, and various governmental entities as a monolithic treatment modality rooted in biology, medicine and the natural sciences.

Whereas individual psychoanalysts and practitioners have long been interested in philosophic questions and developments, organized psychology and psychoanalysis have not felt implicated, much less compelled, to re-examine the presuppositions of the discipline. One of the central questions raised by this book is: How ethical is it to hold each participant in the analytic discourse to healthcare standards when their principled beliefs and values are *other than* those of the healthcare model? For too long, a discourse of meaningful debate about such ethical issues has been marginalized, if not suppressed, by the more politically dominant and institutionalized way of thinking: The medical model of psychoanalysis having its roots in a 19th century worldview.

"Stories From The Bog" is a collection of essays and stories gathered together from over the past forty years of meeting with people in residential treatment facilities, various day treatment programs, and private practice. It is written for all those interested in the questions of madness, philosophy and psychoanalysis and the interweaving of the three. Each of the following chapters is premised on assumptions other than those of the more traditional bio-medical psychologies, the underlying assumptions of which, at once, underlie our identity as healthcare professionals and the pedagogical and practice philosophies that flow from and sustain this identity. Each essay and story speaks in a voice of cultural otherness from the traditional bio-medical psychologies of the analytic community in which madness is assumed to be a mental illness or disease and psychoanalysis is assumed to be a normalized and normalizing discourse. In many respects, the madness revealed in the analytic discourse has to be spoken with outside of the more traditional psychologies of psychoanalysis precisely because they have excluded madness from their discourse. The following essays and stories allow for and encourage the voice of madness to join in both the psychology and conversation of psychoanalysis as we enter the 21st century.

Each of the following essays and stories resituates the analytic endeavor in a literary frame of reference while elaborating its epistemology (chapters 1-10), education (chapters 9 and 10), ethics (chapters 4 and 5), and theory and practice (chapters 1-7) in the realms of philosophy, the humanities and the arts. Further, each chapter hopes to contribute to a more contemporary understanding of psychoanalysis as a science of subjectivity, as concerned with archaic forms of mental functioning, and as premised on the assumption that love is a basic force in the analytic discourse (Lear, 1990). In the continuing story of psychoanalysis, we have only just begun to understand the significance of these three interrelated elements of the Freudian revolution.

PSYCHOANALYSIS AS A SCIENCE OF SUBJECTIVITY

Each of us has a story to tell. And each of us is contained in our life-story as it is contained within us. Whether it is the story of "one of the chronics" on the in-patient unit of an inner-city state hospital who searches over his cup of coffee for the answers to his questions of "Who am I?" and "Where did I come from?" (chapter 2), a young man from a group home who searches for answers as to why he can read his Superman comic book but not his philosophy text book (chapter 3), or a young man who comes to the office looking for a job and eventually makes piles of money in the analytic space (chapter 5), the quest of the subject walks hand in hand with the question of subjectivity. The subjective *I* is at the center of the individual's existence, generates his or her unique and personal reality, and is the ultimate referent in telling his or her story in the analytic discourse: The subjective *I* is ever-present in organizing and communicating his or her life-story. The science of subjectivity is the science of the *I* (Lear, 1990) and is, from this perspective, grounded in the Freudian unconscious understood as an ongoing process of unbroken subjectivity. As a science of subjectivity, the practitioner's appreciation and understanding of the associative-interpretive process and the relativity of reality are at the heart of psychoanalysis.

Our story communicates how we have come to understand and interpret ourselves in the world. In telling our story to another, we reveal something about the history and mystery of who we are, where we come from, and how we have imagined ourselves into being. More than simply a series of facts, events and dates, our story is a three dimensional history that contains the silent and personal knowledge(s) that mysteriously guide us in our movements through life. It speaks our beliefs and emotions, passions and values, and the private and personal madness that is of self. In its telling to another, our story's life and power is unleashed as tissue-traces of historical and personal meanings are re-experienced, repeated, and relived in the analytic space, the understandings of which, often times, lead to a sense-making of that which previously had made non-sense.

The following stories are recounted in the service of illustrating a way of being, presencing and knowing in the intricately complex process of listening, understanding and responding to another's telling of his or her life-story. They are intended as a way of understanding people, madness, and "the stuff of life" in contradistinction to treating patients, psychosis, and "evidences of psychopathology." And, they return again and again to a central idea of the book. Specifically, it is the unique personality of each participant that structures and speaks the singular nature of the analytic discourse; the uniqueness of each participant comes together in some mysterious way to speak the blended uniqueness of the discourse. Taken together, the following stories speak unabashedly to something of the mystery, magic, and muscle of the human being, the human spirit, and the very human discourse of psychoanalysis.

Psychoanalysis has come to be understood and interpreted for myself as being, first and last, a venture into communication via the associative-interpretive process in a contextualizing metaphor from the performance arts, the psychic theatre of the mind. This synthesis and practice underlies each of the stories and essays of this book. In effect, the psychoanalytic discourse is understood as a discourse of moral philosophy, the person is understood as an *historical* and *moral* being, and his or her reality is understood as being semiotically constructed and is ultimately constituted and organized by his or her attitudes and values.

While each chapter is premised on this synthesis and practice of psychoanalysis, chapters 2-5 place their emphasis on the intimate and personal nature of the first of its conceptual elements, … *a venture into communication via the associative-interpretive process*. These three chapters illustrate the complexities of the participants' mutual and interacting subjectivities in the analytic discourse in the context of the enigmatic question of ethics and the associative-interpretive process. In so doing, they speak to how the participants come to know and word something about the wellsprings of madness from which they speak as they immerse themselves in the process of coming to know the silent knowledge(s) that guides their discourse.

The inherent uncertainty of venturing into an individual's dynamic systems of signification and communication is born from the practitioner's deep recognition and appreciation that the person who comes to tell his or her story is the ultimate knower of the *What Is* and the *Why* of the *What Is* of his or her life. Furthermore, that the person's truth and interpretive design of the world is contained in his or her story as recounted and relived in the analytic space. As each person tells his or her story, the practitioner listens, understands and responds to the person's story in ways that are inseparable from the practitioner as a person, his or her assumptions about people and life, and his or her purpose(s) in meeting with the individual in an analytic discourse. As a participant-observer, the practitioner listens with and through all of his or her sensory-based experiences and attempts to understand and respond to the story told by wording the inexplicable in ways that are, at once, helpful, meaningful and furthering of the associative-interpretive process.

Chapters 6 and 7 place their emphasis on the second of the conceptual elements in this synthesis and practice of psychoanalysis, ... *in a contextualizing metaphor from the performance arts, the theatre of the mind.* Whether it is the story of a middle-aged woman who silently and patiently searches through the shoeboxes in the closet of her mind to find the specific memory-experience(s) she wishes to speak about (chapter 6), or a man in his late twenties whose days on the inpatient unit are spent watching over his Virgin Queen Mother and whose nights are spent nursing a never-ending procession of insatiable Venetian babies (chapter 7), madness finds its theatre in the analytic space as it does nowhere else.

The theatre provides the stage onto which the ghosts of one's past can step and speak their dramatic stories. As suggested by McDougall (1985), they await their production until two people are willing to step onto the stage to bring the dramas to life and word, as best they can, their rhythms and rhymes and meanings and purposes. The theatre's stage allows for the dramatization of the person's experiences via the associative-interpretive process, the expressions of which take place in and through all aspects of his or her being. In so doing, the dramas of life come alive, are given voice, and join in the analytic conversation. The analytic practitioner steps onto the stage and ventures into the communications arising from the person's ideothetic story (ideo=personal, thetic=thesis).

Chapters 8-10 call into question the medical model of psychoanalysis as an institutional system of thinking developed during the industrial age of the modern era. These three chapters address positivism as an ideological frame of reference, the underlying positivistic assumptions of the medical model of psychoanalysis, and some of their influences on psychoanalytic epistemology, theory, education, ethics, and practice in the industrialized and industrializing context of the modern era (chapter 8); its largely unexamined notions of competency developed during the industrial age and proposes a different understanding of competency more in tune with the information age of the postmodern (chapter 9); and, deconstructs the premise and assumptions of the medical model while proposing a different identity, educational philosophy and program of study for the analytic practitioner as a poet-shaman in the 21st century (chapter 10).

Contemporary psychoanalysis is characterized in the practice community by a rich and creative diversity in its various ways of thinking, knowing, and being and anticipates, I believe, an equally diverse and creative time in the learning community in the twenty first century. "Stories From The Bog" is written as a contribution to this next chapter in the continuing story of psychoanalysis.

carpe diem,

Patrick Kavanaugh
August 1st, 2011

One

Stories From The Bog
On the Underworld, the Underconsciousness, and the Undertaking

> It would not be too much to say that myth is the secret opening through which the inexhaustible energies of the cosmos pour into human cultural manifestation. Religions, philosophies, arts, the forms of primitive and historic man, prime discoveries in science and technology, the very dreams that blister sleep, boil up from the basic, magic ring of myth.
>
> ~ Joseph Campbell, *The Hero With A Thousand Faces*

THE PROVINCE OF MEMORY: FINDING A PLACE

...and she lives in Connemarra, the province of memory; you know, the province where the old language, ancient customs, and timeless narratives remain most alive. They say that she rules over the mountain range that stretches from the Dingle peninsula up along the coast to Moher where, on a clear day, you might catch glimpses of her silhouette on Hag's Head *(Ceann na Cailleach)*, the most southerly of the cliffs of Moher. And if you travel in the region around Gort, you'll find the greatest concentration of sites named after her, the most legends about her, and the landscape most clearly carved in the stark features of her image (Monaghan, 2003). She lives in many different forms and guises: as Bronach in the lonely, windswept hills of the Burren; as Sionann, the reckless maiden, in rivers like the Shannon; and, as the healer Brigit in county Kildare. She is the Cailleach Bheirre, *The Veiled One*, the Mother Goddess of all other gods and goddesses; she is the old one, the hag, the witch, the rock-faced crone. She came to this island long before the time of the ancient Celts and their traditions, even before the time of written documents and records. She is over six thousand years old and underlies all myth, tale, and tradition in Ireland. [1.]..at least, that's what they say.

In the oral traditions of Ireland, *place* and *storytelling* are inseparable. Each place in Ireland is steeped in history and myth; each place is wrapped in a narrative context that tells its story in song and poetry. They say that Ireland is the land of the poems of place-lore *(dindshenchas)* that tell the mythic meaning of her hills and crossroads, her dolmens and holy wells (Monaghan, 2003). Her poem-stories are forms of memory within the Irish culture. The power of *place* resides in the Irish character and spirit, renewing itself through each storytelling experience. Furthermore, neither place nor storytelling can be separated from she who is the Mother Goddess of Ireland. The rock-faced crone remains alive through the stories that speak the sacredness of her land: She is the place of the cave, the rocks, and the cliffs as well as the womb, the bride, and the gaunt old Hag. Ireland is a *she* and her national consciousness is closely tied to the sacred places of her landscape. Of those places that are of her, the bog is one of the holiest. They say that if you follow the Old Bog Road that crosses Roundstone Bog in Connemara, you walk on one of Ireland's most sacred of places where the Old Cailleach remains palpably alive. ...at least, that's what they say.

In *Finders Keepers*, the Irish poet Seamus Heaney (2002), winner of the Nobel prize in literature, speaks to the magical power and cultural memory that resides in the bog in his poem, *The Bogland.* "We have no prairies...," the poem begins, referring to the frontier and the West as an important myth in the American consciousness, "...but we have bogs," becomes the answering Irish myth. Indeed, much of Irish history is discovered in the material text and remembrances of the bog. The bog remembers and preserves all that it might envelope: bog butter, bog animals, and even bog people are perfectly preserved for centuries under the peat of the bog. ...Bog people, you might ask? They were the people who were part of the ritual sacrifices to the Mother Goddess. The gaunt old hag desires new bridegrooms each winter with whom she can sleep and make love in the hidden places of the bog. When she receives their love, she suddenly and unexpectedly transforms into a beautiful young woman; the Old Cailleach is a shape-shifter. And, her's is an insatiable sexual appetite. Sleeping with her under the stark Burren landscape ensures the fertility of the land and the renewal of life; people are harvested in the winter so that the crops can grow in the spring. The Old Cailleach is, at once, the tomb for those who enter her sacred space and the womb for the crops of spring. She is the goddess of the harvest and fertility, and the endlessly repetitive cycles of life, love, and death (Graves, 1966). The mysteries of death, the underworld, and the bog enfold within the image of the Old Calleach (Campbell, 1991)...at least, that's what they say in their tales and legends of the bog.

"What is the meaning of life in the face of our mortality?" "It all depends..." the chorus replies, "what culture are you referring to?" and "What does mortality and death mean in that particular culture?... the meaning of life is inextricably linked to the culture's meaning of death." Indeed, the stories of our lives are inseparably entwined with our cultural beliefs about mortality, death, and desire.[2.] In Ireland, ancient customs are premised on the Celtic theory of immortality and reincarnation, predate the Christian transcendence of death with its belief in an after-life, and flourished at the time of the Greeks and Romans (Ellis, 1999). Strongly influenced by the Hindu philosophy and culture of India, the ancient Celts were one of the first cultures to evolve a sophisticated doctrine of the immortality of the soul. The soul is immortal and lives after death in the Otherworld until (s)he dies there and returns to this world: Death in this world involves a re-birth in the Otherworld and death in the Otherworld involves a rebirth in this world. In Irish mythology, mortality, death, and desire come together as the eros of the immortal Cailleach entwines in an unbreakable embrace with the eros of the mortal being. In so doing, she achieves a certain transcendence of death by engaging with the erotics of dying as a kind of foreplay to the re-incarnation of life. And the bog is the sacred place where this transformative exchange between life and death takes place. ... at least, that's what they say in their song and poetry.

This chapter is a story about the art of psychoanalytic storytelling as premised on the Irish cultural experience and character. In the context of illustrative vignettes, this story considers the following: first, how Celtic mythology about death and reincarnation on the one hand and the underworld and the bog on the other contribute to a conceptualization of a Cailleach unconscious that organizes and shapes the stories of our everyday lives, and, second, some of the implications that derive from this conceptualization of the unconscious for finding one's storytelling voice in the analytic undertaking.

THE *UNDERWORLD* AND THE UN(DER)CONSCIOUS: FINDING A SPACE

> The myth is the foundation of life, the timeless schema, the pious formula into which life flows when it reproduces its traits out of the unconscious. ~ Thomas Mann, *Freud and the Future*

The Underworld: Beneath the Surface

In Irish mythology and folklore that which is beneath the surface plays an organizing and formative role in shaping her national character and psyche. Beneath the surface of the land, for example, sleeps the energy of one's ancestors; their energy remains palpably alive under the ground. The more family generations that have lived on a parcel of land, the more energy and power generated from those buried beneath its surface, the stronger the spiritual bond that develops to that place, and the richer the stories told about that place (Squire, 2001). This close connection to the land forms the very essence of Irish spirituality.[3.] As the earth receives her dead, the land becomes, at once, the tomb for one's ancestors and the womb of spiritual life. Indeed, the Irish people and their land are so deeply connected that a single word *(tuath)* stands for both (Monaghan, 2003). For the Irish, storytelling is a form of cultural memory in which the family's history is rooted, preserved, and transmitted through the stories told. Storytelling is one of the transformative arts that provides a way of staying close to the land and one's ancestors while calling forth their spiritual energies and magical powers from deep beneath its surface and channelling them into everyday life (Rolleston, 1990).

Beneath the surface of the bog are found the mysteries of death, the underworld, and reincarnation; beneath the surface of the land are found the souls and energies of one's ancestors; and, beneath the surface of a monotheistic Irish Catholicism is found the polytheistic paganism of the Old Cailleach. The special power of place and storytelling in Ireland's national psyche derives from her residual paganism.

> "Scratch a bit at the thin topsoil of Irish Catholicism," the saying goes, "and you soon come to the solid bedrock of Irish paganism (7)."... paganism and Catholicism in Ireland are joined twins that can not be separated. They are not opposites, as archaeologist Proinsias MacCana has pointed out, for in Ireland pagan ways and beliefs formed an "extraordinary symbiosis." ...paganism and Christianity in Ireland need each other to live. (Monaghan, 2003, p. 139)

Christian and pagan beliefs interweave in the cultural fabric to produce a sanctioned way of *being, knowing,* and *perceiving* into which each person is born and of which each is a part (Friel, 1990).

If every culture produces that version of psychoanalysis most needed by the culture, do the mythical stories and archetypal images of the Old Cailleach enfold within an overarching unconscious particular to the Irish cultural experience? That is, does a Celtic understanding of the mysteries of death and the under-world contribute to a mythological un(der)conscious (Adams, 2001)[4.] specific to Ireland? Stories of the Old Cailleach and the bog seem to dance in time with the archetypes of the Irish culture. Although archetypal symbols do not have the same collective meaning for everyone, they do contain the rules of formation (Foucault, 1973) that provide for the discursive rationality and coherence that operates beneath the surface of thematic content in any given culture. As one of the organizing stories of the Irish culture, the story of the Old Cailleach and the bog constructs, contains, and transmits the rules of formation that underlie the fundamental codes of the Irish culture which, in turn, influence and shape their magical and poetical language, the schemes of perception that permit the sightings of fairies and leprechauns, and, the social exchanges, techniques, and values embedded in the stories told at the local pub. As the exterior landscape of the bog influences the interior landscape of the national psyche, mythical stories of the rock-faced crone influence the psychic experiences of the people (Campbell, 1959; 1991). Her story lives within the people and underlies the formation of a Celtic mythological un(der)-conscious. If, as suggested by Christopher Bollas (1999), breasts have become the intellectual property of the British in London while the phallus resides in Paris as the intellectual property of the Lacanians, then "Stories from the Bog..." suggests that the vagina has taken up residence in Connemara in the form of the Old Cailleach not, however, as the intellectual property of a particular psychoanalytical school but, rather, as the lived cultural experience of her mythological unconscious.

The Nature and Characteristics of The Cailleach Unconscious

As our lives are lived, experienced, and recounted in the narrative form of a story, so too, the Cailleach unconscious is conceptualized as remembering, preserving and organizing our life-stories in a three dimensional narrative form.[5.] And in this space that, paradoxically, is not a space, the Cailleach unconscious is understood as having different levels of order and reality, psychically determined but unpredictable dynamical systems, multi-determined, -leveled, and -layered imagery, the juxtaposition of opposites and contradictions, and multiple systems of signification and meaning replete with their various tensions and parallelisms. In this sacred bog-space of her un(der)consciousness is found a psychical province of memory comprised of that which cannot be remembered and, yet, cannot be forgotten.

Beneath the surface of consciousness is found the ancient customs, primitive beliefs, and archaic ways of being, knowing, and thinking that remain palpably alive throughout a person's life. As the analytic practitioner scratches at this thin topsoil of consciousness, he or she enters the spiritual world of the Cailleach un(der)consciousness: An invisible geometry of interrelated and interconnected matrices of meaning organized by the inexplicable something more of the mystery, magic, and muscle of being human. And in this bog space, unconscious memories, experiences and realities are preserved in a three dimensional holographic form, as perhaps best illustrated by Ms. A as she told her story via the associative-interpretive process.

When we first began meeting, Ms. A was a middle-aged woman who had spent much of her previous 22-years in a state hospital diagnosed as a catatonic schizophrenic. Certain of her memories and childhood experiences with mother had profoundly influenced her everyday life as an adult and, also, her ways of communicating in the analytic space. When she was a little girl, for example, her mother would lock her in a dark closet for endless hours at a time where she was to babysit her baby brother. If he made any loud or disturbing sounds, her mother would beat her severely before throwing her back into the closet to continue babysitting. Or, her mother would come into her bedroom while she was sleeping at night and insert her fingers into her vagina to see if she had been "playing around down there." If mother determined that she had been, she would viciously kick her, "down there between my legs." Ms. A's stories were filled with these and other horrific memories of her experiences as she was growing up with her mother.

Shortly after we began meeting, Ms. A stopped talking in words about her childhood experiences. As if in a theatre of the mime, she began recalling and "speaking about" her traumatic experiences through a more primal linguistic: the language of physical movements, expressions and gestures. Her language of space and movement took us back in space-time to the closet of her childhood where, sitting quietly in my office chair, she would reach above her head with her eyes closed and search until she found... a shoebox. She would pull the shoebox off the shelf above her, place it gently on her lap, and remove the lid of the box. We had entered a semiotically constructed, three-dimensional, spatially encoded and enacted representation of her experiences of being in the closet. And inside each shoebox was a memory-experience-event from her childhood central to the telling of her story in the analytic discourse.

While Ms. A's story and her storytelling process can be found in greater detail in chapter six, the focus here is on the process nature and dynamic characteristics of the Cailleach unconscious. In this story about Ms. A's storytelling process, a holographic reality had developed in the analytic space, a shape-shifting reality that, at once, recreated her life-experiences as a little girl, dramatized their profound influences on her life, and shaped her rather dramatic participation in our discourse. Indeed, the unique way and form in which she told her story in the theatre of the mime was integral to its understanding in the present moment of her past.

The memories of Ms. A's phenomenal past were preserved in a three-dimensional holographic form and organized in a narrative format. Within the strange safety of the analytic space, the semiotically constructed reality and context of being in her mother's closet could take place. Moreover, she could put her hand inside of her box, her shoebox that is, and gently explore with her hand whatever experiences might be inside. This most personal and private venture into the unconscious realities of her closeted experiences allowed her to freely play around in her box that had been so viciously and repeatedly violated by her mother's shoe. Each memory-image contained in her various shoeboxes expressed both a part of *and* the whole of her life-world and story. Each partial element of her story contained and communicated the whole story: The part was in the whole and the whole was in each part (Wilber, 1982). The image of the shoebox, for example, was like a psychic stem cell: It contained the whole of Ms. A's life story, the gradual understanding of which took place through the associative-interpretive process.

Ms. A's province of memory is understood as a timeless and spaceless -yet, a time and space-filled- sphere of conflict, dilemma, and the paradoxical. At the intersection where the sacred and profane comingle, time flows backwards. That is, sacred time flows in reverse, enabling the rock-faced crone to shape-shift from hag into maiden, harlot into virgin, and tomb into womb. In the sacred time of her bog space, sequenced notions of time and age have no meaning: Experiences move, at once, backward into the past *and* forward into the future while, at the same time, standing perfectly still in the present moment of the future-past where the stories of our lives unfold: She is timeless. And, her province of memory is time-filled: Her bog-space is filled with the present-tense sensory images that live in the eternal now and contain the stories of our lives. Sleeping beneath the surface of awareness is found the magical and spiritual energies of the soul(s), in this instance, of Ms. A.

Like all the Irelands before the present one, Ms. A's history lives in the present moment awaiting its translation from present-tense sensory-images into narrated stories. Ms. A's memories coexist in the present moment, co-structuring and codetermining the lived-experiences of her everyday life. In effect, the Cailleach unconscious is an ontology of life that emphasizes the process nature of our lived experiences. And at the same time, it conceals as it reveals: It is hidden in plain sight for those who might see its rhythms and rhymes, and meanings and purposes. Had Ms. A been perfectly preserved in deep sacrifice to her own Mother Goddess during her catatonic years in the state hospital? Had she been held captive by her memories, imprisoned and preserved in that place, time, and sensory-based knowledge(s) from whence she had come? Had she become one of the bog people frozen in time, silently screaming her stories from the bog?

As one of the transformative arts, storytelling provides a way of staying close to Ms. A's sacred province of memory and unconscious reality while calling forth and channeling the spiritual energies and magical powers of her phenomenal past into words. In so doing, storytelling provides a narrative context that helps Ms. A make sense of the *non*-sense of her confusing sensory-based childhood experiences. One of the sense-making meanings of her past experiences, for example, could be expressed in the following way: In her mind, her menstrual bleeding was "the curse" in her life that had been caused from being "bwoke down there" by her mother's shoe. In effect, mother was the curse in her life who had caused "the curse" in her life because she, Ms. A, was the fleshed-out embodiment of "the curse" in her mother's life.

They say that the old Cailleach has one purple eye located in the middle of her forehead enabling her to see beyond the world of discrete, sharply demarcated, binary objects into the mystical world of the inter-related and inter-connected. Her polytheistic, or paganistic, perspective is organized around an "and-both" inclusiveness that recognizes the interdependent and interrelated nature of the world of objects and experiences. This purple-eyed polytheistic perspective stands in sharp contrast to a clear and precise monotheistic perspective organized around a world of discrete "either-or" object-based discriminations in which, for example, a shoebox is ...a shoebox, is... a shoebox, objectively speaking of course.

In monotheism, there is but one god; everything else is derived from and is in hierarchical relationship to this one-god essence. From a purple-eyed polytheistic perspective, however, Ms. A's shoebox is, at once, a shoebox as might be found in a closet; *and* a representational image gathering and bringing together the experiences of her mother's *shoe* viciously kicking her "down there" in her *box*; *and* a container that holds these compressed memories and experiences; *and*, a linguistic structure that gradually fills with the multiple meanings and experiences of these memories; *and*, the shoebox is all the above; and...; and ....; and....; *and* from a purple-eyed paganistic perspective, there are many different gods and goddesses and many different narrative stories being told at the same time.

The Cailleach unconscious is conceptualized as an unconscious of the feminine, the poetics of which are characterized by a dynamic and fluid movement of sensory images, comprised of multiple levels of order and meaning interacting in a seemingly chaotic and disordered dynamical system as found in nature, and organized by purple-eyed paganistic notions of time, place, logic and causality. Understood as an interrelated and interconnected mode of being, knowing, and perceiving, the Cailleach unconscious is organized around tissue traces of historical and causal meanings in ways that shape the individual's perception of the world so as to both conform with and confirm certain pre-existing images of self and other. From this perspective, "consciousness" and "unconsciousness" are but different perspectives of an inseparable and mysterious psychological process, in which process anything can stand for itself and anything else at the same time. Indeed, when is a shoebox just a shoebox ... or, for that matter, just another shoebox?

They say that Celtic mythology about death, reincarnation and immortality underlies the rich fantasy, eternal optimism, and "twinkle in the eye" found in the Irish storytelling tradition (Ellis, 1999). If so, how might a Celtic understanding of the underworld and the Cailleach un(der)conscious influence the practitioner's storytelling in the analytic space?

ON THE UNDERTAKING, DEATH, AND STORYTELLING: FINDING A VOICE

> The artist eye, as Thomas Mann has said, has a mythical slant upon life; therefore, the mythological realm -the world of the gods and demons, the carnival of their masks and the curious game of 'as if' in which the festival of the lived myth abrogates all the laws of time, letting the dead swim back to life, and the 'once upon a time' become the very present - we must approach and first regard with the artist's eye.
>
> ~ Joseph Campbell (Primitive Mythology)

In Celtic mythology, the soul of the dead is accompanied between this world and the Otherworld by Morrigan, the goddess of poetry and queen of the underworld, and Ogma, the god of poetry and divine warriors (MacCullough, 2004).[6.] On its journey between worlds, the soul actively searches for an entity with which to unite so as to give expression to itself in a new and different life-form. Like the Old Cailleach, the soul is a shape-shifter finding its expression in different life-forms such as: the white water of the turbulent river Shannon, the carrion crow keeping watch from the gnarled branch of an old oak tree, or the gentle melodic sounds of the wind-chimes caressed by a gentle breeze. Poetry is, at once, the soul seeking new life-forms and the language of the soul that enables its transition from one state of being to the next. The intimate interweave of death, the underworld, and the un(der)conscious on the one hand and the transformative arts of poetry, storytelling, and mythology on the other suggests that the analytic undertaking, of necessity, blends something of the mortuary arts with the literary arts.

The poet's voice speaks the enigmatic, the inexplicable, and the unknown; the poet words the forbidden as (s)he writes about love, sex, and death in ways that resonate with the larger community. Thomas Lynch is unlike other poets inspired by death in that he is hired by the small town of Milford, Michigan to bury their dead; every year, he buries several hundred of his townspeople. Lynch is the town's funeral director in which capacity he serves as his community's voice as both a witness and functionary in the process of death and dying. Indeed, Tom Lynch has buried my father, more recently my sister, and on some day in the not too distant future my mother, as well. Lynch is a poet, a philosopher, and a first-rate storyteller as he reminisces about how as a young boy he had often wondered why his father was called an undertaker (Lynch, 1997). The *under-* seemed quite obvious: the dead went *under* the ground. But to be a *-taker*? A *taker* implies that you actively accompany the person, if not lead the way, as in *taking* someone *under* the ground. As a boy, he preferred the term under- *putter* with the clear implication it was better to stay above ground and put someone else down *under*.

Is the analytic practitioner an under-*taker or -putter*?" And the chorus replies, "It all depends... If he or she is hired by others to give voice to the stories of their lives, then he or she has to be an under-*taker*" with the analytic undertaking understood as a unique psychological discourse by which we "vest the lives we lead against the cold, the meaningless, the void, the noisy blather, and the blinding dark. It is the voice we give to wonderment, to pain, to love and desire, anger and outrage; the words that we shape into song and prayer" (Lynch, 1997, xix).

They say that the daughters of Ireland inherit the poet's tongue (*seanchaid*) while her sons inherit the storyteller's talents (*seanachies*). The art of psychoanalytic storytelling rests on the practitioner listening, understanding, and responding as a "mind-poet" who blends the Irish feminine with the Irish masculine. In so doing, he or she travels with people into their sacred provinces of Memory, speaking to and with and from within the unspeakable from all sides at once. The mind poet is the One Who Remembers in words something about the ideothetic experiences of their own mortality, death, and desire and, further, obligates self to narrate the stories told in the analytic undertaking.

Mortality, death, and desire encircle the analytic undertaking; they are inseparable aspects of our experiences of everyday life. After all, the essence of the essence of any wordly object or experience is its transience or mortality. As we experience the oneness of a desired object, we also experience its anticipated loss; mortality forecloses on the never-ending absoluteness of the desired object's presence (Staten, 1995). In Celtic mythology, however, death is not the ultimate conqueror from whom the soul is to be saved nor is the underworld the dreaded place to be avoided as in Greek and Roman mythology. For the Irish, the reality of death provides a continuity between former, present, and future lives; death is the transitional door to another life. Thus, in undertaking the analytic undertaking, the practitioner has to know the place from where he or she comes, be comfortable with the lived experiences of his or her own dying, and look for meaning and voice in his or her own lives, loves, and deaths.

In the life cycle of birth, death, and rebirth, dying is a part of living as living is a part of dying. In effect, the transience of life is the essence of a dialectic of dying as the transience of death is the essence of a dialectic of reincarnating. This cycle can be seen in the experiences of our everyday lives in which we might catch a glimmer of something dying as something is born. Something dies, for example, as excited parents watch their baby take her first steps, speak his first words, or leave for the first day of kindergarten, highschool, or the military. A dialectic of dying and mourning walks hand in hand with a dialectic of reincarnating and celebrating; something is left behind as something new is embraced. The eternal optimism of the Irish is grounded in there being nothing final about the end: Death is only a change of place and life-form; life is a never-ending process. From within this dialectic one might find their analytic voice...

Finding a Storytelling Voice

In *The School of the Dead*, the poet-thinker Helene Cixous (1993) speaks to the powerful struggle and continuous death of self and other in the creative process of writing. Someone or something must die, she writes, in order for good writing to be born:

> The only book worth writing is the one we don't have the courage or strength to write. The book that hurts us (we who are writing), that makes us *tremble, redden,* and *bleed.* It is combat against ourselves, the author; one of us must be vanquished or die... it's the one I want to write; I tear it from myself.
>
> (p. 32, emphasis added)

Cixous' poetical-narrative style of writing has been described as in some ways biblical, liturgical and mythological. Filled with biblical and mythological imagery, her writing enters a space in which her speaking subject moves from one subject position to another. Such writing enjoys extraordinary freedom, reflecting an eternally present space that emphasizes a fundamental unity and oneness that surrounds her and her readers (Moi, 1991). How can the practitioner as a mind-poet be in relation to the spoken word as Cisoux is to the written text? How does he or she find a storytelling voice that re-tells the story told in ways, "that makes us tremble, redden, and bleed?" The chorus replies, "The mind-poet must bleed in the re-telling of the story as the Old Cailleach bleeds in her fluidity and flow." [7.] Unfortunately, however, -as the chorus knows only all too well- the rock-faced crone is feared in many cultures, psychoanalytic and otherwise, as the source of contamination and taboo; She is considered to be unclean and to be avoided, particularly when she bleeds (Lupton, 1993). As the endometrium, produced and made available through the menstrual process, is the first food in the creation and beginnings of life, however, passion is the endometrium of psychoanalytic storytelling. For the mind-poet to have a story to tell in the analytic undertaking, he or she must passionately believe in what he or she says. Taboos notwithstanding, passion is, at once, the life-blood of the interpretive act and the fluid flow of the associative-interpretive process. The endometrium of passion profoundly alters the mind-poet's state of consciousness, allows a different view of reality to emerge somewhere inbetween the world of consciousness and the Otherworld of un(der)consciousness, and, permits entry into that space where one might find a storytelling voice that "trembles, reddens, and bleeds."

For Seamus Heaney (2002), finding your poetic voice means getting your own feeling into your own words so that your words have your own feel about them. A poetic voice, he says, is probably very intimately connected with one's natural voice. As to how to find one's voice, he advises,

> In practice you hear it coming from somebody else; you hear something in another writer's sound that flows in through your ear and enters the echo chamber of your head delights your whole nervous system in such a way that your reaction will be, 'Ah, I wish I had said that, in that particular way.' This other writer, in fact, has spoken something essential to you, something you recognize instinctively as a true sounding of aspects of yourself and your experience. And your first steps as a writer will be to imitate, consciously or unconsciously, those sounds that flowed in, that 'in-fluence' (p. 17).

For Heaney (2002), putting feelings and experiences into words involves the poet's definitional relationship to reality and life. It involves the discovery within oneself of ways to go outside of one's usual ways of thinking so as to "raid the inarticulate" which involves, "a dynamic alertness that mediates between the origins of feeling in memory and experience and the formal ploys that express these in a work of art" (p. 21). Finding a poetic voice involves plumbing the depths of these memories and experiences while being guided by the euphonics of one's own poetic imagination, vision, and metaphor.

In Ireland, the holy wells are the traditional places of healing. It is believed that the shafts of these holy wells extend deep beneath the surface of the land into the acquifer of the souls of one's ancestors, whose spiritual and magical energies transform into the healing language of poetry and storytelling. Indeed, the holy wells are known as Brigit's places of healing. As a bridge figure for both the Christian and pagan, Brigit is known as 'Saint Brigit' for the Christians, and for the pagans as Brigit, the goddess of the transformative arts of healing and poetry (Monaghan, 2003). Thus, it's not surprising that for Heaney (2002) the experience of translating one's feelings and experiences into words is likened to the turning of the windlass at the well of poetry where

> usually you begin by dropping the bucket halfway down the shaft and winding up a taking of air. You are miming the real thing until one day the chain draws unexpectedly tight and you have dipped into waters that will continue to entice you back. You'll have broken the skin on the pool of yourself (p. 21).

Finding one's storytelling voice is to find the poetical words that serve as the healing bridge-structures to the soul...

Ms. G. was a high priced 'call girl' as opposed to a 'hooker,' as her mother had been. In her mid-twenties, she was quite exclusive in both her clientele and willingness to meet their needs. She had called some three years prior to speak about certain uncomfortable experiences she was having that were interfering with her ability to work: She was having 'flashbacks' that were making it more and more difficult to provide her services to her clients. Increasingly, she had been turning to drugs and alcohol for relief. Over the years of our meetings, Ms. G. had matter-of-factly told of her being born and raised in the housing projects, the youngest of eight brothers and sisters, each of whom had a different father named 'John;' her multiple foster-care placements and the indifference of authorities to the physical and sexual abuses she had experienced in the homes; and more and more, her fear that she was more like a hooker like her mother than what she had first thought. After meeting for three times a week for nearly three years, Ms. G. mentioned at the end of our session that she would like to begin using the couch the next time she came. I agreed.

Ms G. arrived the next session drinking from a two-liter bottle of cold Diet Coke while saying how excruciatingly hot it was outside. As she laid down on the couch, she put the bottle next to her on the floor, saying, "As you can well-imagine, there's a lot of significance for me whenever I lay down in the presence of a man." After several minutes of silence, she took from her shorts' pocket an ornately decorated silver compact case, opened it, and held it back over her head, offering me some of the white powder inside. I was quiet for a moment and mentioned that I was curious -indeed, we might be curious- why it was that she offered me "the classic coke" while she took "the diet coke" for herself?' (In the Irish storytelling tradition, the external drama of everyday life is much more real, relevant and interesting than is an overly abstract and remote focus on the interior landscape of, for example, "the intrapsychic.") Without saying a word Ms. G. slowly closed the compact, put it back in her pocket, and, after a period of silence, said that she had had a dream the night before. This was the first dream she had mentioned since we had started meeting.

In her dream, Ms. G. was lost and wandering in the desert somewhere near Las Vegas; the sun was unbearably hot, her throat was parched and dry, and she was thirsty. After walking for a long time, she discovered the entrance to a cool damp tunnel behind a small bush on a hill. The tunnel led her to the entrance of a cave: "It was huge and beautiful," she said, "I just stood there at the entrance to the cave in awe..." There was a very long silence at this point. Then, she went on to describe the beautiful colors of the stalactites and stalagmites and the gently flowing stream of multicolored waters. As she knelt down and began drinking, however, a flash flood suddenly came roaring through the cave and swept her up. She was drowning; she could not get her breath; finally, she found a tiny air-pocket where she could breathe at the very top of the cave. Then she woke up, sweating profusely. There was a long silence, then Ms G. said, "What do you think the dream means?" I mentioned that she seemed hesitant in asking what I thought and asked what was she thinking. She replied, "When I said, 'I was standing at the entrance to the 'cave in awe,' it sounded like I was saying your last name: "Cave-in awe- Kav-an -augh.."

Some say that the entrances to the underworld are found by springs, caves, wells, and rivers, all of which are carefully hidden in plain sight. Apparently, this entrance was hidden in the "cave-in-awe;" sometimes, like an echo, we hear ourselves coming back to ourselves as we enter the bog. "What do you think it means," she again asked. I began speaking to the significance of her coming and laying down "in the presence of a man" and how that seemed to be related to offering me *the classic coke* while she took the *diet coke*... And I spoke to her deep thirst and high hopes about laying on the couch and finding relief for her life-long experience of feeling lost and wandering about by herself. She had offered me *the classic coke* and feared, her dream and thoughts suggested, that the "cave-in-awe" would, in a sudden rush, "cave-in" to his desires ..., and once again, she'd be lost, overlooked and overwhelmed like the countless times she'd told us about growing-up in the housing projects and in various foster-care homes. Once again, things would get turned around and she would find herself here to meet *my* desires. Better, in her mind, that she be my "mama hooker" and I be hooked on her *classic coke* than she be hooked on me; ...better that she be my 'momma hooker' than I be hers, as signified and communicated by her giving me the classic coke and taking the diet coke for herself.

As the bucket dips again and again into the wellsprings of our memories, experiences, and madness, we reveal ourselves to ourselves as words -precious thirst quenching words- somehow come rushing up from out of the vortex to begin flowing and bridging that space between the mind-poet and story-teller, the consciousness and un(der)consciousness, and the Christian -or, for that matter, the Jew or Muslim - and the pagan. In the bog's space of infinite regress, spirituality and mysticism come together in the form of the carnal and sensuous Old Cailleach warmly nestling with the ghostly images and haunting memories of times past; memories preserved in her timeless tomb wait to be worded and, in so being, re-incarnate into new life forms in her time-filled womb. Memory preserves the ancient knowledge and experiences of where we came from and how we came to be; words are the bucket carriers bringing the history and mystery of our beings to the surface and bridging the space between the there-and-then and the here-and-now.

As "The Veiled One," the Old Cailleach invites the mind-poet into the Otherworld of her bog space to listen, understand, and translate into words the veiled meanings hidden within. The undertaking of such an undertaking requires, however, that the therapist enters the subject's story, images and sounds while permitting them to enter him or herself; he or she walks around in them, smells them, tastes them, knows them, inhabits them, breathes them, and becomes them. The therapist finds his or her poetic voice by entering the sensory experiences of these ancient memories, coming to know them, and wording the shared bodily experiences: Words are like birth canals that lead from the province of memory to a re-incarnated life-form in the lived experiences of self. As a mind-poet, the therapist must be one hundred per cent in the sensory experiences so as to know them and, at the same time, remain one hundred per cent outside of them so as to speak to that place to which words cannot go and from out of which place words cannot come. In effect, the mind-poet must know the story by heart in order to speak it from the heart.

Entering, moving, and speaking from within the incestuous bog-space of the Old Cailleach, however, violates the canons of Judeo-Christian rationality, law, and ethic. More specifically, speaking from within her bog-space of carnality, corporality, and mystical causality runs the risk of being *found under* her *carnal knowledge*, as perhaps best represented by the acronym F.U.C.K.. Thus, most properly speaking, - for those amongst us who are given to speaking most properly -, the mind-poet enters the bog-space where the sacred and profane freely and fluidly comingle to find and speak in one's "mother f.u.c.k.ing storytelling voice" so as to tell the story in all of its sensory aspects. After all, a story not told in its sensory aspects is not a story, much less 'a story told.' - on me sainted mother's grave-to-be, it's true!

Storytelling Purpose

Psychoanalytic storytelling assumes a complex humanity within which there are layers under layers, fictions within fictions, and stories within stories. Contrary to our received psychoanalytic wisdoms, this complexity extends to those who reside in those chemical cocoons known as "accredited inpatient units." *Frankenstein's Genie-ology...* for example, is an autobiographical story of how he came to be as told over a five year period of time by an African-American man on the inpatient unit of an inner-city state hospital (Chapter three). Layerings of his story are enfolded within the ward's milieu structure, dynamic, and process in which his predictably unpredictable violent assaults led to his unofficially occupying the position of "the head man" on the ward. For years, Mr. P. had been wrapped in the analytic fiction of being "untreatable" and "unanalyzable" because of his alleged structural deficiencies, yet his story reflects the palpable experiences and inexplicable processes of psychic transformation in the very telling of his story to another via the the associative-interpretive process.

In this unique storytelling process, a central organizing experience of Mr. P's life came to be known: His living his everyday life as the monstrous fictional creature brought to life by Victor Frankenstein. The layers within layers, fictions within fictions, and stories within stories returned us in some mysterious way to a central organizing experience of his life: His beginning life as a monster-child-man in which image was found the psychic densities and overdetermined realities of how he came to be, where he came from, and who he experienced himself to be. Also contained within Mr. P.'s story was the all-too-often overlooked story of the mystery, magic, and muscle of the human spirit which cannot be quantified, medicated, or manipulated. The retelling of Mr. P's story in words was for the purpose of articulating something about the world as he experienced it to be and around which experiences his life stories were organized. Psychoanalytic storytelling is not for the purpose of enlightening nor liberating, nor is it for medicinal or character building value.

Storytelling Style and Being in the Dark

Like water taking the shape of its container, the practitioner's storytelling style is developed from within the story told. As a shape-shifter, he or she does not have a set style of storytelling that applies to the many different stories told in the analytic space: One style does not fit all. Rather, the practitioner takes on different and unique storytelling styles, each of which fits with the story being told. In narrating a person's life-stories, he or she adopts a "style of no style," the highest level of storytelling style; formulaic ways of listening, understanding, and responding are not part of psychoanalytic storytelling ...except, of course, on those occasions when they are.

Like the ancient Celts, the practitioner has to be comfortable with being "in the dark" while, paradoxically, seeing "the light side" of "the dark side" of human nature. The early Celts had a reverence for darkness and the darkside as reflected in their tribal names such as, for example, the People of Darkness (*Corca-Oidce*), the People of the Night (*Corca-Duibhne*), and the Sons of the Dark (*Hi Dorchaide*) (Squire, 2001). For the Celts, death and darkness always came before rebirth and light; the passage of time began with the night followed by the day and their new year started with the dark period of Samhain (Halloween) when the veil was believed to be thinnest between the souls of the Otherworld and this one (Ellis, 1999). Thus, the analytic practitioner must be comfortable with the uncomfortableness of being in the dark with all the uncertainties, ambiguities, and indeterminancies of "not knowing" as the story unfolds and comes alive through the associative-interpretive process.

Storytelling Perspective

In the best of the Irish storytelling tradition, the stories told might be of a rambling nature, in which instance the practitioner remains fully open to the unexpected discoveries of each moment. Many times, such openness permits a collaborative discovery of things that neither participant might have suspected, much less have known, were even being looked for, as reflected in, for example, the associative material, context, and meanings of the *diet coke* and *classic coke* that unfolded between Ms. G.and myself. A particularly meaningful storytelling perspective is suggested for the practitioner's retelling of the other's story by the magical and symbolic realm of the ancient Irish in which there were five directions: north, south, east, west, and *the center*. The perspective organizing the re-telling of the story is relative to the person's *center*:

> ...for the center is "here" —wherever we stand, orienting ourselves to our world; (we are) centers of a compass whose center is everywhere. *But the center being everywhere is not the same as the center being nowhere* - far from it. The center is not outside us. It is within our innumerable, individual, unique, and irreplaceable hearts.
>
> (Monaghan, 2003, p. 14, emphasis added)

As suggested by the Irish poet-philosopher Patrick Kavanagh (1904-1967), the analyst's retelling of the story told is: in the context of the person's everyday life, from his or herpersonal point of view, and communicates a sense of the uniqueness of the person's life experience (1996).[8.] In this way, the practitioner speaks from the perspective most meaningful to the person. The subject's unique and personal point of view is always at the center of the re-telling of the story....except, of course, when it is not.

For the practitioner to have a story to tell, he or she must passionately believe and trust in *self, other*, and the mystery, magic, and muscle of *the associative-interpretive process*. As considered in chapter two, the mind-poet neither creates nor constructs meaning in the story's re-telling; (s)he creatively discovers meaning in the unseen similarities *within* and *between* the person's poetic images and rhythymic verses. The person's perceptions of the world are not imaginary; they are quite real. The specific similarities *between* and *within* his or her poetic images and verses derive from that which constitute the real possibilities in his or her world. A creative and collaborative discovery takes place when these perceived similarities are seen, spoken, and resonate in ways meaningful for the subject through the interpretive process. Most importantly, however, the storytelling process neither creates nor constructs meaning by cleverly playing with words or emotions.

CONCLUSION

In this spiritual-mystical view of unconscious process and dynamic, the Cailleach unconscious is understood as the essence of human being-ness by which the energies of past memories and experiences, living beneath the surface of our awareness, interrelate and interconnect to form the patterned experiences of our everyday lives. In this way, the stories of our lives are continuously being retold in their reliving. From this perspective, the Cailleach unconscious influences and interweaves with all of conscious thinking and thought; has an elegance of rhyme and reason, and meaning and purpose; and, reveals her radical phenomenality through the fluid flow of the associative-interpretive process. Most importantly, the Cailleach unconscious is not of a one-god essence and does not share in his preoccupations with perversions, pathologies, and ideologies of social control (Kavanaugh, 1997).

As a storyteller, the mind-poet narrates (*seanchaidh*) the personal history,

story, legend and song of the person that he or she has come to know is more like self than otherwise: the other to whom we speak resides, ultimately, within self. It is from this shared recognition of the *other*-of-*self* in the *self*-of-*other* that the powerful significance of the theatre and its drama becomes most valued and appreciated for, like a good funeral, psychoanalytic storytelling

> ... is driven by voices, images, intellections, and the permanent. It moves us up and back the cognitive and the imaginative and emotive register.... In the space between what is said and unsaid, in the pause between utterances, whole histories are told; whole galaxies are glimpsed in the margins, if only momentarily. At wakes and verse, both absence and presence inform the work. What is said and what is unsaid are both instructive. The elegist and eulogist must both ... have a sense when enough is enough.... Good poems and good funerals are stories well told. (Lynch, 2000, p. 257)

And so, enough is enough. I conclude this story about the transformative and healing arts of psychoanalytic storytelling with several questions that only you can speak to, if you so choose:

From what place might you be from?

Who might you be?

What stories might you have to tell?

An earlier version of this paper was first presented on February 20, 2006 in Queretaro, Mexico at the sixteenth annual interdisciplinary conference of the International Federation for Psychoanalytic Education. The theme of the conference was "Psychoanalysis and the Stories of our Lives: Memory, Narration, and Discovery."

NOTES

1. I am indebted to Patricia Monaghan's scholarly recounting of Irish myth, tale, and tradition (2003). Her poetical work provides much of the background context for "Stories from the Bog..."
2. In the United States, for example, our understanding of death and the underworld is closely tied to Greek and Roman mythology. Intellectually, artistically, and politically our genealogy traces to the ancient Greeks and Romans, whose poetic imaginations entered the unknown, humanized the terrors of death and the after-life, and rationally explained the irrational. The terrifying incomprehensibility of death and the underworld were banned from Greece. Those who made the myths disliked the irrational and had a love for facts. "Anyone who reads them with attention discovers that even the most nonsensical take place in a world which is essentially rational and matter-of-fact (Hamilton, 1942, p. 17)." In

many respects, our highly scientific, technological, and materialistic North American culture continues in their scientific-logical vision and world view that reductively explains the soul, happiness, spirituality, and death: For example, the mind is reduced to brain matter, the soul to brain activity, happiness to pre-frontal lobe activity, and death to a physiological condition characterized by the absence of brain activity. In our most technologically efficient way, we push as far away as possible any wareness of death and decay. We arrange for the pre-paid funeral, the pre-scripted eulogy, and pre-grieve the loss of friends and family according to a pre-determined number of sequential steps. The terrors and incomprehensibilities of death are avoided in our lives, thinking, and consciousness as much as possible. In such a cultural context, there is not much of a story to be told or understood. And yet, when death speaks everyone listens.

3. In *The Discovery of the Unconscious* (1970), Henri Ellenberger traces the historical and dynamic relationship between the mysteries of death and the underworld in ancient cultures and the emergence of our contemporary understanding(s) of the unconscious; a culture's understanding of the concept of the unconscious is closely tied to its understanding of death and the underworld.

4. Rooted in the spiritual connectivity to nature is the philosophy of 'systems science' which deals with, for example, ecosystems, ecological lifestyles, and value-systems. As a philosophy, systems science engenders a profound sense of connectedness, of context, of relationship, and of belonging. Its overarching framework generates a new vision of reality in which the world is seen as a network of phenomena that are fundamentally interconnected and interdependent (Capra, 2000). Paganism, or polytheism, sees nature as holy, interrelated, and interconnected in which space chaos theory dances with the intricate and unpredictable possiblities that unfold in nature (Monaghan, 2003).

5. During the past century, the conceptualization of the *unconscious* has gradually broadened from instinctual impulses and wish fulfillments as originally described in the *Interpretation of Dreams* (Freud, 1900) to repressed feelings and ideas and, later, introjected images of people as described in *Mourning and Melancholia* (Freud, 1917). With each conceptual revision, differently textured ways of listening, understanding, and responding to the person entered the analytic conversation. With people coming to populate *the unconscious*, could the organizing stories of our lives be far behind?

6. In the Celtic culture, poetic eloquence is akin to magic and is believed to be of greater power than physical strength (Chaline, 2004). The power of words harkens back to ancient times, when the men hurled their spears at the enemy as the women hurled their powerful curses that guided the spears to their enemy's heart.

7. Luce Irigaray's (1985) "philosophy of flow" violates this tabooed space of the unspeakable in the culture as she dares to touch and taste the flowing fluids. Much like the magical and poetical language of the Mother Goddess, Irigaray's philosophy of flow disrupts, disturbs, and decenters the triumph and privileged position of rationality in the analytic culture.

8. A country poet from county Monaghan, Kavanagh (1996) wrote out of his "Monaghanness" to speak in a passionate earthy voice of his experiences of everyday-life on the farm. His poetry gave permission to speak of the mundane and ordinary of one's life. His poetic was, at once, inclusive and individual; his aesthetic aimed toward increasing the freedom of speech, the linguistic corollary of his poetic. His poetry's emphasis on *place* raised communal consciousness to the specificity and uniqueness of "the local"; every universal epic, he believed, is ultimately local if it is truly universal.

ACKNOWLEDGEMENT

This chapter is dedicated to Sharon Marie.

REFERENCES

Adams, M.V. (2001). *The mythological unconscious.* New York: Karnac Press.
Bollas, C. (1999). *The mystery of things.* New York: Routledge.
Campbell, J. (1959). *Primitive mythology*: The masks of god. New York, Penguin Press.
(1968) *The hero with a thousand faces.* Princeton, N.J.: Princeton University Press.
(1991). *The power of myth.* (B.S. Flowers, ed.). New York: Anchor Books.
Capra, F. (2000). *The Tao of physics: An exploration of the parallels between modern physics and eastern mysticism.* (4th ed.) Shambhala Publications, Boston.
Chaline, E. (2004). *The book of gods and goddesses.* New York: HarperCollins.
Cixous, H. (1993). *Three steps on the ladder of writing.* New York: Columbia University Press.
Conway, D.J. (2002). *Celtic magic.* St. Paul, Minn.: Llewellyn Publications.
Ellenberger, H. (1970) *The discovery of the unconscious: The history and evolution of dynamic psychiatry.* New York: Basic Books.
Ellis, P. B., (1999). *Celtic myths and legends.* New York: Carroll and Graf.
Friel, B. (1990) *Dancing at Lughnasa.* London: Faber and Faber.
Freud, S. (1900). The interpretation of dreams. In J. Strachey, (ed. and trans.) *The standard edition of the complete psychological works of Sigmund Freud,* 24 vols. London: Hogarth Press, 1953-1974. 4: 1-338, 5: 339-627.
(1917). Mourning and melancholia. Standard ed., 14:159-205.
Foucault, M. (1973). *The order of things: An archaeology of the human sciences.* New York: Vintage Books.
Graves, R. (1966). *The White Goddess: A historical grammar of poetic myth.* New York: Farrar, Straus & Giroux.
Hamilton, E. (1942). *Mythology: Timeless tales of gods and heroes.* New York: Warner Books.
Heaney, S. (2002). *Finders keepers: Selected prose.* New York: Farrar, Straus, & Giroux.
Irigaray, L. (1985). *This sex which is not one.* (C. Porter, trans., with C. Burke). , Ithaca, NY: Cornell University Press.
Kavanaugh, P. (1996). *Selected poems.* (A. Quinn, ed.). London: Penguin Books.
Kavanaugh, P.B. (1997, October). *Leaving the Garden of Eden... the codes of the culture, the codes of perversion, and psychoanalysis.* Paper presented at the eigth annual interdisciplinary congress of the International Federation for Psychoanalytic Education, Ann Arbor, Mich.
Lupton, M. J. (1993). *Menstruation and psychoanalysis.* Chicago: University of Illinois Press.
Lynch, T. (1997). *The undertaking: Life studies from the dismal trade.* New York: Norton.
(2000). *Bodies in motion and at rest*: On metaphor and mortality. New York: Norton.
MacCulloch, J.A. (2004). *Celtic mythology.* Mineola, N.Y.: Dover.
Moi, T. (1991). *Sexual textual politics: Feminist literary theory. New York*: Routledge.
Monaghan, P. (2003). *The red-Haired girl from the bog: The landscape of Celtic myth*

and spirit. Novaca, Calif., New World Library.

Rolleston, T.W. (1990). *Celtic myths and legends.* New York: Dover.

Squire, C. (2001). *Celtic myth and legends.* Franklin Lakes, NJ.: Career Press.

Staten, H. (1995). *Eros in mourning: Homer to Lacan.* Baltimore, Md.: Johns Hopkins University Press,

Wilber, K. (1982). *The holographic paradigm and other paradoxes: Exploring the leading edge of science.* Boston, Mass.: Shambhala.

Two

The Dead Poets Society

Ventures Into a Radioactive Pyschoanalytic Space

In pre-literate societies, the poet is the one assigned by the culture to be The One Who Remembers. As the bearer of this terribly important responsibility, the poet remembers the events of yesterday and today out of a deep and sacred respect for the ways of others, helps her or his people make sense of the lives they are living, and provides for those of tomorrow a sense of continuity with the ways and traditions of yesterday (Citino, 2002). In such pre-literate societies, the poet is The One Who Remembers as an historian, mythmaker, and shaman: The poet is the historian who keeps the oral traditions and tells the tribal stories; the myth-maker who weaves the mythologies of the culture through graphic paintings, drama, and theatrical performances; and the shaman who, as the tribal witch doctor, calls upon the spirit world to cure illness. And as Shaman, the poet...

> .... is one who knows that there is more to be seen of reality than the waking eye sees. Besides our eyes of flesh, there *are eyes of fire* that burn through the ordinariness of the world and perceive the wonders and terrors beyond. In the superconsciousness of the shaman, nothing is simply a dead object, a stupid creature; rather, all the things of this earth are swayed by sacred meanings.
>
> -Theodore Roszak, *The Making of a Counterculture* (emphasis added)

Does the analytic practitioner see the world, people, and life through such *eyes of fire*? Does he or she see sacred meanings in the stupid creatures and the green hued faces of the dead as they speak their timeless presence in the analytic space?

In our highly scientific and technocratic North American culture, shamanesque figures and their mystical ways of living are most probably seen as more properly belonging to the magical world of the poet-philosopher than to the medicalized world of the serious-minded psychoanalyst or psychoanalytic practitioner. Indeed in our culture, the traditions of pre-literate societies are most often viewed as superstitious and backwards with the shaman signifying little more than an interesting, iconic figure of a primitive, third world culture. And the Sham(an's) magic represents little more than the ritual and incantation that envelopes the highly suggestible believers of primitive cultural mythologies. And yet, Why is it that the treatment for madness is likely to do much better when provided by a shaman with witch-doctor potions in such countries as India and Nigeria than when provided by a mental health professional with medical-doctor anti-psychotic medications in North America? In the history of medical treatments for madness, outcomes for people in the United States with schizophrenia have actually worsened over the past twenty five years, advances in the neurosciences notwithstanding. What is the mystery, magic and muscle of the shaman's poesy of care - *beyond not keeping people regularly medicated* - that help so many people in these so-called primitive countries? (Whitaker, 2002) And how might these secrets of care contribute to the practitioner's ways of presencing, knowing, and speaking in the analytic space?

Through the ages, various cultures have recognized the poet's sacred responsibility to be The One Who Remembers. In *The Eye of the Poet*, David Citino (2002) takes a look backwards in history to see what was meant by *the poet* at different times in different cultures. In ancient Egypt, the poet was signified by the Arabic *sha'ir*, meaning The Knower; in ancient Greece, by the Greek *poeites*, The Maker; in ancient Rome, by the Latin vates, The Seer; and, in the ancient Celtic nations, by the Gaelic *seanchaidh*, The Narrator. In our more contemporary westernized cultures, is the analytic practitioner not The One Who Remembers in words in the analytic space? Is he or she not a poet of the mind? Indeed, a mind poet? In his poetical attempt to understand poets, Gary Snyder speaks of the Mind Poet in this way:

A Mind Poet
Stays in the house.
The house is empty
And it has no walls.
The poem
Is seen from all sides,
Everywhere,
At once.

(Snyder, *As for Poets, 1992,*
cited in Citano, 2002, p. 203)

As a Mind Poet, might the analytic practitioner benefit from considering the euphonics of poetic imagination, vision, and metaphor as seen through the eyes of *Sha'ir*, from Egypt; *Poietes*, from Greece; Vates, from Rome; and, *Seanchaidh*, from the Celtic lands? This chapter gathers together this multicultural society of dead poets to speak from their respective wisdoms to something of the nature of the analytic space and the poetic utterances and understandings that unfold therein. In the context of process material, the unfinished sketch of the Radioactive Man is considered as it might be fleshed out in words through the eyes of the Dead Poets Society contributing, I hope, to a way of understanding the person's sacred meanings, their links with his phenomenal past, and the poetics of the sense-making of the non-sense-making in the analytic space.

In this chapter, the analytic space is conceptualized as an invisible geometry of interrelated and interconnected matrices of meaning; constituted by determined but unpredictable dynamical systems; and, organized by the inexplicable something more of the mystery, magic, and spirituality of being human. It is a space filled with multi-determined, -leveled, and -layered imagery; the juxtaposition of opposites and contradictions; and, the various tensions and parallelisms of multiple systems of signification and levels of order. The analytic space is understood as a timeless and spaceless —yet, time and space-filled—sphere of conflict, dilemma, and the paradoxical; the poetics of this analytic space speak the ambiguities, indeterminacies, and uncertainties found in everyday life. Those who enter the analytic space enter a dense thicket of meaning; are surrounded by the multiplicity of its imagery and meanings; and collaboratively participate in wording certain life experiences that more fully flesh out the unfinished sketches of self. The following is from the perspective of a skeptical phenomenalist and is intended as a contribution to the study of the psychoanalytic arts.

THE UNFINISHED SKETCH OF THE RADIOACTIVE MAN

> The powerful play of life goes on. And you may contribute
> a verse. What might your verse be?
> - English professor John Keating in *Dead Poets Society*

When we first met, Mr. J. was in his early thirties living in a group home for the mentally ill.[2] He was about six feet tall; had very fine, reddish-blonde hair; and, was quite thin and pale. He spoke and moved as if trying not to disturb the very air around him. He seemed quite shy, lonely, and sad. He was interviewing people to decide with whom he might begin psychoanalysis. During the last semester of his senior year at university, Mr. J. had been hospitalized for a psychotic break which took place, interestingly, during his spring break. He had been in the philosophy honors program and had decided to spend his last spring break visiting Mt. Rushmore. While he was there, the Holy Ghost had appeared and revealed to him that he was Jesus, the son of God. He was to climb the mountain to speak with his heavenly father and the other wise men gathered at the top. Mr. J. had traveled to Mt. Rushmore on his own; he had returned escorted by his earthly father, a much respected minister of the Church. On his return, Mr. J. was involuntarily committed at a local state hospital where he remained for over a year with a diagnosis of paranoid schizophrenia with delusions of grandeur. Upon discharge, he began his odyssey through the aftercare system, participating in various treatment programs and taking each of the new miracle drugs as they made their appearance in the marketplace. Since his first hospitalization ten years prior, he had been hospitalized at various state hospitals some 15-18 times with his length of stay lasting from several weeks to several months.

Mr. J. had decided to enter psychoanalysis. His previous therapies, he said, consisted of responding to questions and following his therapist's directions. He now wanted to talk and see what he was saying. He had made this decision, he said, after conducting a self-designed experiment carried out under well-controlled conditions, for example, at different times of the day or night, after eating different amounts and kinds of food, and after increasing or decreasing his prescribed dosages of medication. His experimental procedure was as follows: Lying in bed late at night in the group home, he would pick up his latest Superman comic book. He was able to see the pictures, read the words, and follow the story line without difficulty. On picking up his philosophy book, however, the words became so blurred he could not read them; the narrative passages could not be deciphered; and inevitably, his mind wandered to Star Trek and the adventures of Captain Kirk, Dr. Spock, and the Klingons.[3] He was a profound disappointment to his philosophy teacher, his much-admired and well-liked mentor. He had wanted to be like him in every way but was unable to read, much less master, his philosophy text. Manipulating the experimental conditions seemed to make no difference: Mr. J could read the comic book but could not read his philosophy book. It seemed to him that if his schizophrenia was the consequence of a bio-chemical imbalance, he would not be able to read either text. It did not make sense to him that a biochemical imbalance could differentiate between his reading of Superman or Nietzsche. He wondered if his *affliction* might be related to something else. What did I think? He seemed quite interested with the idea that maybe his *affliction* was related to *affection*. "Ahhhh", he slowly said, "the A words—*Affliction*, *Affection*, and *Analysis*."

As part of my interview, Mr. J. had prepared a list of questions for me written on a legal-sized pad of paper: *How did I understand delusions and hallucinations? What were my experiences in working in mental hospitals? What did I think of them? and What were my views on involuntary commitments? and medications?* As we concluded with these more formally posed questions, Mr. J. mentioned that for the past several minutes he had been seeing a bouquet of red roses over my left shoulder and a sharpened guillotine over my right shoulder. And then, he fell silent. I responded that I thought that maybe the interview was not yet quite over. It seemed to me that the images of the roses and the guillotine were a way of telling us something more about himself and his experiences of our meeting; the feelings of affection experienced between us; and, perhaps, his wondering if such feelings of affection would have to be cut off as they had been with his father and teacher...or would we be able to talk about them in analysis? He looked at me for a short while, smiled softly, and wrote something down on his pad of paper. And then he said, "When I was a little boy, I was fascinated with the French Revolution. Is this what they mean by 'castration anxiety' - I mean, like cutting off my feelings with a guillotine and all?" I mentioned that it certainly could be. And I also mentioned that, as time was drawing to a close, we were going to have to stop - at the risk of cutting short our budding conversation. He chuckled and said that he was going to meet with some other people on his list and then let me know what he decided. "After all," he said, "it is quite a major decision." I agreed. And we ended our first meeting.

About two weeks later, Mr. J. called. We set up a time, met, talked, and eventually agreed to meet once each week due to his financial situation; payment was from monies saved from his SSI disability checks. And then Mr. J. asked another question, "Can I lay on the couch?" He had read much of the analytic literature and was well aware that the couch was *not* to be used with psychotics because of the development of intense, regressive transferences. "However," he explained, "it *is* my time *and* it's my dime. And besides, What's gonna' happen? Like I've never gone psychotic *sitting down or standing up*?" We talked further and agreed to use the couch. For a long time, Mr. J. continued to bring his list of questions with him to each of our meetings, placing the pad of paper under his hip as he laid down. In a strange kind of way, we seemed to continue addressing the questions Mr. J. had introduced during our first meeting. And the narrative of

Captain Kirk, Dr. Spock, and the Klingons contextualized our venture into deep analytic space.

SHA'IR, THE KNOWER FROM EGYPT AND POIETES, THE MAKER FROM GREECE

> We read and write poetry because we are members of the human race. And the human race is filled with passion.
> - English professor John Keating in *Dead Poets Society*

Often times, a kind of unworded poetry seems to be expressed in the overarching rythyms and patterns of everyday life. If the meaning of poetry extends beyond...*an intricate and careful patterning of words*...to include...*the painting of pictures in a descriptive mode* ..and also, to include... *the language of figures in motion*, then...

> from a psychoanalytic point of view, everyone is poetic; everyone dreams in metaphor and generates symbolic meanings in the process of living. Even in their prose, people have unwittingly been speaking poetry all along. ...Creativity is no longer the exclusive preserve of the divinely inspired or the few great poets.
> (Jonathan Lear, 1995, p. 25)

The meaning of poetry is no longer limited to a genre of expression found in books of poetry. In the poetics of everyday life, words and actions paint pictures that have meaning and purpose, indeed, multiple meanings and purposes. And within the overarching context of life, each element of one's poetic metaphor comes together to create and communicate meaningful patterns and designs, if not a multiplicity of interrelated patterns and designs, that speak to something about the ideothetic nature of one's organizing experiences of everyday life. People are inherently the makers and interpreters of meaning as they go about the business of living their everyday lives.

In ancient Egypt, the poet was *Sha'ir* which literally translates as The Knower. And in the analytic space, *Sha'ir* is the Knower of that which cannot be forgotten but, at the same time, cannot be remembered in words. In ancient Greece, the poet was *Poietes*, the Maker - the Maker who made meaning out of nothing but images, words, and pictures. In the analytic space, Mr. J is *Poietes*, the Maker of Meaning, the artist who conjures reality from illusion through various signs, symbols, and systems of signification. Mr. J actively generates symbolic meanings in the process of living his everyday life; the meaning made is guided by that which he knows but cannot remember. In this way, his interpretive design of the world restructures, repeats, and relives the thematic rhythms of his life. Mr. J. enters the analytic space speaking from within these organizing experiences; he is as contained in his pictures as his pictures are contained in him. And like an artist, he paints these pictures through his words and the more primal linguistic of his movements. In effect, *Sha'ir, The Knower* joins with *Poietes, The Maker* to select the facts of Mr. J's experiences, organize them into meaningful narratives, and interpret the meaning of those facts in ways that confirm and conform to his pre-existing images of self and other. The dynamic constructions of his world and reality *and* people and life are given expression in the rhythms and rhymes of his everyday life. And in the powerful play of his life, Mr. J's associative construction of the world expresses the poetic verse to be worded in the analytic space.

During the early years of our meetings, a central theme emerged in the analytic space organized around hierarchical, spatial elevations in which I would be big and powerful and Mr. J would be small and weak. When I was big and powerful, I would be sitting on top of the Renaissance Hotel, the tallest hotel in Detroit. And with Superman-like powers, I watched Mr. J. as he went through his day: getting up in the morning, eating his breakfast, going to the bathroom, brushing his teeth, driving through the streets, and coming to his sessions. I was watching over him as I literally watched over him on the couch. When I was big, Mr. J. was absolutely terrified that I would unleash my fury at him from on high if he did anything that might displease me. And in this context, his eyes increasingly averted mine as I opened the door to the waiting room. In a short period of time, he began to turn around in the waiting room as I opened the door; walk *backwards* into the office, face the interior wall, and then sidestep down the length of the wall until he got to the couch. He would then sit down, untie and remove his boots and socks, lay down with his pad of paper under his hip, and pull his jacket up around him as if it were a blanket. Indeed for about the first two and a half years of our meetings, Mr. J. did not look at me. When he did steal a glance, it was with a look of absolute terror as he saw me decomposing with jellied-like flesh dripping and hanging from my skeletal face. Paradoxically, I increasingly experienced myself during this time as watching over Mr. J as if he were my little boy coming into his bedroom, getting undressed, laying down, and getting under the covers at night. And then, I would listen to his terrors of the night, spoken from somewhere in-the-space-in-between being awake and asleep. And for Mr. J to speak these terrors out loud was experienced by him as being (like) Captain Kirk and myself as Dr. Spock aboard the Enterprise venturing into deep outer space where no one had boldly gone before.

In his smallness, Mr. J spoke of his father at the breakfast table laughing with his mother, unaware of his presence; of his being a member of the church choir and his father, the minister of music, not noticing how he sang his heart out for him, noticing only when he sang off-key. His father was the King of Song; he was but the Prince of Song. As the little one, he went largely unnoticed by his father. He was forever alone, unnoticed, and secluded. And in the seclusion of his smallness and aloneness, we traveled through the darkness of analytic space to emerge on various inpatient units he had lived on, entered their seclusion rooms, and for many hours watched -and, sometimes spoke with- the cockroaches as they quickly darted across the floor. And in his profound aloneness, we talked with the Klingons who lived at the center of the universe and of whom he kept asking, Was he placed in the seclusion room to be protected or punished? And he seemed to Kling-on to my voice as we spoke with and worded his terrors of aloness. In so doing, Mr. J. began to feel bigger and stronger. And I became smaller and smaller.... and weaker... and weaker.

As he experienced himself as bigger and stronger, Mr. J spoke forcefully of the building collapsing, crumbling, and crushing little me into a finely ground powder; that which was on high would come crashing down on little me as he previously had feared my cosmic fury coming down on little him. And with the wording of these experiences, I bumped into my own wish to have someone to Kling-on to as Mr. J spoke of his intense urges to get up off the couch; bash my head against the wall until my brains were splattered all over; grind my skull and brains into a fine powder with his boots; pack my powdered-brains into one of my pipes on the desk; put-my-clothes-on, see-all-my-patients, cure- them-in-one-session-while-smoking-my-pipe; and then, go home, fuck my wife and raise my kids better than I ever could have done or imagined. And then, spoken in the holiest of ministerial voices filled with genuflected and reverential inflections, they would all go to church "*as a holy family to receive holy communion.*" Mr. J had become the Father of The Holy Family. Had our intense and passionate intercourse in the analytic space resulted in the rebirthing of his *self* as the Father of The Holy Family? Had my brains become the latest miracle drug to be ground into powder and swallowed like a communion wafer to transform him into The ideal-eyes-d Holy Father? To *like me* became *to be like me* which became *to be me* which became *to replace me and be better than me* in every way imaginable.

As the erotics of these intense passions, jealousies, and competitions entered and defined the analytic space, the three A's of *Affliction, Affection,* and *Analysis* seemed to weave together to spell out his intense hunger to incorporatively take me in as part of his interior design and make-up. These incorporative desires were, perhaps, most graphically communicated one day as he lay on the couch with two blue tablets of Haldol that, held out at arms length, looked to him like the blue sky. As he brought them closer, the Haldol-blue-sky turned into blue eyes. As they came closer yet, the tablets became the blue eyes of his father. And then he suddenly popped them into his mouth, so to speak, and swallowed the blue eyes of his father... and the blue sk-eyes of his father were gone forever. And he was left alone to see the world through his own sad and lonely blue eyes. In each incorporative instance, --the inhalation of my powdered-brains, the swallowing of the communion wafer, and the swallowing of the blue-eyed pills,-- the *other* became one *with him,* and *in him*, and, it was hoped, would always remain a *part of him*, transforming his life forever. *To be loved* was to be taken over and swallowed by the other; *to love* was to take over and swallow the other.

Poietes, the Maker of Meaning, and *Sha'ir*, the Knower, join together in the analytic space to express that which is known but cannot be remembered. And for Mr. J, it seemed that that which was remembered but not known in thought or words was expressed through his living and reliving of these archaic feelings of affection for his father and the other wise men gathered at the top of the mountain and, integral to the rhythmic patterns of his life, from whom he must cut himself off from being *with*, being *in like with*, and *being like*. It seemed that Mr. J was quite helpless to experience his relationships to the world and people in any other way. Following our wording of such experiences, he often experienced himself as floating up off the couch with his anus involuntarily opening-up. And I was experienced as a ghost-like figure inserting a light bulb into his anus to see what was going on inside. I became the ghostly Seer, the one who sees the mysterious, unseen and hidden links between, for example, his singing the holy praises of God the Father in the day-time choir *and* his laying in bed late at night terrified of being visited by the Holy Ghost who watched *over* him; *around* him; and, at times, *in* him with an illuminating light bulb. *Praise the Lord!* Were we bearing witness to the holiest of Primal Seens in which *being seen* was experienced as an anal rape of in-light-in-(the)-ment-(al) by the Holy Ghost? Indeed, were we bearing witness to the Immaculate Conception of baby Jesus as seen through the eyes of baby Jesus? *Hallelujah!* Does the sacred and the profane always cohabit the same poetic metaphor? *A-A-A-men!*

VATES, THE SEER FROM ROME, AND SEANCHAIDH, THE NARRATOR FROM THE CELTIC LANDS

In ancient Rome the word for poet was *Vates*, meaning The Seer, the one who could read

> the special correspondences and signs of the natural world. Birds passing over the left shoulder or right, the entrails of those birds, the alignment of planets and stars, other marks by which gods spoke to woman and man. The seer was consulted before any significant undertaking: war, affairs of state and the heart. The seer could read the future in the textures, landscapes, and weather of the present. (Citino, 2002, P. 179)

In a kind of Star Trek adventure from an earlier time and place, *Vates* saw the stars as twinkling dots in the darkness of the nighttime sky and connected the dots to see people like the Archer and animals like the Bull and the Ram. *Vates*, the Seer, had the poet's vision, described in *The Eye of the Poet* (Citino, 2002) as the willingness and ability to push beyond the limits of the senses to become nothing long enough to become something or someone else. In the non-linear matrix of the analytic space, *Vates* sees the mysterious links, patterned experiences, and hidden meanings as they live in the present moment of the past; (s)he sees the unseen, names the nameless, and connects the twinkling dots in the analytic space. Vates is the Seer of the meaning(s) made by Poietes and remembers in words that which Sha'ir cannot forget. In many respects, Vates enters the mysteriousness of the analytic space as a student of Poietes and Sha'ir to see, hear, and read the poetics of the other. In a sense, the analytic discourse is a poetry reading in which Vates listens as if life, itself, depends on it - because, it does.

Vates knows that (s)he does not know in order to be able bear witness to the story being told through the associative-interpretive process - even if, at times, the words of the subject's story have to be spelled out.[4.] Over the years, so many different meanings of words were slowly spelled out by Mr. J. One day out of the clear blue sky, for example, he asked if I had ever noticed how *sunny* and *sonny* sound the same but the words mean something very different if spelled with an *O* or *(yo) U* ; or, with the word *heat,* "like *heat* from the sun," if the *e* is placed after the *at* then *heat* becomes *hate*; not to mention that the word within the word, *ate* becomes the past tense of that hidden word, *eat.* And also, had I noticed that *un*-clear also spells *nu*-clear; it all depends on where the (yo)*u* is placed. In the poetics of the analytic space, as with poetry,

> every component element - word and word order, sound and pause, image and echo- is significant, significant in that every element points toward or stands for further relationships among and beyond themselves. ...each component can potentially open toward new meanings, levels, dimensions, connections, or resonances. ...Each word has a specific place within an overarching pattern. Together they create meaningful and beautiful designs.
>
> (Wolosky, 2001, p3)

As I gradually came to place my (yo)*u* into a sonny *nu*-position, unclear things, indeed, became much more (*nu*)-clear. And sacred meanings seemed to radiate in quantum-like ways. Was I being exposed to tremendous blasts of the *nu*-clear heat of hate radiating from my s*u*nny little s*o*nny boy each and every time we met ? Was Mr. J.'s unclear confusion a way of protecting himself and me from his *nuclear* clarity? Had Mr. J. been secluded in my room for protection or punishment?

As we learned to spell and came to know how one letter changes the meaning of a word -and, reveal multiple hidden meanings-, the *he* and *me* became *We*, a *We* that pushed beyond the senses - beyond the *eyes of flesh* of two people speaking about the relationship between experiences of the past and present- into the *something more* of the *eyes of fire* that see into the darkness of the analytic space somewhere in-between reality and fantasy, history and fiction, and the you and the me. In Gaelic, *Seanchaidh* denotes the Celtic poet, the Narrator-- the One Who Remembers and Narrates the histories, stories, legends, songs, and the poetry of his or her people, the people of whom *Seanchaidh* knows that (s)he is one (Citino, 2002). *Seanchaidh* joins with Vates in knowing that the essence of sacred meanings can only be found, ultimately, in the interrelated networks of conscious-unconscious meanings that unfold in the analytic space. And in which space anything can stand for anything else. By way of illustration, I would like to present some process material from sometime during our fifth year. By this time, Mr. J. and I were meeting twice weekly. The associative context during the session immediately prior to this one centered on the possibility of Mr. J. taking a management position which had been offered to him at work.

THE RADIO ACTIVITY OF THE RADIOACTIVE MAN: POETRY IN MOTION

> I went to the woods because I wanted to live deliberately.
> I went to live deep and suck out all the marrow of life.
> ~Poet-philosopher Henry David Thoreau, read at the opening of meetings of *The Dead Poets Society*

Mr. J came into the office and hung his new wide-brimmed hat on my coat rack while saying, "I wore my adult hat tonight." And as he was lying down on the couch, he continued, "Could you turn off that radio in the waiting room - it's really loud, its drowning out my thoughts; I can't hear what I'm thinking -" After a long pause, he continued: "I said, 'Would you turn off that fucking radio;' the music is too loud. I work too hard all week to save my money to come here to have that God-damn music drowning me out." With that, Mr. J suddenly jumps up from the couch, goes out to the waiting room, turns off the radio, and comes back into the office. Upon re-entering the office, however, he walks *backwards* to the couch, lies down, and begins shaking tremulously. "You're probably sitting there thinking: 'That poor motherfucker's crazy. It's time to call the cops; Get the attendants in here!!!'... This is crazy. I don't want to come here any more." I ask, "How come?" "Things are going too good!!! I got the promotion!!! They really like me! ... What's happening to me?" He goes on to talk about how he is changing. He is becoming too ambitious and powerful at work. He is going to have *too much* power and *too much* influence as to what happens in the work-place. ... I begin to say, "The image of yourself as being instrumental ..." And like a guillotine sharply cutting me off, he says: "My father was an instrumentalist, I can still here that fucking organ music all over the house." Mr. J was terrified that he had crossed over the lines and usurped my authority in turning off the radio. I said, "It seems that you see yourself tonight moving into a position of power and authority over me. And how terrifying it is to feel the excitement of you being seen *by me* as *The Man,... The Man In Charge* in here. And that I wouldn't like it, especially if I see that you do. It's terrifying 'cause you might want to come here twice as often, you might become twice as powerful; - and then, you might want even more."

"I don't like this at all!!" His thoughts turn once again to being a free spirit traveling by himself across the country on his bike wherever and whenever he wanted: East, West, - North, South. He could still model his life after the movie *Easy Rider*. One consistent refrain in the stories about those days was that wherever he went, he- as a dedicated and zealous Marxist- preached for the violent overthrow of the government and any institutional structure which imposed its will on the lives of others. ...And then, he suddenly grabbed on to the sides of the couch and, Klinging-on with a panic bordering on terror, said: "I'm floating up. I'm going higher up; ... I'm up on the ceiling. I can't get down!!!" And I said, "What do you see when you see yourself as my 'higher up'?" He began to laugh loudly and deeply. And in a somewhat measured and detached Dr. Spock-like voice said, "If I can hire you, ... I can fire you!!" Laughingly, he goes on: "Hi, little boy, you look so tiny down there. Have you been a good little boy, today?" At this point, Mr. J takes his glasses off, lays them on his lap, and inhales and exhales very slowly and deeply. Slowly, he begins speaking of memories when he was a little boy of 6 or 7. He recalled how he spent the entire summer sitting on the back porch steps of his parent's home - scared while waiting for the *sun* to get real bright. His parents had a bomb shelter in the backyard in case of a nuclear attack. He would wait all day for the sun to get bright as he knew that that would be the first sign of the attack. And all day, he would practice running to the shelter from different places in the house so as to be sure to get there first. With the birth of his baby brother at the beginning of that summer, he had become quite worried that he would not be able to get in: There were only three bunks in the shelter and there were now four people in the family. If he didn't get in, he would be left outside in the radioactive fallout. If he did get in, however, who would he sleep with? His thoughts then turned to the many seclusion rooms he had been in over the years. He could never figure out if he was put in seclusion to be protected or punished.

It was at this point that I said something like the following, "Wouldn't it be something if in coming here tonight, all of your thoughts and actions have been orchestrated, without being aware of it, to communicate something to us about your experiences of "rising high." You tell us of *rising high* in management, *rising high* in your own eyes with receiving a promotion; and, something about the experiences of *rising high* in my eyes as we sit here on the back porch steps waiting for the sun to get bright. *How bright do you think the sun can shine? How high do you think my son can rise?* What if being *active with the radio*, as in going out into the waiting room and turning it off, is your way of communicating something to us about the experience of seeing yourself as shining brightly as my s(*o*)(*u*)n *rising high* in the sky, *rising so high* as to have power and authority over me - and wanting to have more; not only wanting to be instrumental in everything that happens here but also wanting to be *The Instrumentalist*.... The Main Man. Then I would admire you, fear you, ...*and* hate you ...because you could destroy me... There was a tense, palpable silence in the room... And so, I continued:

And...what if your being *active with the radio* tonight is to become *radioactive* as in caught in the nuclear fallout outside of this protective space. If I found out what you were thinking and feeling about *rising higher than me*, I would keep you out, lock you out and move you out of this space to where it is *radioactive* out there. The anxiety and fear of being locked out of here is matched only by the anxiety and fear of NOT being locked out of here. Being active with the radio seems to be your way of telling us of the same terrifying experiences as when you were 6 or 7 years old waiting for the sun to get bright... Being *in here with me* is to be trapped in that place of being liked by me - not knowing if you would be sleeping here with me as your father...and, would want to touch my organ... or if you would be sleeping with your mother, bringing with it the terror that I would know what you were thinking, call the police, and have you taken away and locked up as a "crazy mother fucker."

There was a long silence... then Mr. J. spoke: "I woke up this morning and I was feeling pretty good. I spent the night with my girlfriend." Quite nervously, he goes on: "I bounced out of bed, I went over to the dresser and, I FROZE. I saw you in the mirror behind me. You were across the street on the roof with a rifle, a high-powered rifle with a scope. You had the cross hairs trained on my back. You could have pulled the trigger any time you wanted. I was paralyzed; I couldn't move. I watched you back there for about a half hour. Then, you just smiled and left." There was another long pause. And I slowly said, "This morning, I was the Marxist, the Marksman with a rifle. If you see yourself as sleeping with your girl fiend and getting 'HIGH MARKS,' then you fear that I would respond to you as you felt when you were a Marxist - when you were 'A MARX MAN.' If I suspected your excitements, accomplishments, desires, and ambitions, then you fear that I would violently put an end to your power and accomplishments - including your rising high over your girlfriend in bed last night." This was followed by squeals of laughter like one might hear from a five-year-old boy. When he stopped laughing, Mr. J said, "Those one-liners are really great! With you sitting behind me, it feels like I'm 'in your sites' when you mirror things back to me and give me your 'insights'." The last five minutes of the session were spent in a comfortable silence. Every once in a while, Mr. J would shake his head and quietly chuckle to himself as if thinking about what had transpired, and where we had traveled in analytic space. At the end of our meeting, Mr. J once again put on his adult hat, said "Good night," and left.

SOME THOUGHTS ON POETIC METAPHOR, MIND-POET, AND THE MAGIC OF *THE ANALYTIC SPACE*

As The Dead Poets Society ventures into this radio-active analytic space, they venture into the semiotic complexities of poetic metaphor which contains, expresses, and conceals the various experiences of being radioactive: *as a little boy sitting on the back porch steps, as me sitting in my chair with flesh hanging from my face, and as an adult man in my office rising high (above me) in management* ...with all of these meanings *compressed into, represented by,* and *echoing* in the same radio-active movement of getting up off the couch and turning off the radio in the waiting room. In the analytic space, the poetic metaphor gathers and speaks to these multiple meanings and experiences, all at the same time.

Mr. J's radio-active movements could be understood as an intricately complex poetic metaphor which, like an elegant compromise formation, gathers the multiple meanings and correspondences of his specific life experiences and expresses them in narrative form. And in so doing, tells us something about the phenomenal story of his life. For example, with the removal of his adult hat Mr. J leaves the sheltered-destructive space of the office space to become radioactive in the waiting room; reenters the office moving backwards in analytic space-time to where little-big-boys sit on the back porch steps day-dreaming about rising high and worrying about sleeping with their girlfriend-like mothers, all the while terrified of being seen by big-little-father-boys sitting behind them, watching their every move and thought - and speaking the images seen in the mirror. Does the English word *mirror* incestuously play with the French word *mere*, meaning *mother*? Is being seen in the image of mother to be caught in the forbidden-sheltered space of *her* affections? And is *being seen* to be captured in (the) sights -and, wrath- of the ultimate Seer looking in the mirror of the present moment of the past? If little-big-boys are seen in the mirror playing *with mere*, must they then be cut off and guillotined from people?...from family? ... from their very being? Such questions are never ending unless, of course, they are never asked, then they never begin.

The eyes of fire that perceive the wonders and terrors in such poetic metaphor do not create meaning in the subject's poetic verse; they creatively discover meaning in the unseen similarities within and between the subject's poetic images. Mr. J's perceptions of the world are not imaginary; they are quite real. The specific similarities between and within his images derive from that which constitute the real possibilities in his world. A creative *discovery* takes place, when these perceived similarities are seen, spoken, and resonate in ways meaningful for him. The associative-interpretive process does not create meaning by cleverly playing with words.

> Metaphoric truth is the primary substance of the poetic imagination. A good metaphor is not merely a clever embellishment of the poet's vision; it is often the only precise embodiment of that vision.
> (Haley, 1988, p. 3)

As a mind-poet, the practitioner steps into the subject's poetic metaphor and verse. In so doing, he or she enters the story, images and sounds while permitting them to enter her or himself. He or she must walk around in them, smell them, taste them, know them, inhabit them, breathe them, and become them. And at the same time, he or she must be outside of them so as to speak them. The mind-poet must know the story by heart in order to speak it from the heart. In a sense, the *self* of the mind-poet enters the analytic space and sketches in words the image of the *other* as the *other* enters and sketches the image of the *self* of the mind-poet, a paradox best represented, perhaps, by the magic depicted in M.C. Escher's lithograph *Drawing Hands* (1948). In Escher's drawing, a hand is drawing a hand while, at the same time, this second hand is busy drawing the first hand. The drawing of the hand drawing the hand as the other hand draws the drawing hand is forever in the process of being drawn. The unfinished sketch of *self* and *other* is forever in the process of being fleshed out in words through repeated interactive experiences with the concretized *other* - of *self*. In the mystery and magic of the analytic space, the mind poet dances with the ultimate in paradox and self-reference in that each participant-observer in the analytic space, assuming that there is an *each*, speaks with her or himself cast in the image of *other*. We speak with whom we are; we are with whom we speak.[5.] In the action of this wording, the prose of everyday life transforms into the rhythms of a poetry that speaks and writes itself. The person's poetic verse is not only *seen* but is *spoken*,

> from all sides,
> Everywhere
> At once.
>
> (Snyder, As for Poets, 1992,
> cited in Citano, 2002, p. 203)

In the poetics of the analytic space, the experiences of past, present, and future creatively gather; freely violate linearized and sequentialized notions of time, place, logic, and causality; and, dynamically fuse together to re-configure various images of *self* and *other*. In a sense, the mystery of the *something more* of being human seizes the moment in a kind of Carpe Diem of the soul.

As Marley spoke to Scrooge, Vergil to Dante, and the Ghost to Hamlet, - or, for that matter, the Holiest of Ghosts with Mr. J - the ghosts of our phenomenal past speak in the analytic space as they coexist, codetermine, and costructure the present moment of the past. As the Dead Poets Society ventures into the analytic space, they speak with these ghostly images, amplify their muted voices, and try to make sense of that which is non-sense. And therein is found the essence of the magic of the analytic space: The deep and abiding sense that self and other can creatively and collaboratively converse. And further, that this conversation takes place sensuously and warmly with a deep and sacred respect of self and other. Perhaps this is one of the Shaman's secrets of care that might contribute to our ways of *presencing, knowing,* and *speaking* in the analytic space. And as we venture ever more deeply into the madness of the analytic space - where, perhaps, no one has boldly gone before - we might catch glimpses of understanding about people and life, ... and ourselves. And in the mystery and magic of deep analytic space, we might be privileged to bear witness to the subject slowly becoming The One Who Remembers - in words.

NOTES:

1. An earlier version of this paper was first presented on October 25, 2002 in Ft. Lauderdale, Florida at the thirteenth annual interdisciplinary conference of the International Federation for Psychoanalytic Education. The theme of the conference was *The Psychoanalytic Space.*
2. In the interests of confidentiality, identifying information or circumstances have been changed or omitted in the material presented.
3. Throughout our discourse, Mr. J. referred to Mr. Spock as "Dr. Spock" which seemed to be a composite figure of Mr. Spock, the Vulcan, and Benjamin Spock, the pediatrician.
4. Derived from the Latin *servare* (to keep safe or preserve) and the prefix ob (over or against), the idea of bearing *witness* refers to someone who is present, *ob-serving* and evaluating through all of their sense experiences that which is given to be seen (Resnik, 2001, p. 121). One's *presencing* in the analytic space carries with it an, oftentimes, unrecognized and unappreciated degree of participation through the very way we listen, understand, and respond in the analytic moment. Participation from a developmental paradigm rooted in biology, medicine, and the natural sciences, for example, is qualitatively different than participation from a holiographic paradigm rooted in philosophy, the humanities, and the arts. In *bearing witness* to what he or she *ob-serves*, the mind poet has an ethical responsibility to physically and morally *watch over* the *other* in the analytic space. This ethic and theory of moral obligation however, is not grounded in a medicalized set of assumptions, beliefs, and traditions about the nature of mind, people, and psychoanalysis. Rather, it is grounded in the associative-interpretive process, a central principle of which is *pre-serving* and respecting the space in which he or she is *ob-serving* as a spectator and participating as an actor. And to *watch over* the *other* includes the moral obligation to oppose and counter the current industrializing trends in psychoanalysis that might compromise the integrity of the analytic space.
5. Indeed, when is it that the mind poet is *not* interacting and speaking with her or his-*other* in the poetics of the analytic space? Are not my observations, experiences, and understandings of the radio-active man, e.g., my-*other*, inseparably interwoven with my observations, experiences, and understandings of my-*self*? These and other such questions raise far reaching implications for psychoanalytic epistemology, ethics, practice and education.

REFERENCES

Citino, D. (2002). *The eye of the poet: Six views of the art and craft of poetry.* New York: Oxford University Press.

Escher, M. C. (1948). Drawing hands. In B. Ernst, The magic mirror of M.C. Escher. New York: Barnes and Noble Books, 1994.

Haley, M. C. (1988). *The semeiosis of poetic metaphor.* Bloomington, IN:

Indiana University Press,

Lear, J. (1995). The shrink is in. *New Republic*, December, pp. 18-26.

Resnik, S., (2001) *The delusional person:Bodily feelings in psychosis.* (David Alcom, trans.) . New York: Karnac.

Roszak, T. (1968) *The making of a counterculture: Reflections on the technocratic society and its youthful opposition.* Berkeley, CA: and University of California Press, 1995.

Schulman, T. (writer), Haft, S. (producer), & Weir, P. (director) (1988). Dead poets society. Burbank, CA: Home Video,.

Whitaker, R. (2002). *Mad in America: Bad science, bad medicine, and the enduring mistreatment of the mentally ill.* Cambridge, MA.: Perseus.

Wolosky S., (2001). *The art of poetry: How to read a poem.* New York: Oxford University Press.

Three

Frankenstein's Genie-ology

The Magical Visionary Experience And The Associative Method

> ... we must be prepared to consider the scandalous possibility that wherever the visionary imagination grows bright, magic, that old antagonist of science, renews itself, transmuting our workaday reality into something bigger, perhaps more frightening, certainly more adventurous than the lesser rationality of objective consciousness can ever countenance.
>
> -Theodore Roszak, *The Making of a Counterculture*-

In our empirical attempts to de-mystify psychoanalysis, the mystery and magic of *free association* has been gradually overshadowed by the grand and reductive rationality of our scientific world view, vision, and reality. Scientific epistemology, method, and theory articulate normative conceptions of people and assert developmental predictabilities with an empirical certainty. In the scientific visionary experience, every psychoanalytic proposition is the consequence of a dialectic that blends science with humanistic values. In so doing, Freud's legacy is fulfilled. Science has cast its spell over the analytic community, fostering the illusion of an unmediated and privileged access to human development and the mysteries of the mind. Organized psychoanalysis remains committed to the authority of the scientific visionary experience which, unfortunately, has led to a shift in interest away from free association as the primary method and process of psychoanalysis. The central focus has become the development of character and character pathologies, their origins in early childhood relationships, and their reproduction and analysis in the transference. As noted by Anton Kris, "Analysis of resistance and transference, now defined in terms of mental structures and their functions, is regarded as the major vehicle of the treatment, while free association serves as the somewhat neglected hand-maiden to those theoretical stepsisters" (1982, x).

An empirical vision of reality and people combines with our increasingly complex structural theories to further psychoanalysis as an empirical science of mind. In these structural theories, free association is largely contraindicated for those diagnosed with the more severe pathologies, having certain structural deficiencies. As the human soul is empiricized, the method and process of free association, the heart of psychoanalysis, falls by the wayside in favor of predictively knowing the objectives, the course, and the outcome of psychoanalysis. In this scientific world view, the objectivizing gaze of science will eventually remove whatever remains of the shroud of mystery surrounding the human condition.

Magic -that old nemesis of science- has its own visionary experience, perception, and reality. Grounded in the Romantic tradition, the magical visionary experience refers to a mode of thinking, perceiving, and knowing in which everything in the world is inseparably and harmoniously interconnected.[2.] The essence of this visionary experience is found in the transactive relationship we have with the world that surrounds us; we make and interpret meaning. In so doing, we actively construct and experience the world in ways that are at once transformative and autobiographical. As human beings, we actively select, organize and construct that which constitutes "the facts" of our experiences. And we interpret the meaning of those "facts" to conform with and to confirm certain ingrained images of *self* and *other*. Our personal histories are always contained in our perceptions of the world; reality is an extension of our flesh. Our dynamic constructions of reality are our unique forms of self-(auto) life-(bio) writings-(graphical). To the Romantic, "we have either known the magical powers of the personality or we have not. And if we have felt them move within us, then we shall have no choice in the matter but to liberate them and live by the reality they illuminate" (Roszak, 1968, p. 257). For those who have known or suspected such powers, the different reality illuminated leads to an understanding of psychoanalysis in which semiotics is inseparable from ontology and *reality* is inseparable from the systems of signification of which we are a part.

From its earliest of beginnings in Anna O's chimney sweeping, *free association* has spoken to a rather mysterious and magical kind of process from out of which unfolds a gradual sense-making of the non-sense-making. Psychic transformations somehow take place as powerful memories and organizing experiences are worded through the associative-interpretive process. As *method*, free association is a most inclusive way of thinking in which all behavior is understood as constituting a multi-level and -dimensional statement; all behavior is communicative having both rhyme and reason and meaning and purpose. As *process*, free association is filled with mystery and magic. At once, it too is transformative and auto(self)-bio(life)-graphical(writing) (Bollas, 1999). As *method and process*, free association's magic lies in coming to know something of the interrelated wholeness of the subject's experiences. And the essence of its transformative magic lies in the sense that self and other can communicate warmly, sensuously, and respectfully as the reality and centrality of the subject's phenomenal past unfolds in the present moment of the past.

Frankenstein's Genie-ology... is the autobiographical story of how he came to be as told over a five year period of time by an African American man on the inpatient unit of an inner-city state hospital. It is a story that reflects the palpable experiences and inexplicable processes of psychic transformation in the very telling of his story to another via the the associative-interpretive process. The story of *Frankenstein's Genie-ology...* rests on the synthesis and practice of psychoanalysis as a venture into communication via the associative method in a contextualizing metaphor from the performance arts, the psychic theatre of the mind. In this chapter, I first describe the context in which our conversation took place, including the ward's milieu structure, dynamic, and process; second, I present some fragments from our conversations during the first month of our meetings-about-*not*-meeting; and third, I consider certain transformative processes and experiences as they unfolded during one of our first mutually-agreed-to meetings. From this and later associative material, a central organizing experience of this man's life came to be known, namely, his living his everyday life as the monstrous creature created by Victor Frankenstein.

In *The Mystery of Things*, Christopher Bollas speaks to the centrality of the associative-interpretive process in psychoanalysis and the profound sense of mystery this mode of presencing generates in self and others. *Free association*, he asserts, is a fundamentally subversive activity. It subverts the assumptions, logical rationality, and authority of: the larger scientific culture, the participants in the discourse, and the analytically acquired truths and ethic of psychoanalysis itself (Bollas, 1999). The story of *Frankenstein's Genie-ology...* is intended as a contribution to this subversion of authority in the larger scientific culture, in particular, to the analytically acquired truth that the associative-interpretive process is contraindicated for the so-called severe pathologies. The focus of this chapter is descriptive and centers on the poetic-artistic perception of the magical visionary experience; its emphasis is on the associative method as the primary mode of *being, presencing* and *knowing* in the transformational conversation. The following story of *Frankenstein's Genie-ology*...is told from the perspective of a skeptical phenomenalist.

THE AESTHETICS OF THE CONVERSATIONAL SETTING

> "...If each of us is a biological mechanism, each poet is a poetic mechanism,"...to which we might add that the mechanism of transformation from the unthought known object that is *the poem to be to the poetic object* is derived from the aesthetic process that goes under the name of poetry.
>
> Bollas, *The Mystery of Things*, (emphasis added)

The aesthetic process that goes under the name of poetry speaks to the spatio-temporal rythyms and rhymes and meanings and purposes that emerge in the patterned experiences of everyday life. From the Greek *aisthesis*, *aesthetics* refers to a discourse of the body which includes the most palpable and private of sensory experiences. In the traditional post-Cartesian dichotomies of mind and body, aesthetics speaks to the experiential world of perceptions and sensations in contrast to the conceptual world of thoughts and ideas. In the sensate experiences of the ward are found the aesthetics of the transformational conversation's *poem to be*.... I turned the key in the lock, pushed on the heavy metal door, and stepped into the world of the ward. It was about 95 degrees that day; it was much hotter on the ward. The air hung heavy, damp, and still; it dripped with the pungent smells of sweat, urine, and shit. It was a 45-bed, locked, adult-inpatient unit which, at the time, was housing over seventy people; mattresses lined the hallways to accomodate the census-overflow. This was an end-of-the-line inner-city state hospital. By state charter, no one in psychiatric need was turned away: Anyone meeting 401 criteria had to be admitted. In effect, there was no control over admissions to the unit. Literally, there was a milling mass of people to move through to get to the nursing station. It was in this space that the euphemized "underserved and underprivileged" materialized into real, sweating people bumping and pushing up against those sweating others known as the "understaffed and underfunded." This was my first day on the ward and I was on my way to meet with Mr. P. [3.]

Known as *one of the chronics*, Mr. P. had been assigned to me as, I was told, he was "a good learning case." Or perhaps more accurately, we had been assigned to each other as there had been no mutual choice, discussion, or agreement in the decisions involved in our working together. On this ward, the in-house disposition for the chronics was, quite simply, to transfer them to the newest staff person as 'good learning cases.' His former therapist had already told him of his impending transference to me, so to speak, and that I would be meeting with him some time shortly after I arrived. Mr. P had been continuously hospitalized at various institutions since he was 12 years old: He was now 26. Several years prior to our first meeting, he had been clerically transferred from a state forensic center where he had been admitted after beating a fellow resident to death at another facility. Since his arrival, he had become a rather central figure on the ward. Everyone knew Tommy, as he was known by staff and residents alike. He had this so-called "bad habit" of unexpectedly striking out and breaking the noses, cheekbones, and jaws of staff or other residents. His was an equal opportunity encounter: He did not discriminate his assaults based on size, gender, age, religion or skin color - or the nature of one's relationship with him. Mr. P. was very intimidating, particularly when his reputation combined with his physical size: He was about 6' 3" and 250 lbs. His well-known reputation for violent and explosive behavior preceded our first meeting.

When I eventually got to the nursing station, one of the attendants directed me to where I might find Mr. P. He was laying on the floor in the corridor not far from the nursing station. His pants were pulled down around his ankles. He was sweating profusely as he slowly masturbated with one hand while looking up and tracing the water pipes under a wall-mounted water cooler with the other. I stood and waited in silence at what seemed to be a respectable distance. He seemed quite aware of my presence. After a few minutes, he looked at me with a cold, menacing look - as if sizing me up - and then he went back to his intense study of the water pipes. After a few minutes, he once again looked at me as if waiting for me to speak. I introduced myself and mentioned that we could meet and talk. Indeed, I went on, we could talk about the water pipes and how they worked to keep the drinking water cool on such a hot day, if he was so interested. He continued glowering at me through narrow-slit eyes while at the same time looking somewhat puzzled by what I had said. He said nothing as he returned to his study of the pipes, clearly communicating that I had been dismissed. I mentioned to him that I would be back the next morning and, if he chose, we could meet then and talk. And I left. Later that day, Mr. P. saw me in the hallway, approached me, and said he wanted to leave the ward for the rest of the day. I told him that it would be necessary for us to first sit down, talk, and decide together about such matters. I again mentioned the time that I could meet with him the next morning. He was quite taken aback. He glared at me for some time, slowly turned around, and walked away obviously very angry.

As I soon came to realize, one of Mr. P.'s unspoken and self-assigned responsibilities on the ward was to accompany the medication nurse as she wheeled her cart through the corridors, dispensing her tranquilizing pills, liquids, and smiles. Mr. P. faithfully accompanied her on her rounds, serving as both her silent protector and medication-compliance assistant: People took their meds without protest in his presence. And in a kind of silent bargain, Tommy received something in exchange; he pretty much left and returned to the ward as he wished. The usual and customary procedures for receiving a weekend or day pass were not necessary for him. Long ago, efforts to understand the meanings and purposes served by his behaviors had stopped: His behavior was what it was and represented nothing more. Furthermore, the staff had somehow come to believe that it was good for him to leave the ward whenever he wanted before the ward routine and pressures "drove him crazy." It was around this question of the pass - his leaving the ward at will - that we were to initially and intensely engage.

The next morning I approached Mr. P. in the hallway and told him that there was an office on the ward where we could meet and talk. He had a look of startled disbelief as he responded with a quick and disdain-filled "Fuck you..," turned, and walked away. Later that day, he again approached me in the hallway. He wanted a pass; he needed to get off the ward. We would have to meet and talk about it, I said. Furthermore, I told him that I had set aside 45 minutes three times each week during which time we could meet and talk. During that time, we could decide about the question of passes. Whether or not he decided to come to those meetings was completely up to him. If he wished to have a pass, however, he would have to take the responsibility to meet me at the office on the ward. And then, we would sit down, talk, and arrive at a decision. I then excused myself, saying that I could meet with him the next morning. And I left.

The Romantic tradition is not to be confused with a romanticized view of self, other, or psychoanalysis. Mr. P. had a sophisticated cunning; he had the street talk, walk, and savvy. He knew the system better than the system knew itself. And he knew how to work it. Over the years, the milieu process and dynamic had constructed a stage upon which certain narratives about power and domination over the other were enacted. It was quite clear, in my mind at least, that the dance developing between us revolved around several very basic questions: What was to be the nature of our relationship and the purpose of our meetings? Were our meetings and decisions to be organized around a kind of psychic blackmail ingeniously and evocatively constructed by this intimidating black male? And was the white male to participate by whitewashing the delicate and intricate steps of this dance of terror, desire, and domination by devaluing the black male's blackmail as simply the by-product of a structural or biochemical deficiency, and in so doing, whitewashing the semiotically constructed real in which Mr. P.'s behavior had real power? His power was that of evocatively creating *the real.* His behavior was *the real*; at the same time, however, it went far beyond the literal meaning of *the real.* Was I there to placate his demands for a pass? Or, were we there to try *to understand* the immediacy of his demands for a pass? We both seemed to realize that each of us had a central part to play in this brutally real and unforgiving psychic drama.

The next morning I went to the office on the ward to meet with Mr. P. He was already there laying on the floor across from the door of the office... sound asleep. I opened the office door, sat down, and watched him sleep in the hallway for about 40 minutes. A few minutes before the end of our meeting time, he slowly began stirring, stretching, and waking. And just as I was closing the office door, he approached me in the hallway and said that he was ready to meet... *timing is everything, they say.* I told him that the time set aside for us to meet had passed. We would have to wait until our meeting the next morning. He was furious and walked away cursing and yelling at the top of his voice, clearly identifying me as the one responsible for his explosive behavior—and by implication, for any violence to be subsequently directed at the staff or other residents. His talent in dividing the staff had been honed to a sophisticated art form.

Over the next several weeks, the suspense and tension kept building as variations on this same script unfolded. He would sleep through our meetings; forget the day or times of the meetings; or, be involved in some other activity that coincided with our meeting times. Invariably, he would approach me later in the day for a pass. After about three and one-half weeks, the dreaded long-awaited took place. As I was walking down the hallway after another brief meeting-about-our-not-meeting, I heard what sounded like a freight train coming from behind me. I vaguely recall hearing a lot of yelling and commotion. I kept walking until the last possible rhythmic moment....and the next thing I knew, I was laying on top of Mr. P. with my knee planted firmly in his crotch, my forearm leveraged against his throat, and I had his head locked in a vise-grip. I was telling him not to move a muscle or I would break his fucking neck.... said in an empathic analytic voice, of course, so as to not contaminate the transference. After what seemed like being suspended in time and space for years, other staff finally arrived. They led Mr. P. off to the seclusion room; they led me off to the seclusion of my office-room ...If we gaze into the abyss for too long, perhaps, as Nietsche once said, the abyss, indeed, gazes back into us.

The next day, I met with Mr. P. in the hallway for a very brief meeting. I related to him that I was willing to meet and work with him to try to make sense of why he had to construct things in such a way so that he had to spend his life locked-up in places like this where he had to be medicated, restrained, and secluded. If he wanted to spend the rest of his life living this way, that was his business. If he wanted to try to do something to make it different, that could be our business. I told him, however, that there were a few basic and necessary conditions for us to meet: When we met, we talked. And we talked in words. And, when we weren't talking in words...we tried to find the words for talking. For my part, I would try to not be attacking, assaulting, or hurtful - physically, emotionally, or verbally, no matter how scared I got. At the same time, I would not tolerate his physically assaulting me. If he ever attacked me again, I would call the police and press criminal charges against him. And, I would do everything I could to transfer him back to the forensic center. The choice was his to make. As I was speaking, he was nodding and seemed to be listening; the ever-present smoldering rage in his eyes seemed to not be as intense. I told him that I could meet with him the next morning and that I expected that he would be there to let me know what he had decided. I took this position as I saw Mr. P. as the responsible author of his life. As such, he had the exclusive right and sole responsibility for making those decisions impacting his life, including the decision to meet with me or not. For me to assume and proceed otherwise, I believe, would be to exercise a profound evil.

THE MAGICAL VISIONARY EXPERIENCE, THE ASSOCIATIVE METHOD, AND TRANSFORMATIONS OF THE REAL

In the sensate world of the ward's milieu dynamic and process something of the aesthetic took root in the gaze and guts where our lives intersected and came together. As I was approaching the office the next morning, Mr. P. was coming down the hallway from the opposite direction. We met at the office door and, without a word, we entered the small office. Two large windows covered with wire-mesh screening kept their silent watch over some old wooden chairs, a rickety table off in the corner, and a much-needed floor fan that didn't work. Mr. P. sat down across from me with a cup of coffee in his one hand and a cream container in the other. He was unshaven, smelled bad, and was dressed in old, tattered pants, a sweat-stained undershirt, and his worn tennis shoes. We sat in silence for quite some time as he stared intensely at me through his narrow-slit eyes. Then he slowly said in a gravelly, defiant voice, "I tripped right before I got to you, you know." It was obviously very important that I understood this circumstance. I nodded and said that I figured that something like that had to have happened for me to be on top. He solemnly nodded: case closed. And then in an intense, icy-flat-evened voice, he slowly said: "You...are...a...crazy...son...of...a...bitch." In a matching tone of voice, I replied that that's probably why we understood each other so well... And, that's probably why we might be able to work together, *if* he was interested. Mr. P. was noticeably startled; slowly he began to smile; and then, he started laughing. We both relaxed - a little. He fell silent and continued staring at me for quite some time. At times, he looked around the room but his eyes never left mine for too very long. After a while, he pulled back the lid on the cream container and calmly poured the cream in his coffee. And then he recoiled in his chair screaming in absolute terror and panic as he stared wide-eyed at the coffee. By way of responding, I talked with him for some time about us meeting and talking and his terrifying experience that my white words would swallow up his blackness, ...that hearing my white words would result in his no longer being black. He would become white like me just as the black coffee had become white-like as the cream blended with its blackness. And I spoke as well to his fear that I would become more black the more I came to know him.

In the magical visionary experience, the poetic-artistic perception takes precedence over so-called objective perceptions. The magic of this mode of perceiving is found in uniting the elements of sensory experiences in ways usually not seen and expressing this alternative reality in ways usually not expressed (Roszak, 1968). This mode of perceiving sees, for example, the interrelationship between Mr. P.'s sensory perceptions of the swirling grayness of the black coffee and white cream and the gray-shaded terror of losing his sense of self as his blackness blended with my whiteness. This alternative reality is understood as present in the immediate moment, expressed through the associative-interpretive process, and, waiting -just beyond our ghostly grasp- to be worded in our conversation. In this visionary experience, there are multiple levels of order, meaning, and reality; the poetic-artistic perception acknowledges the interrelationships between these multiple levels. The seemingly disparate and disconnected elements of Mr. P.'s perceptions in objective consciousness as might be conceived in the classical reality of Newtonian physics are understood as actually linked or unified in an implicit or underlying fashion as might be conceived in quantum physics. The poetic voice narrates from somewhere in the space in between the manifest and the implicate. In so doing, it speaks to the interrelated wholeness of the subject's experience. Psychic reality expressed in one sensory form - for example, the coffee and cream - is acknowledged in another form, such as, the experience of self and other. The seemingly disparate elements of objective consciousness are united in the space in between. In this space, the aesthetic process of the magical visionary experience walks hand in hand with the perceptual-sensory experiences of the associative-interpretive process.[4.]

Mr. P. responded to my talking about *white words* and *black coffee* by staring intently at my left shoulder. And after what seemed like a very long time, he slowly said in a barely audible whispered voice that I had a black head on my shoulder - *his* black head. His gaze was riveted to my shoulder as *his head* began speaking to him-*self*. - A man's head that was his own was on my shoulder speaking to a man who was himself sitting across from his own head speaking to himself...and, to whom he was listening intently. In this archaic transformative experience is *self* not interacting with the *other* of *self*? ...And, is *self* not reflecting on *self*? ....Psychic reality experienced in one form, for example, his *self-listening*, is literally experienced, at the same time, in another form, for example, his *self-speaking* to his *self-listening*. He is in two different places at the same time. Mr. P. is external to himself; he exists in the world. At once, he is both the object *in* and *of* his own visual-experiential field. At this moment in time and space, Mr. P. seems to have a greater access to the wholeness of his experience of self and other.

As he cocked his head to one side listening to his *head man* speaking to him-*self*, I mentioned that sometimes two heads are better than one in trying to sort out and speak to some of the confusing thoughts that come up when two people -one black and one white- get together and try to come to know one another, man speaking to man. He slowly nodded, his eyes never leaving my shoulder. I asked him what was it that his *head-man* was saying; he would have to translate for me. And as he sipped his coffee, I listened as he spoke with and translated what he came to recognize as the voice of his dead grandfather. We both became intensely immersed in their conversation. And we both drank deeply from the rich flow of gray-shaded words that bridged the black and white spaces between us; we seemed enveloped in an associative-interpretive process of two people where only one in privacy had been before (Bollas, 1999). As if interrupting his conversation with his grandfather, Mr. P. suddenly looked at me and asked with a certain urgency, "Where is the chart and the others?" - referring to other staff members. I explained that I would not be bringing the chart or others with me to our meetings; rather, I would be meeting, listening, and talking with him about what he had to say. As time was drawing to an end, I said that we would have to stop. If he wanted to bring it up the next time, however, we could talk more about it. He nodded. ...And he did...And we did...

The central focus of our meetings during the following months was organized around The Chart with its various meanings and significances. Most immediately, The Chart was linked to his so-called "bad habit" of striking out at others. Over the years, a treatment plan had evolved in which his therapist along with members of the ward staff met with Mr. P every morning with chart in hand to review what had happened during the previous 24 hours, confront his negative-aggressive behaviors, and prescribe a "reality-based treatment plan" for the next 24 hours. In Mr. P's mind, The Chart was the all-seeing eye in which gaze his everyday life was monitored, understood, and interpreted; unknown phantom staff members constructed an image of himself and his motivations through their Chart entries. There was no arguing with the image constructed or the motives attributed to him. The Chart stood as both the source and object of his towering rage. Meeting with Mr. P. without The Chart or other staff present became for him an invitation to express this rage during the following months. In this rage-filled context of understanding the meaning of The Chart, grandfather continued speaking through his head on my shoulder, periodically transforming, however, into the images and voices of other members of Mr. P's family who offered him comfort, advice, and encouragement. More specifically, the image of his grandfather who visited him and gave him comfort in hospitals during his early teen years became the image of the father he had never known who advised him in his dealings with the staff. Periodically, the image would transform into that of his older brother, killed in a gang fight, who gave him advice on how to deal with the other residents. ... In a sense, it had become Mr. P.'s turn to bring The Chart and those others who supported him and his reality into the room.

Gradually, it came to be recognized that these were the *head men* in his family; they were his people, his lineage, his ancestry. They were the head men in his genealogy. They each gave him something to be understood in the story of how he came to be: Each of his body parts was experienced by Mr. P as coming from a specific member of his family. His eyes were from his dead grandfather, his penis was from his unknown father, and his hands were from his murdered brother. In these archaic transformative experiences, Mr. P.'s family representations were part of the real; his visual and verbal significations constructed and communicated the real; and the iconic language of his *bodymindthinkingspeakingfeeling* was inseparable from the nature of the reality constructed. As we came to know and translate these experiences, it was as if I, too, had become a member of his family who had said, in effect, "Put your head on my shoulder and we will word the story of how you came to be," and then, had gone on to say, "...you have your grandfather's eyes," "...your brother's hands," and "...your father's penis." Was the objective existence of Mr. P.'s grandfather speaking to him a necessary condition for the appearance of his subjectivity? Was the objective existence of the head men in his family a necessary condition for his genie-ology to be experienced as authentic(ated)? ...And there was something more to the story of how he came to be.

THE EMERGENCE OF AN ALTERNATIVE REALITY: FRANKENSTEIN'S LIFE-WORLD

> If something so monstrous on the outside is human inside, is something so human on the outside monstrous inside?
>
> -Anca Munteanu, *Frankenstein*

Several months after we began meeting, Mr. P. left the ward to spend the weekend with his aunt. He returned early Saturday evening, however, with his aunt and her neighbors quite upset. Apparently, on Saturday afternoon, he had cut off the heads of her neighbor's two German Shepherds, placed their heads on his hands, and chased the children around the neighborhood. As he was later telling me of these events, a kaleidoscopic collage of the recurring images of *the head* kept swirling around in my mind: Cutting the heads off the shepherds; chasing the kids with the heads on his hands: being the head man on the ward; looking for a head job by the water cooler; beating people around the head and shoulders; me ready to take his head off; and, the head men in his family speaking through his head on my shoulder with me becoming the head man speaking...This collage of verbal and visual images of the head seemed to represent more than simply the various derivative expressions and experiences of primitive rage and castration anxiety, or some combination thereof.

Transformation from the unthought known object that is *the poem to be* to *the poetic object* involves a transformation of the psychic reality of both participants into other forms of experience and expression. For me, the images surrounding *the head* connected in my mind with two strands of associative material: The Chart and the image of his self constructed from the perceptions of the phantom staff, and the Head Men of his family and the image of his body constructed from their various body parts. Something came together that went something like this: Were we embedded in living out certain archaic experiences that answered for Mr. P.

something further about his understanding of how he came to be? Did the iconic image of Mr. P.'s monstrous act of severing the Shepherds' heads return us in some mysterious way to an organizing idea about the beginnings of his life as a monster-child-man? Was I experienced as a kind of Dr. Frankenstein robbing archaic memories from the graveyards in his mind, selecting body parts from the dead members of his family, and suturing these parts together with my words to construct him as a monster-child head-man? Was he the monster born of our violent coupling and splitting on the floor of the ward in which I as Dr. Frankenstein laid on top of him whispering sweet nothings in his ear? [5.]

At once, Mr. P. was both the image created by other, that is, the monster, and the creator of the image of other, that is, Dr. Frankenstein. In this image of the monster was found much of the his life story: the psychic densities and overdetermined realities of how he came to be, where he came from, and who he experienced himself to be. The verbal image of Mr. P. as *the monster* not only described who he is, but what he does, and shaped what he can and will do according to an inner image and structure consistent with his being the monster. Contained in this image of the monster were the organizing experiences and meanings around which Mr. P lived much of his life such as, for example, chasing and scaring children as an archaic sub-human *monster* head-man. In many respects, the image of *the monster* seemed to function as a kind of hieroglyph which at once depicted the visual reality that it verbally described. Such hieroglyphs interweave in the fabric of significations that constitute our respective realities; such hieroglyphic narratives as The Creation of the Monster are associated with magic and mystery.

In *The Mystery of Things*, Christopher Bollas (1999) rather elegantly poses the presiding question when he asks:

> What is the intelligence that moves through the mind to create its objects, to shape its inscapes, to word itself, to gather moods, to effect the other's arriving ideas, to..., to..., to...? If there is a God this is where it lives, a mystery working itself through the materials of life, giving us shape and passing us onto others. (p., 195)

The *Genie* in *Frankenstein's Genie-ology* refers to this inexplicable mystery, magic, and muscle of the human spirit that somehow guided our associative-interpretive conversation. The Genie of Mr. P.'s *being* was that aspect of his self that evocatively called forth the various body-memory-experiences from the graveyard of his (-mine) *bodymindthinkingspeakingfeeling* in such a way so that they might be sutured together with words in the interpretive process by a like-minded other of self. The rythymic pacing and evocations effecting our mutually arriving ideas in the associative-interpretive process spoke to a poetry and an intelligence through which the story of how he came to be came to be known and worded. And as we ventured into these dynamic systems of signification, we did so without knowing in advance what changes might occur or how or why they might take place. Indeed, in the magical visionary experience, the purpose of the associative method is not for the production of insight nor the acquisition of a theoretically anticipated outcome. Its purpose is, quite simply to enhance the further expression of the subject's process of free association (Kris, 1982).

In the dynamic constructions of our respective realities, we speak *with* and *to* and *from out of* our internal images of *self* and *other*. And with the awareness of The Creation of the Monster as a central and organizing narrative in Mr. P's life, certain transformations took place in the very matrix of our meaning-making conversation. In effect, we entered a different dimension of reality: the life world of the monster ...and Dr. Frankenstein. In so doing, we turned the key in the lock, pushed on the heavy metal door, and stepped into the *world of the word* in which space such vague abstractions as the *mysteries of life*, *womb envy*, and *omnipotence* materialized into real, sweating experiences bumping and pushing up against each other. In the translation and wording of these experiences, a gradual sense-making of the non-sense making continued to unfold in our meetings over the next seven years, at the end of which time I left the hospital - and so did Mr. P.

CONCLUSION

The magical visionary experience does not aspire to scientific status nor does it posit underlying biological referents for its constructs; it neither seeks nor claims validation from the reductive thinking of a medical-empirical ideology. Transformational experiences are something more than -and, different than- that which can be empirically conceptualized, measured, and validated. In contrast to the scientific visionary experience,

> ...the beauty of the magical vision is the beauty of the deeply sensed,sacramental presence. The perception is not one of order, but of power. Such experience yields no sense of accomplished and rounded off knowledge, but, on the contrary, it may begin and end in an overwhelming sense of mystery. We are awed, not informed. ... we have no interest in finding out about, summing up, or solving. On the contrary, we settle for celebrating the sheer amazing fact that this wondrous thing is self-sufficiently there before us. We lose ourselves in *the splendor* or *the terror* of the moment and ask no more.
>
> (Roszak, 1968, p. 253, emphasis added))

If the practitioner is fortunate, he or she might be invited to bear witness to the magical visionary experiences, perceptions, and realities of the transformational conversation, and thereby, participate in the blending of a black and a white magic and speak from within the various shades of gray that can unite two people in the splendors and terrors of their shared humanity. In such a conversation, a more powerful magic and visionary experience develops, a magic that is something more than what the rationality of objective consciousness can ever countenace .... One has to trust, however, in the mystery, magic, and muscle of one's self and other. And in the uncertainties, ambiguities, and indeterminacies of the associative-interpretive process. In so doing, we might learn more about the world, people, life, ...and ourselves.[6.]

NOTES

1. An earlier version of this paper was first presented on November 8th, 2003 in Pasadena, California at the fourteenth annual interdisciplinary conference of the International Federation for Psychoanalytic Education . The conference theme was *The Transformational Conversation.*

2. In Chinese thought, this interconnectedness is reflected in the Principle of Relationship (*Zheng He Lu*) and constitutes the essence of dialectical thinking: Nothing is isolated and independent; everything is connected and exists in the mystical integration of yin and yang. Entities are opposed to each other and, yet, are also connected in time and space as a whole in time-space. In this worldview, *reality* is a dynamic and ever-changing process and the concepts that reflect reality are also active, changeable, and subjective rather than being objective, fixed, and identifiable entities (Peng & Nisbett, 1999).

3. In the interests of confidentiality, identifying information and circumstances have been changed or omitted in the material presented.

4. In my mind, there is a rather central question to be asked about the transformational conversation: Is this a mutual dialogue between Mr. P. and myself? Yes, it is! and, at the same time... No, it is not! As the aesthetics of the magical visionary experience blend with the mysterious processes of the associative method, the associative experiences of Mr. P. as speaker are inseparable from the interpretive experiences of my-self as listener. Wrapped in the literal concreteness and separateness of objective consciousness, Mr. P. and *I* appear as separate and discrete entities as in classical physics. In the realm of frequencies and interconnected potentialities of quantum physics, however, all things and events are spacelessly, timelessly, and intrinsically one and undivided. In this quantum realm, I am interacting *as listener* with my experience of my-self *as speaker* in the psychic form of Mr. P. In its radicality, the hyphen in the associative-interpretive process signifies a dissolution of the traditional subject/object division of western metaphysics. The analyst is outside of neither the system that (s)he observes nor the process of representation of *other*; there is no perception unmediated by the practitioner's perception. Paradoxically then, the associative-interpretive process provides a means for conceptualizing the participation of both *He* and *I* as: separate and discrete beings in the classical Newtonian sense (Yes! this a mutual dialogue between Mr. P. and myself) and as my-*self* interacting with the *other-of-self* in the mystical-quantum sense (No! this not a mutual dialogue between Mr. P. and myself). It is both and neither at the same time. A concrete example of self interacting with the *other-of-self* seems to be graphically illustrated in the associative material that followed.

5. In the context of this and later associative material, I came to more fully understand one of the meanings and purposes of Mr. P's "tripping" right before he got to me on that dreaded long awaited day: an action orchestrated to relinquish his unspoken position as the head man on the ward. With 20-20 hindsight, it seems that the dance of terror, desire and dom-

ination over the previous month had been a form of both of us coming to know who the other might be. His "tripping" was a form of suicide as the head man on the ward in the service of his desire to be rebirthed, in a sense, and begin a new life. In so doing, he repeated his understanding of how he came to be with the hope that it might be understood and worded.

6. *Frankenstein's Genie-ology...* raises some interesting questions for the analytic educator and practitioner: In our educational institutions, do we sever the heads of our respective psychoanalytic shepherds, for example, Freud, Jung, Klein, Lacan, and others, and act as if we speak 'to the young ones' in the authoritative name of The Shepherd? In the name of science, do we use our normative conceptions of people to shepherd the analysand to a theoretically anticipated objective or outcome? In each instance, wisdom and knowledge received and spoken through "the head of the shepherd" substitutes for critical thinking. And our received *identity, purpose,* and *ethics* as analyst-in-the-process-of-becoming is handed down.

REFERENCES

Bollas, C. (1999) *The mystery of things.* New York: Routledge.

Kris, A. (1982). *Free association*: Method and process. New Hven, CT: Yale University Press.

Peng, K. & Nisbett, R.E. (1999). *Culture, dialectics, and reasoning about contradiction. American Psychologist,* 54: 741-754.

Roszak, T. (1968). *The making of a counterculture: reflections on the technocratic society and its youthful opposition.* Berkeley: University of California Press, 1995.

Four

An Ethic Of Free Association

Questioning a Uniform and Coercive Code of Ethics

> In the question of ethics, the emphasis falls on a continuing process of thinking that diagnoses, criticizes, clarifies by means of questions, destructures the components of meaning and power that silently shape our lives together, and also questions the values and concepts that have rulegoverning and axiomatic power in our culture. ...The question of ethics does not arise outside of ethics, but from within it. Its thought is disciplined by efforts to maintain questionableness, by learning how to ask questions in given settings, and by finding its own heritage and problems. ...There is a subversiveness in such processes vis-a-vis the normal and ordinary, a subversiveness not unlike that of poets and philosophers who are routinely excluded or silenced by totalitarian

> regimes. But subversiveness is neither a goal nor an ideal for the question of ethics. Its goal is to rethink, rework, rewrite, to listen again to the cultural inevitabilities that make us who we are and to affirm the transformative process without sense of origin or teleology.
>
> - Charles E Scott, *The Question of Ethics*

A culture's world view, dominant rationality, and core ideology provide the defining context that speaks to how a culture understands and interprets itself. A culture's ethical doctrine provides the text that speaks to the body of values by which a culture understands and interprets itself with regard to what is good and bad and right and wrong (Scott, 1990). A culture's ethical doctrine is inextricably to its view of people and theory of life. It defines, reflects, and perpetuates that which is held out to be the dignity, the values, and the ideals of human life. Finally, the ethical doctrine reflects the ethos, the underlying system of values, which permeates and colorizes the ideological strands in the culture's fabric. This broad-based understanding of ethics speaks to the inseparable interweave of the culture's world view and ideology with its core beliefs and values. As a doctrine, ethics refers to a grouping of principles that provide the moral foundations underlying legitimate knowledge, sound value judgments, and good conduct in the discourse of everyday life. Ethics, it has been said, is the point at which philosophers come closest to practical issues in morals and politics (Hare, 1997). Ethics, it might also be said, speaks to the practical relevance of moral philosophy in the lived experiences of everyday life as both citizens and professionals.

In the psychoanalytic culture, the legacy of Freud has been described as a dialectic in which every psychoanalytic proposition blends science with humanism (Bornstein, 1985). Historically, this legacy has guided the development of psychoanalysis from the paradigm of biology, medicine, and the natural sciences-a way of thinking that continues to dominate in the analytic culture to this day. In this modernistic mythology, a natural science of the mind is unprejudiced and unmediated by theories, assumptions, or values, and humanism provides the values that humanize the harshness of the science and its objectively discovered knowledges. In this medicalized version of psychoanalysis, the largely unquestioned biomedical objectives of curing and healing various psychic structures are contextualized by the humanistic values of caring and helping to alleviate pain and suffering. Historically, psychoanalytic organizations have actively advanced psychoanalysis as a health care profession, or a specialty thereof. Each of the major psychologies of drive, ego, object, and self have understood people from the organizing conceptual framework of symptomatology, etiology, and pathology, and psychoanalysis has been considered to be a medical technique concerned with the diagnosis and treatment of various mental disorders, diseases, and illnesses. Not surprisingly, the moral foundations for ethical directions, decisions, and conduct for the psychologist-psychoanalyst are to be found in a medical code of ethics such as the American

Psychological Association's (APA, 1992) *The Ethical Principles of Psychologists* and *Code of Conduct.* Succinctly stated, the psychoanalytic culture subscribes to a medical code of ethics and its medicalized ethic of caring. Such medical codes of ethics make certain assumptions as to the basic nature of people, assume a particular theory of life and moral philosophy, and adopt a specific ethical doctrine and theory of moral obligation for the analyst and therapist. They provide the body of values by which the analytic culture currently understands and interprets itself with regard to what is good and bad and right and wrong.

This chapter examines first, the largely unquestioned medicalized assumptions underlying ethics codes that govern the thought, judgments, and conduct of the analytic practitioner. It is guided by three conceptually distinct but interrelated perspectives, as suggested by Callahan (1988): *the metaethics, the theoretical normative ethics,* and the role of *applied ethics* in psychoanalysis. This questioning places particular focus on the moral philosophers of the modern era as exemplified by the philosophy and ethical doctrine of John Stuart Mill's utilitarianism, and particular emphasis is placed on the ethical implications and imperatives that derive for the practitioner from a medical code of ethics and its ethic of caring. Second, the question of ethics is reconsidered from the perspective of an ethic of free association which proceeds from a different set of core values and ethical principles, lays claim to a different ethical standard, and defines a different context for the concept of an ethic of caring.

THE NATURAL SCIENCES, THE SOCIAL SCIENCES, AND THE METAETHICS OF UTILITARIANISM

The ethical doctrine to which the psychoanalytic culture subscribes has been an integral part of the Westernized intellectual tradition-a tradition which is, perhaps, best understood as an argument extending through time in which certain fundamental agreements are continuously defined and redefined through conflict with critics external to the tradition and through internal interpretive debates (MacIntyre, 1988). For example, the tradition of thinking and arguing about ethics and morality in the Westernized cultures finds its foundational framework in Plato's *The Republic* and Aristotle's *Ethics,* extends through time to Aristotle's Christian disciple St. Thomas Aquinas' *Summa Theologiae* and *De Regno,* and moves to the great liberal thinker of the nineteenth century, John Stuart Mill.

In the *Ethics,* Aristotle understood human action in terms of ends and means and claimed that the ultimate end of human action was happiness. Happiness was understood as acting in accordance with reason and logic (Norman, 1983). St. Thomas Aquinas was to give a Christian rationale for the legal enforcement of ethics and morality. His thinking went something like this: What is good for everybody in the end is getting to heaven. The attainment of heavenly beatitude is the central common good and concern of the people, of Christianity, and of government (George, 1993). This Christian contextualization of Aristotelian thinking provided a religious justification for the enforcement of ethics and morality, and speaks to the long and sacred tradition of organized religion joining with government in defining and enforcing the ethical standards of the community, in the best interests of saving the eternal soul of the other. John Stuart Mill extracted this Christian spirit and tradition for his ethical doctrine of utilitarianism, which resembles the structure of a scientific theory and formulary derived from a nineteenth-century world view and set of values (Mill, 1974). Of the modern theories of moral philosophy, perhaps none has been more influential in shaping the ethical doctrine and directions of the helping professions than that of John Stuart Mill, the leading British philosopher of the nineteenth century and one of the founders of the modern social sciences.

First published in 1872, Mill's (1990) *Logic of the Moral Sciences* has been acknowledged as one of the founding documents of the social sciences. This document speaks to the belief that all natural phenomena are governed by predictive and natural laws that could be objectively discovered through the application of the scientific method. People are subject to the same natural laws as are physical events. Consistent with a nineteenth-century world view, the objective of this science of human nature was the discovery and application of natural social laws that govern the acts of people. If we know a person thoroughly and know all the factors impacting upon that person, the social sciences should be able to discern empirical regularities, establish normative standards, and predict behavior and conduct with as much certainty as the natural sciences could predict the ebb and flow of the tides.

The contextualizing *metaethic* for the helping professions is found in Mill's classical utilitarian theory. First published in 1863, Mill's (1962) philosophy of utilitarianism has provided the fundamental underlying principle(s) of morality, the primary source of moral obligation, and the theoretical justification for the largely unquestioned ethic of caring in the helping professions. As an ethical doctrine, utilitarianism rests on the metaphysical assumptions of the mathematical sciences of the modern era, including the assumption that the laws of nature, people, and society are mind independent and value neutral. As a moral philosophy, utilitarianism contains the quantitative and qualitative principles underlying the ethical doctrines, standards, and formulae embodied in current codes of ethical conduct for the helping professions, namely, that we should always choose that which will tend to produce the greatest good for the person or for the greatest number of people. Mill's theory of life as expressed in the "Greatest Happiness Principle" states that "pleasure and freedom from pain are the only things desirable as ends" (Cahn & Markie, p. 347). This theory of life has provided the framework for his theory of morality in which actions are *right* and *good* in proportion to the amount of degree of happiness promoted for the greatest numbers of people. Actions are wrong and bad insofar as they produce the reverse of happiness.

As a philosophy, utilitarianism has been one of the major and defining influences in the development of an ethical code and its ethic of caring in the psychoanalytic culture. Utilitarianism provides the standards and the formulary by which actions of the analytic practitioner are assessed in terms of their ends and consequences, their contribution to human happiness, and the prevention of human suffering. As such, it has provided the precedent, the justification, and the formula for ethical directions, decisions, and actions in which the moral value of an action becomes a function of the consequences of that action. The primary concern of ethics and morality for the analytic practitioner following in the natural science-humanistic tradition can be simply stated: A right moral action becomes that which enhances the well being of others (Prilleltensky, 1997). Utilitarianism has provided the metaethics that contextualize and define the meaning of such moral terms as good and bad and right and wrong.

A THEORETICAL NORMATIVE ETHIC: PSYCHOANALYTIC THEORIES AND GOOD MENTAL HEALTH

The natural sciences were paradigmatic for the social sciences: They provided a model for discovering normative ethical propositions and developing a theoretical normative ethic. The establishment of normative principles central to theories of behavior and ethics proceeds from the basic assumption of self-evident axioms similar to those of mathematical theories from which their theorems are derived (Clarke, 1997). Normative ethical principles are conceived on the model of such mathematical axioms and are thought to be as self-evident to the rational mind. The empirically constructed normative provides a standard for people to which their thoughts, feelings, and actions can be evaluatively compared and to which they either conform or fail to conform (Copp, 1995). Deviations from this normative "Ought-to-be" have been understood in psychoanalytic theories as symptomatic of deeper underlying pathology, the cause of which has been attributed to the lack of development of specific psychic structures and functions. Psychopathology has been conceptualized in binary opposition to the normative. Specifically, the psychologies of drive, ego, object, and self -developed in a health care context- have conceptualized differences amongst people as evidences of pathology. Each of these respective psychologies has assumed that people are lacking something quite basic in their psychic structure necessary for their adaptation and survival in everyday life. That which is lacking has been understood as developmental deficits which cause the symtomatology, explain the etiology, and constitute the psychopathology-all at the same time. These theories provide bodies of knowledge about people, structure certain kinds of conceptions of the analyst and the other, and are largely accepted as natural and self-evident in the psychoanalytic culture. Indeed, there has been a disturbing lack of skepticism about the underlying assumptions and implications of such theories that rest on an organizing conceptual framework of symptomatology, etiology, and pathology.

In this ethos of healing, the psychologies of psychoanalysis have provided the rational justification for a theoretical normative ethic in which psychoanalysis is intrinsically good by encouraging, if not enabling, positive mental health in people who otherwise would continue to lack that which is necessary for their adaptation, survival, or quality of everyday life. Significant underlying ethical and normative dimensions upon which such psychologies are based structure the analytic discourse and experiences. Normative propositions inform, if not direct, the practitioner as to how a person ought to develop, how he or she ought to feel or think, and what he or she ought to do in certain situations. All too often these normatively based views of the other guide the analytic discourse to a theoretically anticipated outcome reflecting how he or she ought to be. In a health care context, getting better in psychoanalysis has come to be understood as making progress toward the idealized normative standards of how the person ought to be as a rational, reasonable, and responsible adult, and good mental health is assumed to conform to these normative standards. A psychoanalysis of conformity has evolved in which the normative principles central to both theories of behavior and ethics assume the empirically established Oughts to be natural, universal, and objective standards.

APPLIED ETHICS: KNOWING WHAT IS BEST FOR THE OTHER AND A THEORY OF MORAL OBLIGATION

Modernistic psychologies of psychoanalysis such as drive, ego, object, and self construct a particular view of people based on the standards of an idealized normative Ought, a view that contains core ethical issues in its very assumptions and conceptions of self and other. Such deficit theories of people are inseparable from the prevailing theory of moral life and ethical obligations of the analytic practitioner. The implications for applied ethics are quite far-reaching. More specifically, the kinds of actions and practices morally permissible by the therapist to resolve specific problematic issues in everyday professional life rest on combining insights from the metaethics of utilitarianism and the principles of its theoretical normative ethic, an ethic that assumes that people who consult with a health care professional are, by definition, not fully capable of managing, choosing, or otherwise functioning in an autonomous manner. It is probably in this space of applied ethics where the underlying principles of a theoretical normative ethic most often collide with the professional ethics of many therapists.

Situated in a health care context, such psychologies of psychoanalysis speak from a particular philosophical, ideological, and political position in the culture at large. They are inextricably linked to the discourse and relations of ethics and power, such as, for example, the power to evaluate the other; the power to signify meaning, purpose, motive, and intent; and directly and indirectly, the power to influence, if not abridge, an individual's political, social, and personal freedoms and responsibilities. In a health care context, the practitioner has the ethical obligation to be a social and moral agent, who acts on behalf of the other who is signified as a helpless, powerless, and passive victim by virtue of consulting with a health care professional - assuming, of course, that it is a virtue. For the mental health professional, the moral logic, the goals of moral conduct, and the theory of moral obligation are organized around the self-evident assumptions of easing another's emotional as well as physical pain (Dougherty, 1996). To the question "Who decides what is best for the other in easing this emotional pain?" comes the reply, those who are competent to judge such matters, are willing to serve as repository figures representing the conscience of the collective, and are willing to serve in the best interests of the other. The mythology of blending amoral scientific proposition with core humanistic values provides the largely unquestioned justification for the moral piety of knowing what is best for the other. In effect, the psychological Haves decide what is best for the Have Nots.

As considered and discussed by Norman (1983), Mill's ethical doctrine emphasizes a distinction between the higher and lower pleasures. Those activities associated with reason and the higher pleasures of the mind such as intellection and mastery of core bodies of knowledge are superior to the lower pleasures. According to Mill's doctrine, that which constitutes the higher pleasures is decided by individuals competent to judge for those not competent to judge. Those not competent to judge are individuals who indulge in that which is considered to be the lower pleasures. The right to judge is grounded on the presumption of what a person's own judgment would be if that person could really experience the alternatives to the lower pleasures. As an ethical doctrine, utilitarianism advocates and institutionalizes a hierarchical dichotomy of psychological Haves and Have Nots. The Haves are assumed to have achieved a higher state of being and a more superior position than the Have Nots. In a health care context, the psychological Haves are hierarchically positioned to evaluate the psychological Have Nots. And the Haves are expected to provide for the pathologized Have Nots via an ethic of caring in which doing what is best for the other is assumed, if not required, by ethic and law.

Endowed through higher education and training, the analytic practitioner as a health care professional has achieved this more superior position, thereby justifying the paternalistic use of power and influence to benevolently guide and persuade, if not direct, the thinking and behaviors of fellow citizens. Such an ethic of caring claims its moral justification and the piety of compassionately knowing what is best for the other from normative theories of behavior and ethics. These normative theories have conceptually contributed to constructing a culture of compassionate altruism and psychological victimization in which the Haves benevolently minister to the Have Nots. This medicalized ethic of caring derives from the Golden Rule of Jesus of Nazareth, instructing people to do unto others as you would have them do unto you. According to Norman (1983), utilitarianism extracts from Christianity the essential spirit of its ethics and attempts to inspire people as an exalted ethical religion, detached from its Christian context. A medicalized version of an ethic of caring walks hand in hand with such deficit conceptions of people and assumes foundational moral values for the mental health professional such as compassion, helping, and altruism. And also, such an ethic of caring justifies and requires the moral obligation of looking out for the best interests of the other.

In the role of applied ethics, enhancement of the well-being of the other translates into a moral theory and set of ethical obligations in which mental health professionals are expected and required to function *in loco parentis* for the individuals with whom they meet. As mediated through a medical ideology, the practitioner's ethical obligation to the patient and society is to assume responsibility for the Other, and in doing so, protect patients from themselves, protect society from patients, and protect patients from society. Such is the nature and role of applied ethics as reflected in the various duties to report, to warn, and to protect. Of course, it is to be recognized that the patient is to be protected from the practitioner. Ethical codes are devised to control the potentiality to do harm based on the assumed universal nature of people as inherently evil. The liberal tradition assumes that, if left to the wants, desires, and interests of the individual, there would be a generalized collapse of society into amoral chaos with individuals feeling little, if any, sense of responsibility to the other. If the social contract breaks down, the obligation to the public good evaporates and only self-interests would remain (Neville, 1989). Thus, the liberal doctrine defines individual freedoms and responsibilities exclusively within the social contract. In the liberal tradition, individual rights are ultimately derived from a consideration of the collective interests, and individual freedoms and responsibilities are defined by the group. Thus, the ethical responsibilities of the practitioner are defined by the interests of the collective, authorized by the social contract, and embodied in the codifications of ethics and law.

The ethical doctrine underlying current codes of ethics is constituted by authoritative, systematic, and instructive ways of thinking by which therapists, psychoanalytic and therwise, are to judge social thought and behaviors and upon which they are to base their ethical decisions and conduct in the applied ethics of everyday professional life. Ethics codes for healthcare professionals assume a common ethical standard and set of common values for the psychoanalytic community in (1) establishing shared moral judgments in the analytic culture, (2) defining the ethical obligations to share that information with other health care professionals, and (3) sharing that information with representatives and agencies of the culture at large when the occasion warrants, such as peer reviews, accreditation audits, quality assurance evaluations, assurances of appropriate treatment plans for diagnostic conditions, judicial proceedings, and the various duties to report, warn, and protect.

In utilitarianism the interests of the collective take precedence over the individual. Individual freedom, rights, and responsibilities are defined and privileged by those who know what is best for the other. Ever wonder what happened to privileged communication? It should come as no surprise in these historical and political times that the personal and lived experiences of the practitioner matter only to the degree that he or she conforms or fails to conform to the prevailing ethical theory and obligations as prescribed in the applied ethics for health care professionals. The authoritative authorities have become morally responsible not only for the social good but for the moral character of the practitioner.

The role of applied ethics collides with psychoanalysis if one's version of psychoanalysis does not assume that individual freedoms, rights, and responsibilities derive from the interests of the collective or the state; does not assume psychological structural defects in the person, and, thus, does not assume the moral responsibility and obligation of functioning in *loco parentis* for a person presumed to be neither competent nor responsible for himself or herself; and, last, does not assume the responsibility to coerce another to conform to the normative expectations of the collective. Such a medicalized ethic of caring is, by definition, coercive and immoral for those analytic practitioners and analysands whose principled systems of thinking, beliefs, core values, and personal ethic are otherwise. For them, such codes of ethics and psychoanalysis collide. For these practitioners and those people with whom they meet, ethics collide with psychoanalysis when an institutionalized ethical system presumes, perpetuates, and sanctifies the moral piety of knowing the Truth, the Right, and the Good for the Other. Indeed, for many of this group, fundamental civil liberties are violated when they are required to report fellow citizens to the proper authorities when certain behaviors unacceptable to the collective are suspected. For them, the ends do not justify the means, no matter how virtuous and noble the ends might appear to be when wrapped in the cloak of a compassionate ethic of caring. Are we moving closer to Fascism? Or are we already there and just beginning to catch glimpses of it?

The study of ethics and moral philosophy has been often undertaken as if the underlying principles of ethics and morality were timeless, natural, universal, and unchanging, as if these underlying ethical principles exist independently of the historical and political context in which they first make their appearance (MacIntyre, 1988). Ethical codes, however, are the creation of a particular historical-political community; its doctrine, tradition, and theory of life must be understood in that context. And its historical-political context includes the lived antagonistic relations mediated by the power struggles rooted in its structural and ideological oppositions. For example, the industrialization and commercialization of the health care professions of our own historical moment provide the unique opportunity to see, firsthand, how economic and political forces combine to redefine the very concept of ethical and the meaning of that which constitutes integrity, quality, and caring for the health care professions.

The so-called managed care threat with its emphasis on a business ethic and profit motive redefines the standards of ethics, of practice, of care, and of education. As Farber (1993) has rather succinctly stated: "The two medical models which dominate in the field today are the psychoanalytic model and the biochemical imbalance model; the former is rapidly losing ground to the latter" (p.117). It is of more than just passing interest to note that utilitarianism, as a social philosophy, provides the basic assumptions for cost-benefit analysis and other formal methods of assessment for technological decisions to be made in our health care delivery systems (Barbour, 1993). Those rules and practices that will tend to produce the greatest good for the *greatest number* tend to be chosen in our national healthcare systems. According to a rules utilitarianism (Callahan, 1988), the most ethical decision to be made is that which produces the greatest net balance of social good. The well-being of the larger community takes precedence over the individual.

The professional community of psychoanalysis as a whole is affected by the complex processes, the changing social structures, and the redefinitions of core values by the health care industry and governmental entities. Changing professional standards are being incorporated into an increasingly uniform, coercive, and instructive medical code of ethics. The issue confronting the psychoanalytic practitioner, however, is neither the managed care threat, the business profit motive, or national healthcare. The defining issue is a medicalized psychoanalysis and a theory of moral obligation embodied in a metaethics, a theoretical normative ethics, and an applied ethics premised on outmoded nineteenth-century ways of thinking about people, the world, and life. Ethics in psychoanalysis have become subordinated to the political ideologies and power alliances of our current historical and political moment.

Any consideration of the question of ethics of psychoanalysis moves far beyond an interesting academic debate as the ethical principles (American Psychological Association, 1992) by which we are to abide rest on a supposedly "common set of values upon which psychologists build their professional and scientific work" (p.86) and constitute "enforceable rules for professional conduct and decision making; and, may be applied by state psychology boards, courts, and other public bodies" (p.2). A theory of moral obligation resting on these gratuitous assumptions and this authoritative rationality has evolved in which the questions of legal exposure for the practitioner are decided by the degree and severity of violations of assigned duties, questions of legal responsibility are defined by the standards of a medical ideology, and questions of legal liability are determined by those with the "deepest pockets".

In many respects, ethics has become a remote, specialized, and marginalized body of knowledge separated and far-removed from the lived experience of the therapist's everyday professional life. In its very codification, ethics has been distanced from the realm of individual ethical systems and personal moral issues and has transformed ethics, itself, into a set of instructive, technological rules to be implemented for the presumed good of the other. The practitioner has been transformed into a repository figure of moral conscience, an advocate of the prevailing political ideology, and an agent of social engineering and control.

A uniform code of medical ethics, in and of itself, raises certain ethical and political questions about our freedom to question, to conceptualize, and to practice outside of a prohibitive health care context. It is this very capacity to question certain practices that constitutes our freedom as citizens and professionals (Rajchman, 1985). Like other professionals, analytic practitioners have the ethical obligation to question the received wisdom, values, and pieties of conventional morality established by tradition and directed by customary rule (Callahan, 1988). In a reflective morality, we are obligated, individually and collectively as citizens and professionals, to continuously reflect on what principles will govern our actions. This reflective morality speaks to the therapist as an autonomous moral agent who questions his or her received wisdom and knowledges and acts on the basis of his or her principled convictions. "The way it has always been" serves as little, if any, justification for unreflectively continuing an ethical tradition, perpetuating a theory of moral obligation, or forming a committee to revise, update, or otherwise fine-tune an ethical code based on the model of a mathematical science and the humanistic values of an exalted ethical religion from the nineteenth-century. If we do question our received wisdoms and moral pieties based on a set of principled beliefs, values, and convictions, is there a moral justification, if not a moral requirement, to transgress current law or the current code of ethics?

The industrialization and commercialization of the health care professions has generated a maze of oftentimes contradictory ethical rules, regulations, and instructions to be unquestioningly followed by the healthcare professional. In these political and historical times, it has become increasingly prohibitive and difficult for one to speak easy and to listen easy in the analytic discourse. During the 1930s in the United States, an earlier time of prohibition in the social order, underground speakeasies were developed for those who might choose to frequent such places. In many respects, it seems to me, the analytic practitioners of current times operate a similar kind of establishment when they provide a space and place to which a person might come to speakeasy in confidence in the analytic discourse. They do so, however, at risk of breaking the law and violating the code of ethics by which they have been subsumed as healthcare professionals.

SOME THOUGHTS ON AN ETHIC OF FREE ASSOCIATION

An ethic of free association speaks to the question of freedom and moves far beyond the narrowed definitional concept and meaning of the fundamental rule in psychoanalysis of free association. An ethic of free association speaks to the foundational and implicit meanings of an individual's political, personal, and social freedoms. This view of freedom is premised on the recognition that the authority for a person's thoughts and actions is inalienably his or her own (Neville, 1989). Each person is the responsible author for himself or herself, for his or her own actions, and for the public good. The seat of responsibility is found in the speaking subject.

An ethic of free association recognizes, acknowledges, and appreciates that we are born into preexisting systems of meaning and signification., This understanding, however, does not in any way abrogate or remove notions of individual self-reliance, self-directedness, self-determination, individual choice, or personal responsibility. An ethic of free association values this fundamental principle of freedom and its core values in the individual's political, social, and personal spheres. The fundamental nature of freedom to which I speak is the freedom that flows from the constituted experience of self (Bergmann, 1991). The abridgement of this freedom and responsibility constitutes a deep and profound evil and does violence against the person.

An ethic of free association speaks to this question of freedom and, above all else, the freedom to question. This freedom includes the freedom to question the structures of our traditional social institutions, the assumptions of our received knowledges, and the self-evident truths in the forms of our experiences. This freedom includes the freedom to question the received wisdoms, values, and pieties of the institutionalized truth and ethic of psychoanalysis, the constituted experience of the culture, of the individual, and in the analytic discourse of ourselves as analytic practitioners. This freedom to question is central and basic to a psychoanalysis situated in philosophy, the arts, and the anthropic sciences. From this perspective, psychoanalysis derives from philosophy, is contextualized by philosophy, is fundamentally concerned with philosophical issues, and its discourse is a discourse of moral philosophy.

Essentially, psychoanalysis is considered to be an intellectual discipline for understanding the interplay of human values (Bowman, 1996), wherein reality, good and truth ultimately reduce to the values of the subject (Vattimo, 1988), and each image of self and other is a moral construct expressing what has been forbidden, allowed, and expected in the individual's experience and construction of a social context (Margolis, 1998). As such, psychoanalysis is fundamentally concerned with the moral issues and matters of the enunciating subject and the moral issues and integrity of the practitioner. Situated in philosophy, psychoanalysis is concerned with the soul and the mind in contrast to biochemical imbalances and the brain.

In the *philia*, or friendship, of the philosophers of ancient times, there was found a way of life dedicated to persuing the *sophia*, or freedom in Knowing and Being through their questions and games of language (Rajchman, 1991). It is this *philia*, or friendship, and this *sophia*, or questioning, that speaks to the philisophical friendship found in the analytic discourse. It is this philosophy that contextualizes the discourse of psychoanalysis. As a discourse of moral philosophy premised on a radical subjectivity, psychoanalysis speaks to a way of thinking by which and in which an individual might question the fundamental "What is" of his or her world and life, and the "Why" of that "What is," and in such questioning attempt to make that world more comprehensible, coherent, and meaningful. As a moral philosophy, the focus and purpose of analysis is found in listening, understanding, and responding in the interpretive moment to the quest(ion) of the subject. The practitioner attemps to understand the nature of the Truth, Goodness, and Beauty according to the subject. Psychoanalysis speaks to the something more of spirtuality and the unknowable mystery, magic, and muscle of people as both participants in the discourse are mutually searching and questioning. This unique psychological discourse is understood as a friendship in difficulty, a friendship that contextualizes the struggle and difficulty of questioning the natural order of things in one's world and life, one's personal ethic in the lived experience of everyday life, and in seeking one's identity. This passionately held freedom to question derives from and leads to a different understanding of the dignity, the values, and the ideals of human life. It reflects a much different understanding of the analytic discourse and its ethic of caring.

Friendship in this most intimate and difficult of struggles speaks to an ethic of caring in which one cares enough to attempt to understand the enunciating subject's construction of reality, the interpretive design of his or her world, and his or her interpretive theories as to the nature of that world and the laws by which it operates. Furthermore, this ethic of caring extends to caring enough to attempt to symbolize in words in the interpretive moment the as of yet unsymbolized; to elaborate further in words concealed dimensions of experiences not yet known, revealed, or recognized; and to explain certain discontinuities in the person's experiences from his or her world of significance, meaning, purpose, and internal adaptation. This ethic of caring rests on a different view as to the basic nature of people and a different theory of life and moral philosophy, and has a different theory of moral obligation for the practitioner.

It is certainly recognized that this ethic runs the risk of violating many of the traditional health care values, objectives, and standards of the helping professions such as helping the less fortunate, healing the pathogenic, caring about the alleviation of pain, and curing that which causes the suffering. Such medicalized assumptions, values, objectives, hierarchical orderings, and normative standards of the Ought-to-Be, however, are repudiated by the very conceptual framework and discourse of analysis as a moral and ethical philosophy. Indeed, this ethic of free association is inherently incompatible with such health care and accreditation standards and ways of thinking. Human suffering and pain are understood, appreciated, and accepted as integral aspects of the human condition and life, the experiences of which are to be understood in the analytic discourse - if one so chooses.

An individual's decision to participate in such a discourse serves as its own justification and rests on a fundamental social freedom in which the opportunity to freely associate in the social order is a constitutional right in a democratic society. The authority for one's own actions and decision to participate in such a discourse is inalienably one's own and reflects the individual's claim on authorship and responsibility. Political, social, and personal freedom entails this responsibility for one's decisions and actions. Furthermore, and most importantly, this ethic of free association recognizes that the analytic discourse is of a much different epistemological order than is the social discourse of everyday life: One speaks easy and listens easy in a much different way in the analytic discourse about whatever comes to mind as reflected in the fundamental principle of free association. An ethic of free association involves the freedom to think, the freedom to speak easy and the freedom to live in a permanent state of questioning the "What is" and the "Why" of that "What is," if one so chooses. In such a discourse one may speak easy as the principles of strict confidentiality extend to the very existence of the analytic relationship itself.

It is in the very freedom to think, speak, and question in such a discourse that a different relationship to self is possible, one in which there might be new possibilities for thought or action (Rajchman, 1985). Therein is to be found one's personal freedom in the capacity to choose amongst these possibilities. Freedom, power, and possibilities intersect in this most personal of freedoms: The freedom to choose from various possibilities is power, and the power to choose amongst these possibilities is personal freedom. This personal freedom includes making those political, social, and personal decisions with which society, family, or therapist might individually or collectively disagree. Differences amongst people in the decisions they might make, however, are considered to be "the stuff of life" in contrast to "evidences of psychopathology." The tolerance for such differences amongst people is respectful of a fundamental political freedom arising from the nature of responsibility as subjectively located in the individual. Authority and responsibility for one's own decisions and actions are inalienably one's own. Personal responsibility walks hand in hand with such personal freedom.

From this perspective, the question of ethics in psychoanalysis has a plurality of complex principles and is not reducible to a set of uniform rules, universal laws, or abstract master principles modeled after a nineteenth-century view of science. Psychoanalysis is understood as art rather than science and is conceptualized as an ideographic enterprise without nomothetic laws. As a unique psychological discourse, the analytic discourse is constituted by ethical principles internal to it, the principles of which derive from the context that structures the specific meanings of the discourse. In such a discourse, the character and the moral integrity of the practitioner is central and fundamental. In such a discourse, the practitioner's personal ethic is his or her professional ethic. Such a discourse is regulated only through the ethical integrity and mutual agreements of the practitioner and the other, both of whom are assumed to be capable of deciding, determining, and managing the best and most appropriate parameters of the discourse.

CONCLUSION

In the United States, the identity of the analytic practitioner has been inextricably linked by history and politics with the ethical duties and responsibilities of a healthcare professional. This identity has shaped a medical code of ethics with its largely unquestioned ethic of caring. Such a code of ethics, with its implicit and explicit theory of moral obligation to the collective, coercively erodes individual responsibilities and freedoms in the analytic discourse. Furthermore, attempts to bring the unique discourse of psychoanalysis in line with other forms of rationality, normative principles, and scientific propositions may be at the cost of divesting psychoanalysis of its essence.

Ethics in psychoanalysis has become inseparable from a medicalized system of logic, beliefs, and values. Questions not consistent with this core ideology have been discouraged and suppressed. Questions consistent with and perpetuating the dominating rationality of symptomatology, etiology, and psychopathology have been encouraged and sanctioned. A uniform code of medical ethics is however, by definition, inherently antithetical to those versions of psychoanalysis dedicated to the development of psychoanalysis as a science of subjectivity. There is an absolute incompatibility of psychoanalysis as a science of subjectivity with our current healthcare and accreditation standards. This is not to suggest, however, an abandonment of ethics. To the contrary, ethics as values and judgments returns again and again in the very question of ethics in the lived experiences of the analytic discourse.

The practice of psychoanalysis is the practice of morality and ethics and involves the freedom to continuously place into question the morality and ideology of the culture as well as the very personal identity and ethic of the practitioner and other. Rajchman (1991) encourages making the question of ethics an unavoidable part of ethics and, in doing so, no longer separating who we think we are as practitioners from what we think is proper in analysis, or what the good is presumed or prescribed to be in its discourse. If the question of ethics is to be an integral aspect of ethics, then the practitioner, it seems, must resituate himself or herself in a place in which identity as an analyst or as a health care professional is neither assumed, nor sought, nor received. In this place, identity as an analyst, itself, must be continuously questioned. Such questioning reintroduces the question of our bonds with one another and our communal understanding as to the question of ethics; disrupts and disturbs the complacency encouraged by medicalized traditions, assumptions, and ways of thinking; and serves as the impetus to reconsider, reexamine, and rethink our received ethical doctrine and its values. In doing so, we speak to the as of yet unspoken and unexamined ethical questions in psychoanalytic theory, practice, and education. And, there is a pressing urgency to do so.

REFERENCES

American Psychological Association.. (1992, December). Ethical principles of psychologists and code of conduct. *Amer. Psychologist*, 47(12):1597-1611.

Barbour, I. (1993). *Ethics in age of.technology: The Gifford lectures* (Vol. 2). New York: HarperCollins.

Bergmann, F. (1991). *On being free*. Notre Dame, Ind.: University of Notre Dame Press.

Borstein, M. (1985). Freud's legacy: Science and humanism. Psychoanal. Inq., 5: 499-500.

Bowman, M. R. (1996). On the idea of natural science as a resistance to psychoanalysis. *Psycho-anal. Contemp.* Thought, 19: 372-386

Cahn, S. M., & Markie, P. (1998). *Ethics: History, theory, and contemporary issues.* New York: Oxford University Press.

Callahan, J. C. (1988). *Ethical issues in professional life.* New York: Oxford University Press.

Campbell, A., Charlesworth, M., Gillett, G. & Jones, G. (1997) Medical ethics (2nd ed.). New York: Oxford University Press.

Clarke, D. S. (1997). *Philosophy's second revolution:* Early and recent analytic philosophy. Chicago: Open Court.

Copp, D. (1995). *Morality, normativity, and society.* New York: Oxford University Press.

Dougherty, C. J. (1996). *Back to reform: Values, markets and the health care system.* New York: Oxford University Press.

Farber, S. (1993). *Madness, heresy, and the rumor of angels: The revolt against the mental health system.* New York: Open Court.

George, R. P. (1993). *Making men moral: Civil liberties and public morality.* Oxford: Clarendon Press.

Hare, R. M. (1997). *Sorting out ethics.* Oxford: Clarendon Press.

Macintyre, A. (1984). *After virtue: A study in moral theory.* Notre Dame, Ind.: University of Notre Dame Press.

____ (1998). *Whose justice? Which Rationality?* Notre Dame, Ind.: University of Notre Dame Press.

Margolis, D. R. (1998). *The fabric of self: A theory of ethics and emotions.* New Haven, Conn.: Yale University Press

Mill, J. S. (1974). On liberty. In Mary Warnock, ed., *John Stuart Mill: Utilitarianism,* On Liberty, and *Essay on Bentham.* New York: Signet.

____ (1962). *Utilitarianism.* LaSalle, Ill.: Open Court. (Original work published 1863)

____ (1990). *Logic of the moral sciences.* LaSalle, Ill.: Open Court. (Original work published 1872)

Neville, C. (1989). Freedom, tolerance, and Puritan commitment. In L. S. Rouner, ed., *On freedom.* Notre Dame, Ind.: University of Notre Dame Press.

Norman, R. (1983). *The moral philosophers: An introduction to ethics.* Oxford: Clarendon Press

Prilleltensky, I. (1997). *Values, assumptions, and practices:* Assessing the moral implications of psychological discourse and action. *Amer.*

Psychol., 52:517-535.
Rajchman, J. (1991). *Truth and Eros: Foucault, Lacan, and the question of ethics.* New York: Routledge, Chapman, and Hall.
____ (1985). *Michel Foucault: The freedom of philosophy.* New York: Columbia University Press.
Scott, C. E. (1990). *The question of ethics: Nietzsche, Foucault, Heidegger.* Bloomington: Indiana University Press.
Vattimo, G. (1988). *The end of modernity.* Baltimore: Johns Hopkins University Press.
Wolf, S. (1990). *Freedom within reason.* New York: Oxford University Press.

Five

Wang Fo and an Ethic of Free Association

Poetic Imagination, Mythical Stories, and Moral Philosophy

> The myths as we have them are the creation of great poets... written in a rich and subtle and beautiful language... in their own image. ... In the earliest Greek poets a new point of view dawned, never dreamed of in the world before them, but never to leave the world after them.
>
> -Edith Hamilton, mythographer

In the *Psychoanalysis of Fire,* the French philosopher Gaston Bachelard (1968) notes that science normally begins empirically with observations of reality that gradually lead to an intellectual construct. The arts, however, begin with a constructing power, the imaginative dimension, and embody it in forms that make them objects of perception to others and, as applied to the external world, provide a way to understand its phenomena. In Greek mythology, for example, Zeus, the King of the Gods, ruled the heavens and universe from the cloud-wreathed heights of Mount Olympus. The lesser Gods and the merely mortal looked to him for protection, justice, and assistance in times of distress. At his side, Zeus kept the symbols of his rule as a Sky God, a mighty eagle and a stockpile of thunderbolts which he would hurl down from the heavens to strike down those who angered him (Seton-Williams, 2000). The constructing power of the poet's imagination helped explain the jagged bolts of lightning, the deafening claps of thunder, and the awesomely destructive power of a ferocious summer storm.

In earlier times, the poets' analogy making helped to order, explain, and understand our experiences of the world and life through their mythical stories of the Gods. Furthermore, their imaginative dimension contributed to our understanding and interpretation of ourselves as human beings. For example, in the mythical tale of Eros, the archer of love, and Psyche, the beautiful Greek mortal, Eros accidently scratches himself with his own gold-tipped arrow, falls in love with the beautiful Psyche, and brings her back to life with his kiss (Hamilton, 1942). The tale of Eros and Psyche speaks to the magical powers of love and the mysterious passions of the soul. In so doing, the complexities of our human desires, passions, and experiences became more comprehensible.

In time, the poet became the one selected to receive and translate for others the sacred messages from the gods. And metaphoric truth became the primary substance of the poet's imagination.

> For whatever reason, God stopped speaking to the Hebrews, so the prophet came into being, a man or woman who could hear the words of heaven and speak them to the people of the earth, often in poetical units called oracles. A good part of what Christians call the Old Testament - especially the prophetic books - is poetry, pure and simple. Either the prophets were poets or God is. (Citino, 2002, p. 182)

The Bible contains the prophetical, historical and religious poetry that has played such a powerful role in shaping our history and culture. Poetic imagination has shaped our mythical stories, influenced our various images of God, and helped define the Judeo-Christian ethic of the westernized cultures, for example, the system of values and beliefs, the ethos, by which we determine the *good* and *bad* and *right* and *wrong* in our everyday lives.

Gradually, the poet's analogy making shifted from mythical narrative stories to the realm of literature. With this shift, the poet's constructing power, based on analogy and symmetry in the mythical story, appeared in literature as simile and metaphor (Bachelard, 1968). In time, mythical stories and literature brought psychoanalysis into existence by naming and giving narrative meaning to many of our most human of experiences. In speaking of the relationship between literature and psychoanalysis, Shoshana Felman (1993), professor of French at Yale University comments that

> from the very beginning, literature ... has been for psychoanalysis not only a contiguous field of external verification in which to test its hypotheses and to confirm its findings, but also the constitutive texture of its *conceptual* framework, of its theoretical body. ...Literature...is the language which psychoanalysis uses to *speak of itself* in order to *name itself.* (p. 9)

Literature is the inherent frame of reference by which psychoanalysis names its findings and itself. Psychoanalysis, for example, derives: its key concepts from Greek mythology (Echo and Narcissus), its central theories from literature (the tragic figure and complex of Oedipus), and many of its interpretive insights from the lives of historical figures (Leopold Von Sacher-Masoch and the Marquis de Sade).

While deeply rooted in the humanities, philosophy, and the arts, psychoanalysis turns -rather paradoxically- to the natural sciences for its philosophy and to medicine for its ethics (Lear, 2000). Premised on the Judeo-Christian text, a medical code of ethics defines the system of values and beliefs by which psychoanalysts determine the *good* and *bad* and the *right* and *wrong* in their everyday lives as healthcare professionals. But what about those who understand and interpret themselves outside of a healthcare matrix? Does the mythical story as an imaginative enterprise articulate an ethic for those whose identity is that of a mind-poet, artist, or philosopher? As poetic imagination is central to the development of the mythical story, is the mythical story central to the articulation of a moral philosophy for those who situate psychoanalysis in philosophy, the humanities, and the arts?

Martha Craven Nussbaum, professor of philosophy, classics, and comparative literature at Brown University, considers morality as a form of practical reasoning, or *phronesis*, as suggested by Aristotle in the *Nicomachean Ethics.*[1] She believes that as a form of practical reasoning moral knowledge stands closer to poetic imagination and to those modes of knowledge transmitted through mythical stories than to "formal rules'" as in Kant's morality or "the results of actions taken" as in Mill's utilitarianism. Her conception of moral philosophy and life finds in literature its most appropriate realization. The mythical story, she maintains, is itself a moral achievement; moral life is like a literary work of art (Nussbaum 1987). Nussbaum's view of literature as a form of moral imagination speaks to the imaginative dimension of literature as an essential component of moral life. In much the same way that literature is resistant to paraphrase, moral life is resistant to formulation in universal and formal rules (Kant) or instructive and quasi-scientific abstractions (Mills). Her conception of moral philosophy and ethics requires that attention be given to the particulars of a situation rather than simply to the application of formal rules or abstract principles.

This chapter has a three-fold purpose: First, it examines the Taoist fable from ancient China, *How Wang Fo Was Saved*, in terms of the ethic and values embedded in its central organizing themes: the master-student relationship between Wang Fo and his disciple, Ling, the nature of their relationship to the world, and achieving a harmonious balance between the forces of *good* and *evil.* Premised on the Zen Buddhist and Taoist texts, these themes and values suggest an emotional, ethical, and intellectual attitude that complements and is enfolded within the associative-interpretive process, the very heart of psychoanalysis. Second, consideration is given to an ethic of care and theory of moral obligation as suggested by the mythical story of *How Wang Fo Was Saved* and as illustrated in the narrative story of "Small Change Makes Cents," the analytic conversation I had with a young man I began seeing shortly after his third psychiatric hospitalization. Third, I present some thoughts regarding an ethic of free association premised on the Zen-Taoist text, an ethic more consistent with our inherent frame of reference, the literary arts.

The following story is from the perspective of a skeptical phenomenalist and is intended as a contribution to the study of the psychoanalytic arts.

WANG FO, LING, AND THE KINGDOM OF HAN

> Right now a moment of time is fleeting by! Capture its reality in paint! To do that we must put all else out of our minds. We must become that moment....
>
> -Paul Cezanne, artist

> The old painter Wang Fo and his disciple Ling were wandering along the roads of the Kingdom of Han. They made slow progress because Wang-Fo would stop at night to watch the stars and during the day to observe the dragonflies. They carried hardly any luggage, because Wang-Fo loved the image of things and not the things themselves, and no object in the world seemed to him worth buying, except brushes, pots of lacquer and China ink, and rolls of silk and rice paper. They were poor because Wang-Fo ....paid no attention to pieces of silver. Ling, his disciple, bent beneath the weight of a sack full of sketches, bowed his back with respect as if he were carrying the heaven's vault because for Ling the sack was full of snow-covered mountains, torrents in spring, and the face of the summer moon. (Yourcenar, 1938, p. 3).

So begins the story of *How Wang Fo Was Saved*, an eloquent tale of love, conquest, murder, passion, erotics and jealousy. And, there is something more... Embedded in this tale from ancient China is a system of values and beliefs that contextualizes Wang Fo's way of being in the world, organizes his life experiences, and guides his wanderings through the Kingdom of Han. These values and beliefs are expressed in two of the tale's most central themes, that of the master-student relationship and the nature of their relationship to the world.

> [Wang Fo and Ling met when] one night in the tavern Wang Fo shared Ling's table...The rice wine undid the tongue of the taciturn craftsmen, and that night Wang Fo spoke as if silence were a wall and words the colors with which to cover it (. p4)... At the end of the night, they walked away together with Ling holding a lamp whose light projected unexpected fires in the puddles... And that evening, Ling discovered with surprise that the walls of his house were not red, as he had always thought, but the color of an almost rotten orange. ...In the courtyard, Wang Fo noticed the delicate shape of a bush no one had noticed until then and compared it to a young woman letting down her hair to dry. And Ling realized that Wang Fo had presented him with the gift of a new soul and a new vision of the world (p. 5).

The relationship between Wang Fo and Ling speaks to the master-student relationship central to many forms of Buddhism, particularly Zen Buddhism, in which mentoring is not merely helpful, it is essential. Whereas Wang Fo's ethic cannot be taught, received or regulated, it can be learned. In the Zen-Buddhist tradition, the words and actions of the mentor are far more important than Buddhist scripture as a way of encountering the mind of the Buddha (Levering & Stryk, 2000). And so, Ling apprentices himself to Wang Fo to learn more of his wisdom, vision, and values.

> One after the other, Ling sold his slaves, his jades, and the fish in the pond to buy his master pots of purple ink that came from the West. When the house was emptied, they left it, and Ling closed the door of his past behind him... (p. 6).

And as they travelled the Kingdom of Han, their spirit fully embraced the lived experiences of everyday life.

As Zen follows the breath in meditation, Wang Fo follows the breath in his sketches and paintings. It was said that "they were the most vivid, intense, and alive of pictures. It was murmured that Wang-Fo had the power to bring his paintings to life by adding a last touch of color to their eyes" (p. 7). Again and again, he returns to the breath in his sketches as "he paints the farmer's watchdog, the lord's best warriors, and the delicate young woman who hung herself from the branches of a pink plum tree with the ends of the scarf that were strangling her floating in the wind, entangled with her hair" (pp. 6-7). As an artist and poet, he breathes life into his renderings of the world; his sketches are palpable extensions of his flesh. His ethic flows from his *being* as he interprets and paints the lived experiences of his everyday life. His is an *ethic of being* that moves with the natural rythyms and rhymes of life's natural cycles. Each aspect of living and dying is his subject matter; everything evokes an open, childlike, and innocent curiosity: the green-hued faces of the dead, the rotting carcass of the dog by the side of the road, and the ant wandering aimlessly into a crack in the wall. His *ethic of being* translates into a *presencing* and *knowing* that freely violates our more westernized taboos regarding suicide, death, ugliness, and the profane. Wang Fo's heightened awareness of this world permit his entry into a space where the mysteries of the sacred and profane co-exist, flow through his veins like rivers, and are revealed through the magic of his brushes as he sketches his interpretive encounters with the world.

In Wang Fo's world, everything is harmoniously interrelated and interconnected; everything is sacred and respected as part of the deeper pulse of life; and everything is in the never-ending process of becoming. His world is a matrix of non-linear and dynamic inter-connections, a dynamic totality in which each individual aspect is, at once, affected by and affects the whole system of interrelationships. His universe is in a dynamic flux of perpetual co-creation in which nothing has an independent existence or an essential nature that separates it from all other things. Things obtain their *being-ness* by virtue of their connection to other things; all beings exist and are defined in relation to one another. This principle of dependent co-origination is central to the Buddhist text (McMahon, 2003). It premises Wang Fo's mystical mode of being, presencing, and knowing the world as an artist and poet-philosopher. In his world, everything posseses a form of awareness; everything has the capacity for sensation and feeling. His interpretive encounters with the world reveal his most fundamental mode of relating in which everything has sacred meaning, is deserving of dignity and respect, and moves far beyond the ordinariness of everyday life.

At the core of the Zen-Taoist text is the belief that all things are comprised of the completely impersonal and natural principles of yin and yang. These cosmic forces are understood as originating in one another, and as inseparably interdependent with each other, yet as existing as the opposite to the other (McMahon, 2003). In the inseparable complexities of their relationship, the sacred (yin) is found in the profane (yang), as the profane is found in the sacred. In this relationship, yin is associated with darkness, passivity, and femininity, whereas yang is associated with light, activity, and masculinity. Evil results from disharmony or imbalance in the Tao, yet one force is not to be opposed and overcome. Yin is not *bad* and yang *good*; one force is not privileged over the other. Both yin and yang are necessary and have to be balanced for the optimal functioning of nature; harmony or goodness exists when the forces of yin and yang achieve the state of dynamic equilibrium as illustrated in the symbol of the Tao (McMahon, 2003).

As the tale of Wang Fo unfolds, the imbalance between the forces of *good* and *evil* emerges as its most central theme:

> One day at sunset Wang Fo and Ling reached the outskirts of the Imperial City whereupon they sought out an inn where they might spend the night. At dawn, heavy steps echoed in the corridors. Soldiers carrying lanterns entered their room, bound their hands, and dragged them stumbling to the Imperial Palace where the air was so thin and the silence so deep that not even a man under torture would have dared to scream....They entered a small chamber in which the Celestial Master sat on a throne of jade, his hands were wrinkled like those of an old man, though he had scarcely reached the age of twenty. On his right was his Minister of Perfect Pleasures and on his left his Counselor of Just Torments. Wang Fo had been summoned because he had gravely offended the Son of Heaven: Wang Fo was an insane impostor who had lied with his paintings. The Kingdom of Han was not the most beautiful of kingdoms as depicted by Wang Fo's pictures: mud and stones paved its roads, village vermin spoiled the beauty of the rice fields, the flesh of mortal women disgusted him like the dead meat hanging from the butcher's hook, and his soldiers' coarse laughter filled him with disgust. The only empire worth reigning over was that which Wang Fo alone could enter... And then, like a cut flower, Ling's head was severed and his remains carried away. And Wang Fo's eyes -the magic gates through which one enters his kingdom- were to be burned out. His hands - the two roads of ten forking paths leading to the heart of his kingdom- were to be cut off. Before the punishment was to be carried out, however, Wang Fo was to complete an unfinished painting in the Celestial Master's possession. Unfinished, it was but a sketch of the seascape and mountains. Finished, it would gather the final secrets and capture the mysteries amassed during Wang Fo's lifetime. Refusal would bring the burning of his lifetime of paintings. Wang Fo began working feverishly to finish his unfinished sketch. His impending death increased the sensuality of his desires and the vividness of his colors (p 8-16)..

ENFOLDING THE ETHIC OF WANG FO WITHIN THE NARRATIVE STORY OF SMALL CHANGE MAKES CENTS

> Yin and yang are everywhere. In front and behind. To our left and to our right. Above us and below us. Darkness is the same as diminished light. Light is the same as diminished darkness They are complementa-

> ry. Universal counterparts. Yin does not exist without yang and yang does not exist without yin. Two in one and one in two.
>
> -Cheng Yi, Song Dynasty (1033-1107)

As Wang Fo lives and moves in the deeper pulse of life, so do the participants in the analytic conversation. In many respects, the lived experiences of everyday life are, at once, the beginning point of the analytic conversation, the medium through which the conversation takes place, and the context in which the narrative story of psychoanalysis unfolds and develops, as the following vignette illustrates.

Mr. G. called because his mother told him to do so: He had to get a job and move out of the house.[2.] I suggested that we meet so that we could talk further about his situation. He agreed and we met several days later. He appeared quite nervous as he introduced himself in the waiting room. And as we sat down in the office, he reiterated that he needed help in getting a job, making some money, and moving out of the house. With little hesitation, he went on to relate that he had been hospitalized for hallucinations and delusions on three separate occasions since graduating from high school, some four years prior. Embedded in the details of his story was the recurring notion that each hospitalization took place when he was thinking of leaving home, more specifically, when he was thinking of attending university, moving to another state, or getting a job other than working with his father. I asked Mr. G. if he had noticed that leaving home and getting a job seemed somehow connected to his going into the hospital?. He was surprised. No, he hadn't noticed that, he replied earnestly. He was a hard worker, he said. He didn't think it was because he was scared of work. By way of elaboration he went on to say that since he was six or seven years old, he had worked as his father's helper after school, on weekends, and during the summer. As he spoke about working with his father, Mr. G would sometimes pause with his head tilted to one side as if listening to someone provide him with details he had either forgotten or had inadvertently left out of his story.

Mr. G. had worked with his father for a long time, but he couldn't seem to make enough money to move out on his own. I mentioned that his getting a job seemed to have a lot of meaning for him: not only would he be leaving home, he would be moving out of his very close relationship with his father. He was noticeably sad as he nodded, yes, he had thought about that. As the time of our meeting drew to an end, Mr. G. seemed increasingly frustrated that he did not yet have the solution for his dilemma, but, yes, he would be interested in meeting again to talk some more. Over the next couple of weeks, we met several more times, eventually deciding to meet regularly each week for the purpose of trying to understand more about his leaving home and getting a job. As we more explicitly formalized the purpose of our meetings, we also agreed that he would have the responsibility for keeping track of how many times we met during each month and would bring a check for the amount due on the last session of the month. So began the story of "Small

Change Makes Cents," the narrative story of this young man's struggle to get a job, make some money, and leave his home.

> If you can't find the truth right where you are, where else do you expect to find it?
> -Dogen, *The Enlightened Mind*

As Wang Fo, Mr. G. sketches his interpretive encounter with the world via the associative process; Mr. G. selects the experiences, organizes the facts of those experiences, and communicates his understandings and interpretations of their narrative meanings. If the mind-poet is interested in listening, understanding, and responding in ways meaningful to Mr. G., then (s)he must apprentice her- or himself to Mr. G. as Ling does to Wang Fo, bending beneath the weight of a sack full of sketches, bowing her or his back with respect as if carrying the heaven's vault because the sack is filled with the unknown possibilities of possibilities of the analytic conversation. As Ling, the mind-poet listens with respect to the tissue traces of historical meaning embedded in what might seem to be the most trivial and ordinary of life's experiences, as seemingly trivial, perhaps, as an ant wandering into a crack in the wall. As Ling, the mind-poet knows that the essence of the subject's meaning and truth can only be found in listening to the interrelated networks of conscious-unconscious meanings unfolding in the discourse, in which discourse anything can stand for anything else. At times, each participant embodies the role of the master; at other times, that of the student; and, at times both are, at once, master and student. At all times, however, both are continuously sketching the pictures, mixing the colors, and wording the meanings in the margins of the text of the other (of self) via the associative-interpretive process. In so doing, the analytic conversation provides the opportunity to see the unseen, hear the unheard, and word the unworded - and in this way, move beyond the ordinariness of everyday life.

> Where there are humans you'll find flies, and Buddhas.
> - Issa, *The Penguin Book of Zen Poetry*

About two months after we had been meeting, Mr. G. called about five minutes into our session to say that he did not think that he would be coming that day. He was in the emergency room of a local hospital where his father had been taken following a massive heart attack. He was going to stay with his father. We talked for a few minutes and it was left that he would call back when he knew more about his father's condition. About twenty minutes later, he called to say that his father had just died. ... Was it possible for us to meet later that day? he asked? We found a time for later that evening. When he arrived, he was painfully wracked with sadness and grief, consumed with an overwhelming sense of loss. He sobbed uncontrollably for a long time; his father had been unexpectedly ripped from the fabric of his life. He knelt on the floor in front of me, praying in a whispered voice as if I were God the Father and at other times as if I were his daddy, with whom he pleaded not to leave him. He wanted to die, he sobbed; he wanted to kill himself, he could not go on living without his daddy. I spoke with him about the horrific experience of losing his father and wanting to be with him and talk with him, as well as wanting his father to watch over him, take care of him, and keep him safe. We talked and worded as best we could the very deep, empty hole in his heart. As the time came to end our meeting, he cried, saying that he could not leave. We talked more about his experiences of his father's leaving and that we could continue talking the next time we met. Mr. G. asked if we could meet the next day and talk some more, and I agreed. We met early the next morning and continued listening and responding to his profound sense of loss and sadness.

The mind-poet bears witness to the story told. A story not told in its sensory experiences, however, is not a story... much less, a story told.

AN ETHIC OF FREE ASSOCIATION: "SMALL CHANGE MAKES CENTS"

> You say my poems are poetry? They are not. Yet if you understand they are not- then you see the poetry of them.
>
> - Ryokan, *"Dewdrops on a Lotus Leaf"*

As Zen follows the breath, the mind-poet pursues the desire to translate into words the radical *other of self* as expressed in and through the evocative images of the associative-interpretive process. The following material is from the third meeting after Mr. G's father had died, the session at which the fee was due for the previous month. Mr. G arrived on time carrying two money bags, the kind used at banks to carry coins. He sat down in the chair across from me and opened one of the bags. It was filled with half-dollars, quarters, dimes, and nickels. Without saying a word, he began counting the small change into neat stacks on the table between us. As he counted, he slowly began speaking about his father's coming to this country as a small boy during the Great Depression, the hardships he had endured during his early years, and how, as a young man, he had married and started his own landscaping and construction business. His father was a self-made man; he was a survivor, he said proudly.

> The whole of life lies in the verb seeing.
>
> -Teilhard De Chardin, *Jesuit Philosopher*

Mr. G.'s reverie gradually turned to how his father had advised him to live his life according to two very basic principles. First: *He should never become involved with anyone unless he had the opportunity to make money in the relationship.* This was, quite simply, an essential fact of life - and of survival. There was a very palpable and poignant silence. I spoke into the silence by inviting him to consider that we could, perhaps, understand his desire to adhere to his father's guiding principle during these very hard times of his own Great Depression. It was as if he, himself, had entered the construction business, literally *making piles of money*, even as we met. In so doing, I went on, he was experiencing his father's approval for his participation in this relationship with me, as he made these piles of money. ...With tears in his eyes, he went on to say that his father's second principle was: *He was to never invest his money unless there was a guaranteed return on his investment.* A picture-thought hanging around somewhere in the back of my mind slowly began coming to the forefront. I inquired as to how he thought we should proceed, given that we had agreed that the fee would be paid by check. While bringing all this change was filled, no doubt, with rich meaning should we not, I asked, keep to our agreement? He was silently thoughtful for some time. Then he said, yes, he would bring a check the next time we met. As he returned the half-dollars, quarters, dimes, and nickels to the money bags, I quietly mentioned that it looked like he was getting a 100% return on his investment. He nodded, smiled sadly, and left with the second of his father's principles fulfilled.

> When you meet a master swordsman, show him your sword. When you meet a man who is not a poet, do not show him your poem.
>
> -Lin-Chi, *Zen and Zen Classics*

Mr. G brought the check the next session. Following an *inter-pret* having to do with his coining a phrase regarding the check, I inquired, "Does that make sense?" There was a long pause and he replied "S-E-N-S-E" or "C-E-N-T-S". And we both laughed. ... In that compressed moment in space-time, small change seemed to make imminent (s)(c)en(t)s(e). It seemed that we had made a kind of abstract sense (SENSE) of his previously concrete experience of making piles of cents (CENTS). And then, in the experience of the interpretation, Mr. G received a return on his investment ... if that makes (s)(c)en(t)s(e)? Had Mr. G found a job in the analytic space in which he could make piles of (s)(c)en(t)s(e) and get a return on his investment with the hope that some day he might be able to move out on his own? As we continued meeting, we gradually came to understand that the small change brought in that day was money received from his father when Mr. G was a little boy for his lost tooth, his weekly allowance, and receiving good grades on his report card. Each coin represented a very specific memory-event-experience. In one sense at least, our conversation was for a very long period a time of recollecting (re-collecting) each of these memories, making CENTS/ SENSE of them, and saying goodbye to them. In a very concrete sense, we had plenty of time to do so.

What is Buddha? "Dried shitstick"
-Yun-men, Zen

Mr. G's father had died in early November. He could not be buried, however, until the early spring. His funeral services were to take place in Michigan's upper peninsula where the ground remains frozen deep below the frostline during the cold winter months. Burials took place in the spring with the softening of the ground with the spring thaw. As we awaited the coming of spring and the time for the new beginnings of life, Mr. G. gradually assumed more and more of the managerial responsibilities in his father's landscaping and construction business. As the time approached to bury his father, his thoughts were filled with "working the dirt," by himself, and digging holes for various spring plantings such as small trees and bushes. With the images of his father being lowered into his grave and planted in the ground, there arose from deep within the hole in Mr. G's heart his perfectly preserved rage with his father for leaving him behind as if he were nothing more than ... small change. His anger was experienced and expressed quite directly in conversations we had with his father in the analytic space, about which we were able to make piles of sweet-smelling (s)(c)en(t)s(e). In so doing, we violated deeply ingrained taboos against playing in such sweet-smelling dirt-shit (feces=money= financial cents = intellectual order=control=intellectual sense = piles of sweet-smelling shit scents). A series of questions are posed: What are the implications for the question of ethics premised on the Zen-Taoist text? Does (s)(c)en(t)s(e) = Sensei? Do the interrelated and interconnected multiplicity of meanings of (s)(c)en(t)s(e) come together to speak something more than their individual meanings? Does (s)(c)en(t)s(e) embody the Sensei of this unique psychological discourse?

SOME THOUGHTS ON AN ETHIC OF FREE ASSOCIATION: AN ETHIC OF CARE AND THEORY OF MORAL OBLIGATION

> In America and Europe, God is perceived as the creator of the universe who is in control of everyone and everything. In order to change our fate, we need to pray to Him and He may or may not respond. The Zen view is that the tao is the cause of all being; the universe exists in an orderly form according to three principles originally derived from the concepts of Taoism and Confucianism: *li, zi ran,* and *wu wei.*
>
> A. Yen Mah, *Watching the Tree*

Given Mr. G's delusional and hallucinatory experiences, his profound sense of depression, and his desperate wishes to kill himself to be with his father, what is the mind-poet's ethic of care and sense of moral obligation to Mr. G? It all depends on how the practitioner understands and interprets *self, other,* and *psychoanalysis.* It also depends on the mutually agreed purpose for meeting. Ethics are inseparable from the mind-poets's *identity* and *purpose*. Their genealogy is traceable to the broader historical, social, and political context in which her or his theory of life takes root. Ethics are an unavoidable and inseparable aspect of the mind poet's interpretive context and experience; the lived experiences of his or her ethical life are embedded in the interpretive-enunciative act itself.

THE HEALTHCARE PROFESSIONAL: DO NO HARM

> Without the ten commandments, how will you know what is good and what is evil?
>
> - A. Yen Mah, *Watching the Tree*

In this country, psychoanalysis is understood by history and politics as a healthcare profession or specialty thereof. The analyst is educated and trained to conceptualize in the framework of symptomatology, etiology, and psychopathology; the *Diagnostic and Statistical Manual of Mental Disorders,* fourth edition (DSM-IV); and curative factors. Understanding one's *self* as a healthcare professional situates ethics in a medical context of caring in which the *right* -ness or *wrong*-ness and the *good*-ness or *bad*-ness of the analyst's actions and decisions are determined. Derived from a law based interpretation of the Judeo-Christian text, our medical codes of ethics are organized around an overarching "ethic of saving" the other as in saving the other's soul in religion, the other's life in medicine, and the other's mind from psychotic and depressive illnesses in psychology and psychoanalysis. A medical standard of care for the analyst derives from the physician's cardinal principle: *Do no harm.*

In this medical tradition of caring, the psychoanalyst is expected to function as the psychoanalytic equivalent of Aristotle's *phronemos*: He or she is expected to have the appropriate psychological wisdom and foresight to determine in any given set of circumstances what psychological, ethical, and practical decision or course of action should be taken to ease the pain and suffering for those in their care (Lear, 2000). The exercise of such ethical wisdom and decision making requires, however, that the analyst know the future consequences of her or his actions before acting and, further, that the *right* ethical decisions are those made consistent with our culture's "ethic of saving." To this end, the analyst assumes a certain authority *over* the patient in terms of his or her power to signify the patient's meaning, motive, and intent. And as a psychoanalytic *phronemos*, the medical analyst is ethically and legally required to abridge the patient's personal, social, and political freedoms if he or she poses a danger to *self* or *other*; or, is unable to meet certain basic needs.

The medical principle of *Do No Harm* enfolds within a theory of moral obligation in which the analyst assumes responsibility for the patient's doing no harm to themselves or others, resting on the assumption that the patient does not have the capacity -and, thus is not responsible- for decisions regarding him- or herself or his or her actions. In effect, the analyst is expected to function in *loco parentis* on behalf of -and, in the best interests of- the patient.

As a mind-poet, artist, or philosopher, the psychoanalyst has a different understanding of psychoanalysis, its purpose, and ethics. Embedded in Mr. G's life story, for example, are the moral principles, values, and wisdoms by which he came to understand and interpret his self and other. Ultimately, his moral values are understood as constructing and organizing his objective reality and that which constitutes *the good* and *bad*, *the right* and *wrong* and *the truth* of the lived experiences of his everyday life. From this perspective, the practice of psychoanalysis is the practice of morality and ethics. Its discourse is a discourse of moral philosophy in which the mind poet's moral task is to render -as best as he or she can- Mr. G.'s experiences into descriptive words and nuanced tones organized around his interrelated and harmonious wholeness as a moral and historical being. Understood as a discourse of moral philosophy, the analytic conversation is guided by a very different ethic of care and theory of moral obligation. In contrast to the physician's, *Do No Harm*, the analyst as a mind-poet is guided by the metaphysician's cardinal principle, *Mirror (Reflect) the Suffering.*

THE BODHISATTVA: MIRROR (REFLECT) THE SUFFERING

> The *tao* is the ancestor of all things. It is powerful but it is also invisible and inaudible. It is hidden and nameless *dao ying wu ming* and operates by non-action (*wu wei*) which means non-interference, or letting things take their own spontaneous course.
>
> Lao Zi, Tao Te Ching

From a Zen-Buddhist perspective, individuals do not presume some special authority over nature or others. In the analytic context, the mind poet is not privileged over the other. He or she does not presume to know what is *good* or *bad* or *right* or *wrong* for the other; life, death, suicide, pain, happiness are all aspects of the life cycle. As such, the mind-poet embraces, understands and words the experiences of the subject - as best he or she can -, however they might unfold and wherever they might lead in the associative-interpretive process.

Guided by an ethic of free association, the analytic discourse is understood as a collaborative conversation characterized by a deep respect for self and other, in which conversation the analyst's identity as a mind-poet, artist, or philosopher provides the interpretive context from which he or she understands and speaks to the radical other (of self). Such an identity might structure the purpose of analysis as, for example, more fully fleshing out in words the unfinished sketches of the self (of other) via the associative-interpretive process. And in so doing, tying the question of ethics to the associative-interpretive process, the very heart of psychoanalysis. In the associative-interpretive process, the interpretive act takes root in the mind-poet's view of Mr. G as the maker and interpreter of meaning. As a human being, Mr. G continuously organizes his world in terms of that which has meaning to him. His most basic activity of everyday life is that of interpreting the world and the objective real (as his senses reveal it to be) into forms previously taken to be meaningful. This structuralizing form of interpreting and understanding the world is understood as a basic modality of human existence.

In contrast to a medical ethic premised on the Judeo-Christian text, Adeline Yen Mah (2001), a Chinese physician and author, implicitly suggests a Zen perspective for the analyst as a mind-poet, artist, or philosopher when she states that

> Zen has no creed and does not involve committing oneself to certain definite rules of behavior. It is concerned not with faith but with wisdom, knowledge and experience. Unlike Christianity, which has a creed and a code spelled out in the Ten Commandments, Zen suggests certain principles of action that *help people to discover for themselves* the meaning lying at the root of Buddhism.
>
> (p. 85, emphasis added)

Zen does not follow rule-like commandments. The aim of Zen is to awaken the student (of self) to the realization of her or his own enlightenment. In the Zen view, the universe exists in an orderly form according to the three basic principles of *li, zi ran,* and *wu wei,* concepts originally derived from Taoism and Confucianism. As translated by Yen Mah, *li* means "principle" or "order of Nature." The Zen interpretation of *zi ran* is "to act according to the order of Nature (*li*), inherent in the *Tao.*" And, *wu wei* translates as "taking no unnatural action."

Since the Tao is the cause of all being, all things are in order according to these three principles of the Tao. There is a rythym and rhyme to the universe and to the life world and experiences of people. As the universe is perfect in itself and should not be "coerced" or "forced" to conform to human desires, these three principles of the Tao - *li, zi ran, and wu wei* - combine to speak a radically different emotional, intellectual, and ethical attitude for the associative-interpretive process, a mental posture that could be described as: "Let everything do that which is of itself." In the contextualizing world view of the Tao, *li, zi ran,* and *wu wei* come together to form the conceptual and intellectual foundations for an ethic of free association.

Letting everything do that which is of itself speaks an ethic of care premised on the mind-poet's recognition and appreciation that there is a deeply harmonic purpose and sense to Mr. G's experiences: *What Is*, as perceived by Mr. G, is. An ethic of care arising from the Zen-Taoist text speaks to a deep and abiding respect for understanding this *What Is* of his life world and story. As Ling, the mind-poet travels with Mr. G. for the deceptively simple purpose of understanding the *What is* of his story and experiences and more fully fleshing out in words his interpretive encounter with the world. Wording the experiences of his story, however, is not for the purpose of changing, normalizing, managing, or making better, as assumed by our medical psychologies and ethics. Nor is it for the purpose of saving the life, soul, or mind of the other, as assumed by the Judeo-Christian text. Rather, from a Zen perspective, the mind-poet ventures into *What* (ever) *is* for the purpose of embracing the lived experiences of Mr. G's everyday life (his father's dying, for example), speaking to the various discontinuities between his *self* and the desired *other* (of *self*) (his father being alive and with him), and more fully awakening this *other* (being alive and with him) to life as it actually is, as perceived by Mr. G (his father being dead and gone from him). In so doing, dissolving the duality brought about by Mr. G's clinging to the illusion of permanence of his father being alive as he steps away from the permanence of his being dead.

> Look within, thou art Buddha.
>
> -The Voice of the Silence

Consistent with the cornerstone of Buddhist philosophy - the principle of dependent co-origination (*pratityasamutpada*), everything in the analytic space is understood as somehow harmoniously interrelated and interconnected in an invisible geometry of interrelated and interconnected matrices of meaning; constituted by determined but unpredictable dynamical systems; and, organized by the inexplicable something more of the mystery, magic, and muscle of being human. Everything is in a dynamic and perpetual state of flux; nothing is permanent in the analytic space (*anicca*):

> ... our world is neither static nor absolute. Everything is relative, as in the duality of *yin* and *yang*. Change is the only given, nothing remains the same, and all standards are relative. We are born, we mature grow old and die. Then the cycle begins again.
>
> (Mah, 2001, p. 23)

The conceptual and intellectual foundations underlying the emotional, intellectual and ethical attitude of *letting everything do that which is of itself* are formed by the three basic principles of the Tao: *li, zi ran*, and *wu wei.* The Buddhist's Three Signs of *anicca* (everything changes), *anatman* (there is no self), and *dukkha* (suffering is universal) come together to suggest that all of human life is filled with a shared, ongoing experience of suffering which derives in this instance, for example, from Mr. G's clinging (*tanha*) to the ideas and experiences of permanence (his father in his life) and self (as his father's helper). The mind-poet translates conscious-unconscious process and dynamic, and in so doing mirrors (reflects) Mr. G's suffering so as to help him discover for himself the personal meaning(s) lying at the root of his reality and suffering, however he experiences it to be.

The Buddhist ethic is embodied by the mind-poet who has reached her or his own awakening, which involves touching, breathing, tasting, smelling, and feeling the naked truth of her or his own tabooed objects and experiences. Further, he or she chooses out of compassion to guide others (of *self*) out of suffering. In Zen-speak, the analyst as mind-poet is known as a *bodhisattva* (Brannigan, 2002). As the embodiment of a Zen philosophy and ethic, the analyst as *bodhisattva* speaks the "right speech" of the Eightfold Path that one needs to undergo in order to free one's self from suffering. In the instance of Mr. G, the "right speech" attempts to word his organizing experiences and the depths of his suffering as related to his father's sudden and unexpected death. Understanding Mr. G. as an historical and moral being, the mind-poet attempts to understand his historically developed set of moral values, their role in constructing his objective reality, and, their influence in organizing certain of his life experiences and choices, such as his bringing small change into the analytic space. Thus, the mind-poet's interpretive act is concerned with understanding the personal meanings of the storylines that organize Mr. G's everyday life.

In many respects, the fundamental spirit of an ethic of free association is to wander amongst, gather together, and speak to Mr. G's experiences of his everyday life, fully understanding that the seat of responsibility and decision-making power is situated with him. Mr. G is the responsible author for himself, his life, and his actions, even those decisions made that the therapist or society might not be in agreement with such as, in this instance, the tabooed possibility of his taking his own life. Tied to the associative-interpretive process, the question of ethics in psychoanalysis lies outside the medical and social construals of *ethics* and *the ethical.* It is in this way that psychoanalysis departs most radically from the ethical of everyday life. The analytic conversation is not organized around achieving "happiness," or "the greatest good." Nor is it organized around living "the good life" through the promotion of "virtue" (Aristotle), living according to universal rational rules (Kant), or instructive or quasi-scientific abstractions (Mills).

In this unique psychological discourse, the associative-interpretive process is constituted by ethical principles internal to it, the principles of which derive from the context that structures the specific meanings of the discourse. The mind-poet fulfills her or his moral task by responsibly attending to Mr. G's world of action and consequence and finding the descriptive words and nuanced tones appropriate to its rendering in ways meaningful to him. The interpretive action of translating unconscious process and dynamic into words becomes a lived experience of moral conduct and psychodynamic reasoning, the articulated expression of which relies on a fine sense of the particular details, qualities, and experiences of Mr. G's story. The mind-poet's translation is itself a form of moral action - the action of fulfilling the moral obligation of keeping to the purpose for which we had agreed to meet - to do otherwise would be unethical.

...AND HOW WAS WANG FO SAVED?

> The fundamental delusion of humanity is to suppose that I am here and you are out there.
>
> - Yasutani Roshi, *philsopher*

...There is something more in the tale of *How Was Wang Fo Saved*, something vital and necessary in considering an ethic of free association:

> Ling was dead and Wang Fo was to finish his sketch for the Celestial Master before his execution. Wang Fo began by adding a touch of pink to the very tip of the wing of a cloud perched on a mountain. He then began painting the surface of the sea. And as he painted the liquid greens and blues, the jade floor in this deep inner space of the Celestial Master's chamber became increasingly damp. Water began deepening on the floor, as the strokes from Wang Fo's brush brought life to a fragile rowboat. And the rythmic sounds of its oars rose suddenly, quick and eager like the beating of a bird's wings with the sound gently filling the whole room. The water kept rising, extinguishing the red-hot iron waiting to put out Wang Fo's eyes. The silence of the jade blue sea was so deep one could have heard a tear drop as Ling, wearing a strange red scarf around his neck, suddenly appeared and stood next to Wang Fo who said to him softly, ... "I thought you were dead." And Ling replied, "You being alive, how could I have died." Ling then helped his Master into the rowboat, and fearing for his life, Wang Fo sadly said, "What are we to do ..." "Master have no fear," Ling replied, "these people are not the kind to lose themselves inside a painting." The sound of rowing filled the room again, strong and steady like the beating of a great heart. As the rowboat slipped into the distance, the level of the water began to drop in the inner space of the Celestial Master's chamber. The beating of the oars grew fainter, as Wang Fo's boat sailed away 'til it veered around a rock in the distance. And Wang Fo and Ling vanished forever on the jade blue sea that Wang Fo had brought to life through his painting of the unfinished sketch. (Yourcenar, 1938, pp.17-19)

When the student is ready, the teacher unexpectedly appears in the form of Ling. Wang Fo was saved as Ling speaks and quiets his fears, helps him into the rowboat, and sails away with him into a strange and non-sensical space. They lose themselves inside the painting wherein they speak from out of where they are not and from within the madness of where they do not think. An ethic of free association invites the subject to reveal who he or she is by fully entering the text of his or her reality of the present moment at the deepest level of existence. And an invitation is issued to the mind-poet as well: He or she must also be willing to enter into the most sacred and profane experiences of the present moment and lose him or herself inside the painting. The mind-poet must enter that solipsistic space that taps on the wellsprings of madness that is *of self* and from which the We of the analytic discourse drinks deeply from the intoxicating taboo(ze) of madness. In this space, the mirrored reflections of the multiple meanings of (s)(c)en(t)s(e), indeed, mysteriously transform the *We* of *self* and the *other* (of *self*) into a mystical kind of Sensei that, at once, surrounds and guides the discourse while speaking from deep within. In so doing, the mind-poet uses the actuality of her or his own existence, however it is experienced to be, as the field in which he or she deepens the capacity for presencing with the radical *other* of *self* (Magid, 2002).

> ... Your poetry arises by itself when you and the object become one.
> - Basho, Poet (1644-1694)

As a mind poet, the analyst enters and loses *self* in the images and pictures sketched by the radical other of *self*, in this instance, Mr. G. Like Wang Fo, the analyst must love the images of things and not the things themselves; the things themselves are, at once, "illusions of the real" as they are "the objective real." In the analytic space, there is no external world; there is simply a series of images of things that are illusionary and provisional, many of which are experienced as objectively real. As succinctly stated by Michael Brannigan, professor of philosophy at La Roche College and director of the college's Center for the Study of Ethics, "The mind enslaves us when we become attached to illusion, when we convince ourselves that the world we see and reflect on is the real world" (p. 107).

Indeed, reflecting on one's observations creates the illusion that things are separate and exist independently; one's reflections creates obstacles to understanding. The observational ego's rational reflections creates the very duality that Zen seeks to dissolve, a duality structured by the Cartesian premise of the westernized cultures: *I think therefore I am*. A Cartesian worldview dichotomously organizes experiences of *self* and *other* into sharply demarcated, independently existing, thing-like objects or categories such as *mind* and *body*, *man* and *woman,* and *neuroses* and *psychoses*. In order to enter and lose one's self in the picture, the mind-poet must free him- or herself from the illusion of an independently existing fixed self (anatman = no self) and, in so doing, free her or his mind (mushin = a state of no mind) so that he or she does not *think*, but, rather *knows*. Yet, paradoxically, the analyst as mind-poet must reflect and be skeptical while neither reflecting nor being skeptical. Go figure. Or better yet, don't. When one knows rather than *thinks*, then one knows through the oneness of *bodymindthinkingspeakingfeeling*; words never substitute for human experience. The human psyche has an enormous capacity to heal its spirit: The associative-interpretive process has the enormous potential to allow that possibility to take place. To allow for that possibility, the mind-poet must be where he or she does not think and, at the same time, think where he or she is not.

> Zen is the unsymbolization of the world.
> - R.H. Blyth haiku, Eastern Culture

As a constructing power from the literary arts, poetic imagination weaves the mythical story of *How Wang Fo Was Saved* from the Zen Buddhist-Taoist text. In so doing, this tale from ancient China provides psychoanalysts with a way of thinking about the enigmatic question of ethics and the associative-interpretive process. From within the interiority of this ancient tale is suggested an ethical, emotional, and intellectual attitude that enfolds within the narrative story of "Small Change Makes Cents." In so doing, it articulates further an ethic of free association in which making sense of that which appears to make *non-sense* is a moral act that is right, and understanding the organizing purposes and meanings of one's life is *good*, even if it might appear to the outside observer as resulting in only small change(s). As the author of his life, however, Mr. G is the only one who can determine the worth and significance of such, seemingly, small change(s).

An earlier version of this paper was first presented on November 5, 2004 at the 15th annual interdisciplinary conference of the International Federation for Psychoanalytic Education in Chicago, Illinois. The conference theme was *Ethics, Ethos, and Taboos.*

NOTES

1. Aristotle's "virtue ethics" has come to the forefront in recent years due, in part, to the impoverishment of moral philosophy (Lear, 2000; Rorty, 1980). In the Aristotelean tradition, the ethical life is grounded in the development and expression of character. The attainment of moral wisdom is an ongoing lifelong process and is inextricably linked to the development of the individual's character and "practical reasoning." As a form of practical reasoning, *phronesis* is attained through apprenticing oneself with a *phronemos*, or *person of practical wisdom*, who serves as a role model and from whom one learns moral wisdom; *phronesis* is not attained by classroom instruction through a traditional teacher-student relationship. Virtue develops and evolves; the *phronemos* -or role model- is someone helpful in that development.
2. In the interests of confidentiality, identifying information and circumstances have been changed.

REFERENCES

Bachelard, G., (1964). *The psychoanalysis of fire.* Boston: Beacon Press.

Brannigan, M. (2002). *There is no spoon*: A Buddhist mirror. In W. Irwin, ed., *The matrix and philosophy: Welcome to the desert of the real* (pp. 101-110). Peru, IL.: Open Court.

Citino, D. (2002). *The eye of the poet: Six views of the art and craft of poetry.* New York: Oxford University Press.

Felman, S., ed. (1993). *Literature and psychoanalysis; The question of reading: Otherwise.* Baltimore, MD: Johns Hopkins University Press.

Hamilton, E. (1942). *Mythology: Timeless tales of gods and heroes.* Boston: Little, Brown.

Kavanaugh, P.B. (1999). *Thinking about psychoanalytic thinking: A question(ing) of identity, purpose, and ethics.* President's Address, International Federation for Psychoanalytic Education, 10th annual interdisciplinary conference, San Francisco, CA.

Lear, J. (2000). *Happiness, death, and the remainder of life: The Tanner lectures on human values.* Cambridge, MA: Harvard University Press.

Levering, M. & Stryk, L. (2000). Zen: *images, texts, and teachings.* New York: Artisan.

Magid, B. (2002). *Ordinary mind: Exploring the common ground of Zen and psychotherapy.* Boston: Wisdom.

Mah, A. Y. (2001). *Watching the tree: A Chinese daughter reflects on happiness, tradition, and spiritual wisdom.* New York: Broadway Books.

McMahon, J. L. & Csaki, B.S. (2003). Talking trees and walking mountains: Buddhist and Taoist themes in the *Lord of the Rings.* In G. Bassham, & E. Bronson, eds., *The Lord of the Rings and philosophy: One book to rule them all.* (pp. 179-191). Peru, IL: Open Court.

Nussbaum, M. C. (1987). "Finely aware and richly responsible": Literature and the moral imagination. In A.J. Cascardi, ed., *Literature and the question of philosophy.* (pp. 167-191). Baltimore, MD. Johns Hopkins University Press.

Rorty, A.O. (1980). *Essays on Aristotle's ethics.* Berkeley: University of California Press

Seton-Williams, M.V. (2000). *Greek legends and stories.* New York: Barnes & Noble, Rubicon Press.

Yourcenar, M. (1938) *Oriental tales.* New York: Noon Day Press, 1994.

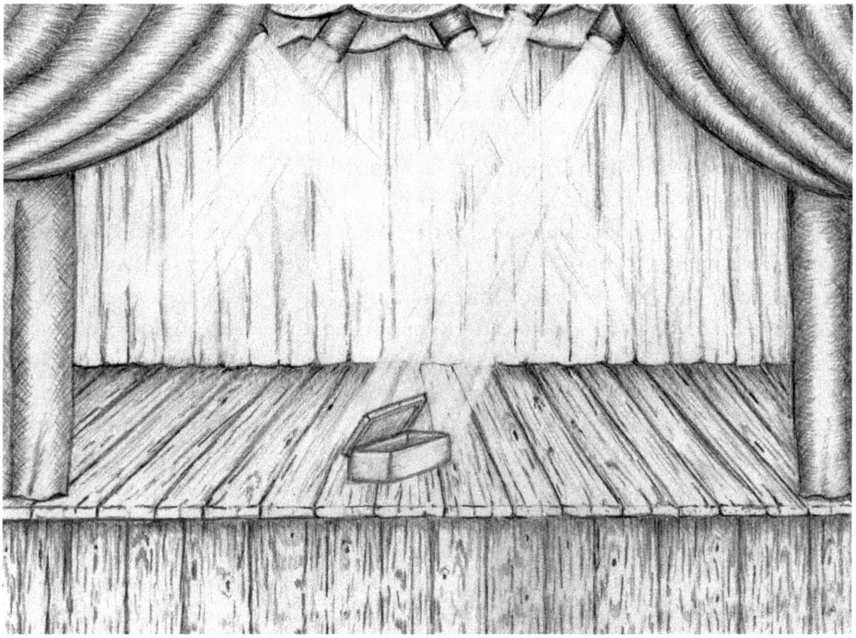

Six

The Dramatic Meaning of Madness in Psycho(analy)sis

The Ear-Rationality of Treating Illusion as Reality

> Ruse and new triumph of madness: the world that thought to measure and justify madness through psychology now must justify itself before madness, since in its struggles and agonies it measures itself by the excess of works like those of Nietzsche, of Van Gogh, of Artaud. And nothing in itself, especially not what it can know of madness, assures the world that it is justified by such works of madness.
>
> Michel Foucault, *Madness in Civilization*

Conceptually rooted in biology, medicine, and the natural sciences, contemporary psychology continues in its quest to scientifically measure and explain the human psyche. A science and pathology-driven psychology understands differences amongst people as the result of neuropsychic deficiencies, diseases, and disorders which are inscribed in the empirical language of our diagnostic and statistical manuals such as, for example, the DSM-IV. Infused with a medical ideology, the various meanings of madness are subsumed by psychology's bio-medical notions of *psychosis*. Madness as a complex social phenomena is, unfortunately, understood and interpreted within the organizing conceptual framework of symptomatology, etiology, and psychopathology. In the larger picture, our bio-medical traditions, beliefs, and values provide the bases for the largely unquestioned articulation of our professional standards in the learning and practice communities. Indeed, a science and pathology-driven model of understanding people continues to provide the standards for psychoanalytic education, training, and practice; produce the psychoanalyst as a mental healthcare professional; and, prescribe the core competencies to be mastered and measured in order to receive a government-issued license to practice.

If the scope of psychoanalysis is to continue to widen as a viable discourse for the understanding of madness as a socially complex phenomena, then its rethinking must also include the rethinking of its conceptual foundations and professional standards. The positivist assumptions underlying the monolithic psychoanalysis of yesteryear are no longer valid for the diverse psychologies of contemporary psychoanalysis. The rich and creative pluralism of our contemporary psychologies speaks to a world of differences between the various theoretical and methodological positions that derive from, for example, the existential-humanistic, relational, phenomenological, transpersonal, hermeneutic, and philosophical ways of thinking, knowing, and being. Many of these psychologies premise different understandings of the basic nature of people, posit different methods of knowing, have different understandings of the concept of the unconscious, and, assume different purposes, objectives, and understandings of the analytic discourse. Acting as if they share the same underlying assumptions, raises serious questions about the institutional power and ethics of organized psychoanalysis in the professional community; perpetuates the illusion that all psychoanalylic practitioners conceptualize and practice as healthcare professionals; and treats this illusion as reality, which becomes little more than an institutionalized form of madness within our psychoanalytic institutions.

While deeply rooted in the humanities, philosophy, and the arts, psychoanalysis turns -rather paradoxically- to the natural sciences for its philosophy and to medicine for its ethics (Lear, 2000). As a contribution to rethinking our conceptual foundations outside of a healthcare matrix, "The Dramatic Meaning of Madness..." resituates psychoanalysis in a philosophy of language and phenomenalism, (e.g., *reality* is whatever the senses reveal it to be; Eaker, 1975), the humanities, and the arts. Thus, this chapter understands psychoanalysis as "a venture into communication via the associative-interpretive process in a contextualizing metaphor from the performance arts, the psychic theatre of the mind" (Kavanaugh, 1995, p. 6). This synthesis and practice rests on the assumption that there is an inextricable link between the theatre, everyday life, and psychoanalysis.

Wherever culture exists, there are forms of theatre that, understood as one cultural system among others, has the general function of generating meaning. People live in a signifying world in which the meanings of particular sounds, actions, and objects come to have meaning in the context of the culture in which they are produced. (Fischer-Lichte, 1992). In our culture, everyday life can be viewed as an instance of people performing culturally prescribed roles and in so doing meeting certain social expectations. These lived-experiences of everyday life are culturally designed as continuous, ongoing, spatio-temporal theatrical performances, the meanings of which are shaped by the historical and cultural context of the times, the person's different social roles, and his or her unique life-experiences. Indeed, in a very real sense, all of life is but a stage upon which each person plays his or hir part. And, there is a living and breathing link between everyday life and psychoanalysis. The internal psychic drama that many times unfolds but gradually within the analytic setting is the same drama that unfolds in each significant relationship in a person's everyday life. It is neither the appearance nor presence of this drama that distinguishes psychoanalysis as psychoanalysis. Rather, it is how the practitioner listens, understands, and responds to its various meanings in the analytic discourse.

In contrast to *psychosis* conceptualized as a bio-medical condition, this chapter speaks to *madness* as a complex socio-cultural phenomenon having, at once, its adaptive and protective purposes, expressive and communicative dimensions, and ideothetic and multiple meanings generated from the person's unique life-world and experiences. Whereas a medical-scientific understanding of *psychosis* rests on conceptual foundations rooted in biology, medicine and the natural sciences, this alternative conceptualization of *madness* is deeply rooted in philosophy, the humanities, the arts, and the anthropic sciences.

The assumptions underlying a medical-scientific understanding of psychosis lead to the conceptualization that *mind* is a function of the physiological processes of the brain. From a philosophical premise of radical subjectivity, however, an alternative conceptualization emerges, one that is more suitable for engaging with the voice of *madness* in the analytic space and discourse: The *brain* is a function of mind. Situated in this alternative paradigm, this chapter places its emphasis on the dramatic meaning of madness in which the theatre develops its truth: illusion treated as reality (Foucault, 1965). Its focus is on several questions basic to this truth of the theatre: First, if madness is illusion treated as reality then how does one's philosophical premise and theoretical assumptions influence, if not determine, how one might listen in the analytic discourse? And second, how might one understand and respond to such communications in the analytic moment? The truth of the theatre -illusion treated as reality- speaks quite directly to the ear-rationality by which the practitioner might listen, understand, and respond to the madness of interacting illusions in the analytic discourse. One's assumptions structure the analytic outcome:

Resting heavily on hermeneutic thinking and McDougall's (1989; 1985) notions of psychic theatre, this chapter considers each of the aforementioned questions in the abstract-theoretical and the concrete-specific in the overarching context of an analytic conversation with a woman who was looking to understand something more about who she was and where she had come from.

The following story is from the perspective of a skeptical phenomenalist and is intended as a contribution to the study of the psychoanalytic arts.

ON THE TRUTH OF THE THEATRE; ILLUSION TREATED AS REALITY

> ...our society does not wish to recognize itself in the ill individual whom it rejects or locks up; as it diagnoses the illness, it excludes the patient...
>
> Michel Foucault, *Mental Illness and Psychology*

THE DRAMATIC MEANING OF MADNESS...

A woman calls and asks for an appointment. We find a time to meet later that week. When she arrives, I meet her in the waiting room and introduce myself. She wordlessly acknowledges me with a slight nod of her head, rises from her chair, and, clutching her purse in front of her, walks rather stiffly into the office. She sits in the chair across from me, staring at the purse she holds so tightly in her lap.

Ms. A. seems about 75-100 lbs. overweight; her hair is cut unevenly and jaggedly, as if she had cut it herself with a pair of scissors; and although a very warm day in early May, she wears a winter jacket which seems two or three sizes too small for her.[1] She is quite literally tight-lipped, seems very nervous, and waits for me to say something.

I ask her to tell us about herself. A long silence follows, during which time she intensely and searchingly looks at me, until after some period of time, the intensity of her gaze slowly fades into a vacuous, empty, and listless stare. After about ten minutes, she replies in a flat-lined tone of resigned dejection that she is in her early forties and that she's schizophrenic. And then there is another very long silence.

I mention to her that in her saying that she's schizophrenic she seems to communicate that she feels that there is simply nothing more to be said, as if she has said everything by saying that she is schizophrenic. I go on to say that I wasn't sure what she meant by schizophrenic and invite her to tell us more about what it means for her. She sits silently and motionless while staring at the purse in her lap. Slowly, she begins speaking. She's been a schizophrenic nearly all of her life, she says. Beginning when she was about 20 years old, she's been hospitalized several times each year for the past 22 years. Her first hospitalization, she says, was shortly after the birth of her baby. She was then hospitalized continuously for about

$4^{1/2}$ years at a state hospital, during which time she describes herself as "just existing in a catatonic stupor." And then with a certain measure of satisfaction and pride in the discovery of a major and defining aspect of who she is, she looks at me and says, "I'm a *catatonic* schizophrenic."

Ms. A. states that she would like to meet for a while to talk. I ask her, how come? And she says that her friend in the hospital, her roommate, had told her that talking with someone about her childhood would help her. Is that true?, she asks. I reply that I really don't know, but if she were so inclined we could meet and talk about her childhood and then she could tell us if it had been helpful. As time is drawing to an end, I ask Ms. A. if she might be interested in meeting again and talking further about it. There is another very long silence. She nods her head yes, she would like to meet again.

I mention a time at the beginning of the following week when we could next meet. She seems quite surprised that it would be so soon. She thought we might meet again next month, a frequency of meetings more consistent with the various aftercare programs she has been involved with. I mention to her that the more frequently we could meet, the more opportunity we might have to speak to those issues of importance to her concerning her childhood. She thinks about it for a few minutes. Yes, she says, lets meet next week.

During the next four or five meetings, we mutually agree to meet three times each week at a fee realistic to her circumstances. Furthermore, we agree that our purpose in meeting is to talk about and attempt to understand her childhood, a deceptively simple agreement, purpose, and undertaking. And also during these meetings, Ms. A relates something about her rather extensive 22-year history of psychiatric hospitalizations. She appears somewhat confused that I would be neither sending for her hospital records nor having contact with anyone outside of herself, including her family or psychiatrist regarding her history or medications. She was quite disbelieving, if not distrustful, that she could, or would, or should speak to certain of her memories as throughout her years in the mental health system she had been told to not talk about the terrifying images she saw or the frightening voices she heard. Nonetheless, she slowly began telling her story.

Ms. A is quite soft spoken, cautious, and frightened as she relates, "My mother use to beat me and I don't know why." She describes how her mother use to lock her in her bedroom closet with her baby brother for endless hours at a time when she was three or four years of age: She was to babysit her $1^{1/2}$ year old brother in the closet. If he made any noise that disturbed her mother, the closet door would suddenly open and her mother would viciously beat her, throwing her repeatedly against the wall. Just as suddenly, she'd be thrown back into the closet, the door slammed shut, and she would be left enveloped in the eerie, quiet darkness of the closet. And she goes on to relate other childhood memories and events. She would be sound asleep in her bed, for example, and the lights would suddenly go on; her mother would pull back the bed sheets, tear off her pajama bottoms, and insert her fingers into her vagina to see if she had been "playing around down there." Mother then would jump on the bed and begin to viciously "kick me down there between my legs," she says in a little girl-like voice. Any attempt to protect her self would serve only to infuriate mother to even greater rage and assaultiveness. Then, just as suddenly, mother would stop, the lights would go out, and she would once again be left, enveloped in a blanket of quiet and darkness. Indeed, "playing around" of any kind was not tolerated. She was not to speak or interact with her schoolmates on the playground during lunch or recess; neither toys nor playmates were permitted. For the most part, these memories are haltingly yet 'factually reported' with little, if any, emotion. At times, however, her voice would suddenly change to that of a little girl's as she would say, "I don't like going to the doctor's office. I don't want to go anymore! Every time I go I find another bone that's bwoke; I didn't know they was bwoke."

THE MADNESS OF INTERACTING ILLUSIONS IN THE ANALYTIC SPACE; THE EAR-RATIONALITY OF A MUTED TEXT

> The scenarios are written in an unknown language; the dialogue is inaudible, sometimes reduced to mime; the characters are as yet unnamed. The psychic dramas of the theaters of the mind thus await production on the analytic stage. In the hope of finding meaning and easing pain, two people step out on that stage to bring the drama to life as psychic reality.
>
> -Joyce McDougall, Theatres of the Mind

Increasingly, Ms. A. would sit down in the chair across from me, close her eyes, and speak few, if any, words during the session. She would speak, however, through her actions as she would sit in the chair, reach above her head with her eyes closed, and begin searching with her hands until she found what I gradually came to understand to be ... a shoebox. She would then pull it out as if taking it off a shelf, bring it down from the shelf, put it on her lap, and open it up. Sometimes, her search for the desired shoebox might take five to ten minutes, during which time she might take down different shoeboxes from the closet shelf, look inside with her hand, and then replace the box back on the shelf where she had found it, possibly to be reopened at a later time.

As a child, locked for long periods in her mother's closet, she had occupied her time by taking down and looking inside different shoeboxes. She could see in the dark by feeling around and touching whatever was inside with her hand. In her mind, she would secretly play in the closet with the shoeboxes. And inside each shoebox was a different memory-event-experience. In our meetings, we had traveled back in space-time to the closet; we had entered that dark closeted space of her childhood.

Upon finding the desired shoebox with the particular memory-experience she had been looking for, Ms. A would then become one of the images in her memory-experience and I would become one of the concretized others: Sometimes I became mother, sometimes baby brother, sometimes her... and, at the same time, it seemed like I became the shoebox containing her memories and experiences. There gradually emerged from these various shoeboxes a certain constellation of memory-experience-events which, in a linearized and historicized way of understanding, went something like the following: At times, for me to speak or make any sound was experienced by Ms. A as my becoming her baby brother making sounds in the closet, precipitating a vicious and horrible assault on her by the voices in her head (Shhhh!!!... be very quiet, baby brother...). At times, for me to begin speaking to her was experienced as my becoming her mother, viciously and violently assaulting her and her head would snap back from my words and crack loudly against the wall behind her. And at times, for me to say nothing came to be understood as my becoming her father sitting in his easy-chair doing and saying nothing, experienced by her as my permitting, if not tacitly encouraging, these atrocities through my withdrawal of self.

At the end of each session with her eyes still closed, she would gently take the thing-like memory-experience-event in her hand, as if it were a baby doll, and gently place it carefully back in the box on her lap where her purse always rested. She would then replace the lid and carefully place the box back on the shelf above her, open her eyes, and leave the office. It was not until years later that Ms. A more clearly and continuously experienced herself as becoming that aspect of her mind called Mother. As mother, she became the embodiment and personification of the statement: "I am she who is nice, good and kind" and I became, in a role of complimentarity, her little girl. As her little girl, I became the embodiment of the statement: "I am she who is little, nasty, and evil," the embodiment of all that is horrible and despicable. I became the personification of the discourse of the ugly, despicable other. If madness is the reality constructed by interacting illusions, then being back in the closet set the stage for its dramatic meanings to unfold on the stage of our psychic theatre.

As Ms. A came to recreate and relive certain archaic patterns and experiences of self with other, we more frequently entered that space where dichotomized distinctions between past and present, her and I, and fantasy and reality dissolved as our interacting illusions evocatively and continuously played on the object hungers, fears, terrors, and desires of the self-of-other. More specifically, at times, I did not have a thought or clue as to what was going on in the session, feeling completely in the dark, so to speak. At times, I felt absolutely confused and paralyzed, catatonic-like in thought, word, and action. At times, I felt helplessly trapped in this space with her with no way out, as in boxed-in and relentlessly battered by her silent accusations, hatred and screaming. At times, I felt absolutely furious and enraged with her, seeing my own rage-filled madness in our interacting illusions of madness in this play of the play of our theatre. And at times, there was my wishing to receive –or wishing to offer her- a helping hand during these dark-filled early months of our meetings, a set of experiences that presaged a blistering childhood memory awaiting its symbolization in words at a later time.

The madness of the analytic discourse includes the object hungers that develop from tolerating the collapse of the real, at which times I found myself existing at moments in an in-between space and place in which, for example, I could not say exactly where I was or we were, who I was or we might be; where I or we had been, much less, where I or we might be going, if anywhere; there was a deeply felt dread that there might not be a transitional space enroute to anyplace. In this psychic theatre, these were the sensory experiences and issues to be understood, symbolized, and translated into words as they were in the associative material and in my experiences, as I slowly came to understand them. I certainly felt that I could understand from a much different perspective something about what catatonic might have meant for Ms. A in her statement "I'm a catatonic schizophrenic" mentioned towards the end of our first meeting.

In this psychic drama, we played with life and death in the play in the closet; the play in the play is the thing! Had Ms. A. brought all these memory-experiences with her, clutched in her purse, hidden behind her tightly pursed lips that very first time we had met? Could it be that within the strange reality of this semiotically constructed space of the closet, Ms. A. could put her hand inside of her *box* (her *shoebox*, that is) and freely explore with her hand whatever might be inside? - a most personal and private venture into the *mindbodythinkingspeakingfeeling* of playing around in her *box* which had been experienced as having been so traumatically violated by her mother's *shoe*? The process of repeating and reliving these experiences is understood as a form of remembering and communicating that which cannot be forgotten but cannot be recalled in words. In the struggle to be detached and observing while immersed and experiencing, the mind-poet historiographer attempts to wrap words around these experiences and, in so doing, symbolize the not yet symbolized. The mind-poet is, however, always part of the history (re-) constructed; the history told is a function of the context and process of the telling, the listening, and the retelling of the story. In the process of listening, we produce meaning. It is here that our primary *identity*, as either a mental healthcare professional or as a mind-poet-historiographer provides the contextualizing field for our interpretive acts which then become integral aspects of the associative-interpretive process.

Ms. A. had taken us back in time to the closet of her childhood where we entered a semiotically constructed, three dimensional, spatially coded representation of her various childhood experiences. A holographic reality had developed in the analytic space, a shape-shifting reality that reflected, at once, the different experiences of her life as a little girl and the nature of her participation in the analytic discourse: The very silent form in which Ms. A. told her story was integral to its understanding. Meaning is, however, not so readily grasped in the theatre of the mime. The mime-play occupies that space in-between text and performance in which semiotic constructions speak a language of the stage which privileges movement over mimesis, space over speech, spectacle over meaning, and vision over voice (Oswald, 1989). And in so doing, the uncertainty and un-knowingness of the mind-poet increases as

> the mime suspends the traditional primacy of the written text over performance and reveals a weak point in the classical interpretation of mimesis as the imitation of living speech. Since the mime does not breathe dramatic life into discourse but creates meaning by manipulating contortions of his body, his performance suspends the ideal closure between being and meaning in speech, placing in question *the unity and the identity of the speaking and spectating subject.*
>
> (Oswald, 1989, 123, emphasis added).

As we ventured further into the closet of her childhood by wording the mime-play, Ms. A seemed to come further out of her closeted memory- experiences. After approximately 4 1/2 to 5 months, there gradually developed more of a sense of calm and stability in the analytic space, a relatively peaceful quiet with less emotional volatility and intensity. Ms. A's eyes opened and came alive; she spoke in words with greater articulation and spontaneity; and she seemed to be increasingly more comfortable. I know for sure that I was. During this time, other vivid memories of her relationship with her mother were related through words, an example of which was a childhood memory that seemed of particular relevance, given my recently having wanted to receive a helping hand in the more immediate psychic drama. The memory was as follows: Upon arriving home from school, her mother might ask her, "Would you like a surprise?" Ms. A. recalled her anticipation and excitement as she said to her mother that she would. "Then close your eyes and hold out your hand," her mother would say. Whereupon, her mother would place a hot iron in her waiting hand. As Ms. A. was recalling this memory with her eyes closed and her hand extended towards me, her palm turned a bright, blistering red, as I perceived it to be; so much for wishing to receive a helping, loving hand. If ever she did not want to play this game with mother, she would be slapped across her face and told that obviously she was *not* a little girl as every little girl wanted a surprise from her mother.

As we continued to meet, Ms. A. began speaking of her growing excitement about the upcoming Christmas holidays and looking forward to being with her children and celebrating her family's various Irish traditions. Her anticipation and excitement, she said, was unlike that which she had known previously. The following material is from our first meeting after Christmas.

RHYTHYM AND RHYME IN THE EAR-RATIONAL NARRATIVES OF MADNESS

> There is no madness except as the final instant of the work of art- the work endlessly drives madness to its limits; *where there is a work of art, there is no madness*; and yet madness is contemporary with the work of art, since it inaugurates the time of its truth.
>
> Michel Foucault, *Madness in Civilization*

As I open the door to the waiting room, I am quite startled and taken aback by Ms. A's physical appearance. She is sitting in a chair as if in a stupor, blankly staring down at the floor in front of her. Her hair is matted and tangled; her face is pale and expressionless. She has lipstick on her face in the shape of lips but it is placed high up on her cheek. Her blouse is misbuttoned in that she apparently misaligned the buttons on the one side with the button holes on the other. Her appearance immediately takes me back to my experiences on the backwards of various state hospitals. As I stand at the waiting room door, I have the fleeting picture in my mind of me buttoning up her blouse "like it should be." Ms. A sits motionless in the chair for what seems like a long time before standing up and slowly coming into the office, at times stopping to hold onto the wall for support. Upon sitting down, she says in a barely audible voice and with a feeble attempt at humor, "It's been a six thorazine trip to get here." Closing her eyes, she begins sobbing uncontrollably. At times, she holds her hand up as if to keep me away and, at times, holds her hand out palm-side up, as if wanting to receive something from me. I begin speaking with her of, once again, being in the presence of her mother waiting to be burnt with an unexpected surprise. I stop as she opens her eyes and says that she has not slept for the past four days.

Once again, she begins crying as she relates that she has never been to the cemetery to see her son. Her son had been born with multiple birth defects in early May, she says, and for the first seven months of his life she had to be with him every $1^{1/2}$ hours around-the-clock to feed and watch over him. He was not expected to live. Month after month he slowly got better, however, until, without warning, "he suddenly took bad just after Christmas." She describes taking him to the hospital and staying with him around-the-clock for three days and three nights until she could barely stay awake any longer. The doctor told her to go home and get some rest, she says, with his assurance that her baby would be okay. She went home, laid down around midnight, and fell fast asleep. About 1:30 A.M., she awoke with a terrified start and a desperate sense of urgency to get back to the hospital as fast as she could. She tearfully describes the ride to the hospital and running up to the nursery, only to find her son's crib empty. She goes on to describe the sinking, deadening feeling of talking to the nurse and discovering that her son had died. The Doctor had sent her home so that she could get rest before he told her the next day: burnt with the helping hand of another unexpected surprise!

At this point, I communicate to her that maybe we could both understand her feeling that if she had to do it all over again, she would have stayed up longer. She would have sat and waited quietly with her son for *four* days and nights, for *four years*, for *fo(u)r*-ever, if necessary, so as to not leave her son, based on her belief that it was her leaving him that night that had caused his death. He would not be sleeping forever if she would have been a better mother by staying awake forever, quietly watching over him as she had with her baby brother. I communicate how guilty she feels that her baby boy died because of her; that she had been kept in the dark about it; and, how badly burnt she had been by the Doctor's unexpected surprise. Ms. A begins sobbing and with great difficulty says that she never had a chance to bury her son. Indeed, she never saw him again because she then went into labor and her baby girl died 9 days later. I was more confused than usual... She explains that, at the time of her little boy's death, she was 5 months pregnant with her little girl. As she speaks, she begins rocking in the chair with her arms folded across her lap forming, it seems to me, an empty cradle as she relates that her daughter, Colleen, was born and died later that same day. She never held, nursed, or rocked her baby girl. Nor had she buried her. Indeed, she was taken to the state hospital where she remained in a catatonic stupor for the next $4^{1/2}$ years.

There were only a few minutes left in the session as Ms. A quietly cries and slowly rocks in her chair. And I communicate to her how it seems that her experience of not having time for either her little boy or little girl is brought right into this present moment of the past between us and how it seems that we do not have enough time to say 'Hello,' much less 'Good-bye' to her son or her daughter, as much as we might want to, *just as there had not been enough time before.* If she chooses, however, we could take time for both her son and daughter the next time we meet. Ms. A. continues rocking in her chair for several minutes and very slowly gets up and leaves... and she comes back the next time to continue talking about her babies dying… and the next time… and the next time. And the endless series of next times.... With each telling and retelling of her story, there seems to be a further historification between what she experiences as *the present* and what is experienced as *the past.* With words, Ms. A's. memories did not need to be endlessly repeated through her *bodymindthinkingspeaking* in everyday life. Her words became like shoeboxes; that is, they were like linguistic structures existing as empty containers waiting to be filled with the experiential meanings from her life story. As they filled with meaning, she was more able to walk through the hallways of her time-past and her time-present, at the same time.

SOME THOUGHTS ON VENTURING INTO MS A'S COMMUNICATION

This version of psychic theatre rests on the radical semiotic that considers every entity, including the human entity, as potentially a sign *of* and a sign *for* something else. In this theory of meaning and interpretation, anything can stand for itself and anything else, at the same time. Thus, one conceptualizes the various multi-determined levels and layers of meanings in the analytic discourse as one might conceptualize the visual imagery of dreams. In the narrative of this ear-rational discourse with Ms. A, for example, could the first seven months of our meetings from May through December, including her getting better and suddenly taking bad just after Christmas, be understood as an exquisitively delicate restructuring, repeating, and reliving of the first seven months of her son's life and death? And also, of the pregnancy, birth, and death of her daughter? During the session just recounted, were we not mourning Ms. A's death as a mother? and her death as a baby-boy and brother-son? and her death as a baby girl? Were we not mourning the death of herself as a little girl who felt she had died before she was even born? Only much later was it learned from Ms. A that Colleen, in Gaelic, means *little girl.* ...

At the same time, from a slightly different perspective, might her rocking in her chair toward the end of this session relate in some way to the beginning of the session and the fleeting picture in my mind of buttoning up her blouse like it should be as I stood at the door of the waiting room? Did she wish for me to rock her and comfort her at the end of the session as a good mother might do, as I had had the image of buttoning her up in the waiting room as a good mother might have done? At the same time, might this desire for her (m)other to rock her be related to the terror of her going off her rocker if she were to be held in my tentacled embrace? After all, her experience of her mother, her doctors in the hospital, and the countless others was that they wished to button her up so that she would not speak on the outside about the horrific experiences closeted on the inside. They would then not have to see her rage, her despair, and her profound loneliness and madness. ...Did I see myself as *buttoning her up* in the waiting room so I would not have to see *my own* rage, *despair, loneliness*, and *madness* in this intimate discourse with my secret other? ...Perhaps the secret psychosis of self (Searles, 1965) is one of the dramatic meanings of madness that leads to psychology's preoccupations with the scientific measurement and explanation of the human psyche that produces the bio-medical diagnosis of psychosis for the other of self.

SOME THOUGHTS ON THE POSSIBILITY OF POSSIBILITIES

> There is very good reason why psychology can never master madness; it is because psychology became possible in our world only when madness had already been mastered and excluded from the drama. And when, in lightening flashes and cries, it reappears as in Nerval or Artaud, Nietzsche or Roussel, it is psychology that remains silent, *speechless*, before this language that borrows a meaning of its own from that tragic split, from that freedom, that, for contemporary man, only

> the existence of 'psychologists' allows him to forget.
> -Michel Foucault, *Mental Illness and Psychology*

Situated in philosophy, the humanities, and the arts, psychoanalysis is understood as art rather than science. As a humanistic discipline, it's discourse is concerned with the understanding of *madness* as a complex social phenomena as opposed to *psychosis* as a bio-medical condition. Premised in a philosophy concerned with language, semiotics, and cultural systems of signification, psychoanalysis ventures into the individual's dynamic process of signification, in which process reality is conjured from illusion. As the theatre develops its truth in illusion treated as reality, the dramatic meanings of madness in which Ms. A. developed her truth were found via the associative-interpretive process in which her reality was treated as illusion for the purpose of understanding and wording her life's story, as she perceived it to be, and in which process the complexity of the subjectivity of both participants was embraced and understood as integral to the process. In the rhythms and rhymes of her story, Ms. A. is understood as orderly in her unique complexity rather than lawful in some formulaic simplicity.

In this synthesis and understanding of psychic theatre, there is a one time only nature to the discourse and an only one time nature to the associative-interpretive process, the creative significance of which can neither be categorized nor conceptualized in abstract symbols and nomothetic laws. As a theatrical experience, "every performance is unique and unrepeatable, understood by whatever codes are available to that audience at that specific cultural moment" (Carlson, 1990); the analytic discourse is conceptualized as an ideothetic enterprise without nomothetic laws. From a phenomenalistic perspective, reality is, at once, whatever the person experiences it to be (Eacker, 1975) and the reality to be understood in the analytic discourse, the objective of which is to understand the *What Is* of a person's life and something about the *Why* of that *What Is*, as communicated through the associative-interpretive process. Thus, the mind-poet historigrapher is not meeting with the person so that he or she might get better, to cure his or her mental illness, or so that he or she might become a more productive or happy citizen. Nor is he or she meeting with the person to bring about some other theoretically anticipated outcome. Indeed, to abstract into conceptual categories or pre-configured ways of thinking about what something might mean, from whence it derives, where the analytic discourse ought to be headed, or how the person ought to develop contradicts the uniqueness of both the person and the discourse. Furthermore, to do so limits -if not curtails- the potential for realizing the possibilities of that which might be. In speaking about this human potentiality and possibility, Jonathan Lear (2000) states that "to live with human possibility, one has to tolerate a peculiar kind of theoretical anxiety; the willingness to live without a principle. Only then can we begin to grasp the peculiar possibility for possibilities that human being opens up." (p. 165). The mind-poet has to know that he or she does not know in order to begin knowing the (hi)story of the subject. To do so, however, requires that he or she trusts himself or herself, the other, and the associative process. In so doing, paradoxically, certain life altering changes might come about in a most mysterious and unpredictable kind of way as a by-product of the work-play of wording the dramatic play of the psychic theatre.

The possibility of possibilities speaks to the mystery, magic, and muscle of the human spirit and to what is possible in the analytic discourse and in one's life. Ms. A and I met, for example, for the deceptively simple purpose of talking about and attempting to understand her childhood. In so doing, Ms. A assumed the responsibility for arranging for her own transportation to and from our sessions during the thirteen years of our meetings even though she did not own a car and had very meager financial resources. During this time, she did not miss any of our sessions. As she found employment and began working, we mutually agreed to increase her fee. Over the years, she seemed to develop a much more comfortable relationship with herself and others in her life. In contrast to her previous 22 years of multiple hospitalizations each year, Ms. A was readmitted to the hospital but once during the years of our meetings for a weekend shortly after the session just recounted. It has been my experience that the possibility of possibilities that human being-ness opens up provides a continuing source of wonderment, admiration, and awe.

Finally, the madness involved in treating illusion as reality can only be found by two people passionately engaged in the mutual struggle to find the words that monumentalize the other's passage in time. In listening, understanding and responding to the *ear*-rational, our historical sense is a privileged sense if we refuse to entertain and search for the certainty of empirical absolutes and formulaic notions of what the historical antecedents must have been or what the outcome of analysis ought to be. Rather, we listen with an ongoing skepticism about conclusionary facts as the story told is always in the process of being told. In so listening, the hidden movements of the multi- leveled, -layered, and -determined explode from their compressions into their many different and contradictory meanings. As we listen, understand, and respond *with* and *through* this historical sense to the telling and retelling of one's personal story, there emerges the potential for a creative synthesis of the phenomenal past with the experience(s) of the present moment of the future-past. With this synthesis, the possibility of possibilities for new and different thoughts and actions becomes possible. And we might contribute to the chapter of our history waiting to be written. As stated by Foucault (1965), "We have yet to write the history of that other form of madness by which men, in an act of sovereign reason, confine their neighbors, and communicate and recognize each other through the merciless language of non-madness" (p. ix).

An earlier version of this paper was first presented on March 3rd, 2001 in Mexico City as the keynote address at the international congress of the Instituto de Investigacion en

Psicologia Cllinica Y Social, A.C.. The theme of the congress was Psicosis Intersubjetividad (Psychosis and Intersubjectivity).

NOTE

1. In the interests of confidentiality, identifying information and certain circumstances have been changed or omitted in the material presented.

REFERENCES

Carlson, M. (1990. *Theatre semiotics: Signs of life.* Bloomington: Indiana University Press,.
Clarke, D.S. (1997). *Philosophy's second revolution: Early and recent analytic philosophy.* Chicago: Open Court.
Eacker, J. N. (1975). *Problems of philosophy and psychology.* Chicago: Nelson-Hall.
Fischer-Lichte, E. (1992). *The semiotics of theater.* (J. Gaines & D.L. Jones, trans.) Bloomington: Indiana University Press.
Foucault, M. (1965). *Madness and civilization.* (Richard Howard, trans.) New York: Random House.
(1987) *Mental illness and psychology.* Berkeley: University of California Press.
Kavanaugh, P.B. 1995). *Influences from philosophy, the theatre, and the poets on psychoanalytic theory and technique* MSPP Newsletter, 5: 6-10.
Lear, J. (2000) *Happiness, death, and the remainder of life: The tanner lectures on human values.* Cambridge, Mass.; Harvard University Press.
McDougall, J. (1985). *Theaters of the mind: Illusion and truth on the psychoanalytic stage.* New York: Basic Books.
(1989). *Theaters of the body: A psychoanalytic approach to psychomatic illness.* New York: Norton.
Oswald, L. (1989). *Jean Ginet and the semiotics of performance.* Bloomington: Indian University Press.
Sarup, M. (1993). *An introductory guide to post-structuralism and postmodernism* (2nd ed.). Athens: University of Georgia Press.
Searles, H. F. (1965). *Collected Papers on Schizophrenia and Related Subjects.* New York: International Universities Press.
Strenger, C. (1991). *Between hermeneutics and science: An essay on the epistemology of psychoanalysis.* International Universities Press, Madison.
(1998). *Individuality, the impossible project: Psychoanalysis and self-creation.* Madison, Conn.: International Universities Press.

Seven

Escaping the Phantom's Ghostly Grasp

On Psychoanalysis as a Performance Art in the Spirit World

> Those who have seen your face draw back in fear...
> *I* am the mask you wear. My spirit, my voice in one combined.
> The Phantom of the Opera is there...inside my mind...
> -Christine Daae and the Phantom, *The Phantom of the Opera*

He often comes to her in her dreams at night, gently calling her name. She never actually sees him; she only hears his hauntingly beautiful voice speaking to her until, one evening, he quite unexpectedly materializes in the full-length mirror in her dressing room. As her father had promised her before he died, the Angel of Music had come to teach her to sing the music that she herself had inspired him to compose, the love story told in *The Music of the Night.* His face half-obscured by a white mask, he tells her to look at her face in the mirror and there she will see him inside. And he then invites her inside the mirror. As she enters, she is led by her ghostly guide and guardian through a gloomy maze of passages beneath the Paris opera house, across a great subterranean lake, and into the deepest and darkest regions of his inner world where she comes to know him and why he must hide behind his mask. And so begins the powerful and passionate story of *The Phantom of the Opera*, a journey into the wellsprings of desire and passion, innocence and tenderness, and darkness and hatred found deep within the phantom's obsession with Christine.

First published by Gaston Leroux (1910) as a dark tale of suspense and obsession, *The Phantom of the Opera* was later adapted to Andrew Lloyd Webber's *Music of the Night* (Levan, 1990).[1] In so doing, the minds of author and composer came together to reach deep inside the old Paris opera house, enter the shadow-image of Christine's phantomlike other, and unleash the power of this basic human drama. And through the magical interweave of the transformative arts of storytelling, song, and poetry with the performance arts of the theatre, they invite the audience to join with Christine in looking beneath the mask and witnessing her escape from her phantom's ghostly grasp.

Wherever there is culture there are forms of theatre. And as a cultural phenomenon, the theatre is generally seen as a source of entertainment or as a diversion from real life (Fischer-Lichte, 1992). Rarely is the theatre thought of, however, as being necessary for sustaining life itself. A very different meaning, function, and significance emerges when the mind of the analytic practitioner reaches into the theatre, steps onto its stage with another human being, and blends the transformative arts with the performance arts to speak with the ghosts of the person's spirit world. In *Theaters of the Mind*, for example, McDougall (1985) considers the theatre as a metaphor for the human dramas of everyday life, a way of understanding the psychoanalytic process and psychic reality, and the stage upon which these dramas can be re-constructed, re-lived, and re-experienced in the analytic space. In her *Theaters of the Body*, McDougall (1989) reaches even further to include those people accustomed to speaking their stories through their bodies and, in so doing, giving expression to their psyche's primitive messages in the form of allergic, gastric, cardiac and other such physical symptoms. Both her books trace their genealogy to Anna O's private theater and her mysterious "chimney sweeping" through which process her deafness, visual disturbances, and muscular paralyses gradually disappeared as she expressed her experiences surrounding her father's death; chimney sweeping had somehow enabled her escape from her phantom's ghostly grasp. This chapter poses the question. Is there another stage onto which the analyst might step, reach even further into the spirit realm and, in so doing, speak with the phantoms that reside therein?

Described as a madman-philosopher, a poet-dramatist, and a theorist-playwright, Antonin Artaud (1895-1948) wrote a collection of essays on the theatre during his nine years in various mental asylums in France in the 1930's. Published in 1938, *Le Theatre et Son Double* (*The Theatre and Its Double*) presented a revolutionary theory in which his metaphysical theatre replaces the psychological theatre of the West (Artaud, 1958). In so doing, Artaud broke with the Aristotelean tradition in which theatre: is an act of catharsis, speaks from a scripted narrative text, and appeals to the intellect by providing psychological insights into the human condition. Influenced by an Oriental philosophy of theatre, Artaud's metaphysical theatre neither assumes nor imitates an objective reality, nor does it seek to portray universal psychological truths about people (Zinder, 1980). As embodied in his *Theatre of Cruelty*, his theatre represents an imitation of *internal* experiences; is spoken in a unique language of the stage, for example, a language of space and movement; and enters a more dangerous kind of reality that looks beneath the mask of the civilized and demands that the audience viscerally see and speak with the more barbaric, primitive, and real aspects of self and other (Artaud, 1974; Bermel, 1977). In effect, his *Theatre of Cruelty* reveals social reality as an elaborate masquerade of the civilized, places the human subject on the stage in the place of scripted characters, and is characterized by the terrors of freedom, the surreal, and the mysterious.

"Escaping the Phantom's Ghostly Grasp" enters the Theatre of Cruelty as found on the in-patient unit of an inner-city state hospital to consider the beginnings of a conversation with "The Man From Venus." In so doing, I hope, first, to contribute to a more radical poetics of psychic theatre in which the stage of Artaud's theatre presents us with another reality and space – a spiritual reality and space- from which we might speak with the ghosts of the spirit realm. Second, I consider in the context of process material some of the philosophical and theoretical issues involved in speaking from this more dangerous reality, as the phantom of Mr. W's private theatre materializes on the stage in the form of his Virgin Queen Mother as (s)he prepares to nurse me as one of her insatiable Venetian babies.

THE THEATRE OF CRUELTY, THE MAN FROM VENUS, AND THE MUSIC OF HIS EBONY-BLACK NIGHT

> Night time sharpens heightens each sensation
> Darkness stirs and wakens imagination...
> Silently the senses abandon their defenses.
>
> -*The Music of the Night*

Artaud's Theatre of Cruelty does not refer to a sado-masochistic form of cruelty –although at times, it might- nor does it refer to physical or spiritual maltreatment as the words might suggest. Rather, it artistically expresses and exposes what he calls the "rigor," "necessity," or "implacability" of suffering in life and, in so doing, shatters the false reality of the civilized (Artaud, 1974; Bermel, 1977). His theatre assumes that the normal experiences and processes of life such as love and loss, happiness and sadness, and aging and dying involve suffering and cruelty; cruelty is inherent to human existence (Knapp, 1969). From a philosophical and especially a metaphysical point of view, Artaud (1974) says of his theatre, "I use the word 'cruelty' in the sense of hungering after life, cosmic strictness, relentless necessity, in the Gnostic sense of a living vortex engulfing darkness, in the sense of the inescapable necessary pain without which life could not continue. Good has to be desired, it is the result of an act of willpower, while evil is continuous" (p. 78). Artaud's theatrical presentations were designed to reject form and incite chaos by hurling the spectator into the turbulence of the unfolding drama and, in so doing, committing an act of cruelty upon the audience (Jamieson, 2007).

In many respects, I found myself on the stage of this theatre of cruelty when I joined the staff of an inpatient unit at an end-of-the-line inner-city state hospital. By state charter, no one in psychiatric need could be turned away. Anyone who constituted a danger to self or others, or could not take care of their own basic needs because of mental illness had to be admitted. In effect, there was no control over admissions to the unit. In chapter three, I described something about the world of this ward and its milieu structure, dynamic, and process. Suffice it to say that the ward was a 45 bed, locked, adult-inpatient unit which at the time was warehousing over seventy people. Mattresses lined the hallways to accommodate the census-overflow. Understaffed, underfunded, and overcrowded, the foul-smelling stench of urine and shit mixed with the smells of sweat-drenched bodies in the stifling 95-degree heat, the stench of which spoke unequivocally to the presence of people, life and mortality.

In this theatre, the dynamic actions of the ward took place on all levels and dimensions at once in ways that assaulted the senses and dissolved the boundaries between audience and actors. On its stage, the primitive anxieties, terrors, and experiences of both staff and residents alike were palpable as they dissolved the separation between the stage and the spectator. As the spectator became immersed in the turbulence and intensity of the ongoing psychic dramas, the principles of civilized life seemed to move just beyond one's ghostly grasp.

As I was becoming oriented to the rules, routines, and rhythms of the ward, I noticed Mr. W from a distance, before I knew we would be working together. He was an African American man in his late twenties or early thirties. He was about 5'6" tall with a deep bluish-black ebony-toned skin that sweat-glistened in the heat of the ward. His head was shaved, his front teeth were gold-capped, and he had a silver ring in each ear. His physique fairly rippled with muscles defined within muscles. Endless hours of lifting weights had transformed his body into a beautifully sculpted art form - like, perhaps, something Michelangelo might have freed from a block of marble. He always wore a white shirt, the front of which was pulled up through the top giving the impression he was wearing a halter; the sleeves were cut out, accenting his muscular biceps and forearms. And, he wore a pair of extremely short shorts with an unmistakable attitude of seductive invitation while, at the same time, daring anyone to respond to the invitation. Always quietly floating and gliding on the outer margins of the ward's groups, activities and happenings, the visual erotic of his appearance and movements at once colorized his way of being-in-the-world, set the stage for our meetings, and spoke to something of the dangerous reality and space of his private theatre.

Along with several other people, Mr. W had been clerically transferred from the state hospital for the criminally insane, as it was then known, to the locked inpatient unit at this inner-city state hospital. Due to budget cuts in the mental health system, the forensic unit had been closed several years prior and the people housed within its walls were transferred to other lock-down units in the system. Known as *one of the chronics*, Mr. W had been assigned to me after about a week of my orientation as, I was told, he was "a good learning case." Or perhaps more accurately, we had been assigned to each other as there was no mutual choice, discussion, or agreement in the decisions involved in our working together. As mentioned in chapter 3, the in-house disposition for *the chronics* was, quite simply, to transfer them to the newest staff person as "good learning cases."

I was told something of Mr. W's psychiatric history which was essentially the same as for the others transferred from the forensic center. He had a long history of psychiatric hospitalizations precipitated by delusions, hallucinations, and violent assaultive behaviors. His life on the ward was characterized by his seemingly random and explosive assaults on both other residents and staff. As was my custom, I did not read his social history or records before we met, as I believed he would tell us in his own ideothetic way everything that would be important to know. The social worker did communicate one aspect of his history before we met, however: Mr. W was known on the ward as The Rat Baby. As an infant, rats had chewed on him in his crib. Indeed, life is filled with suffering, pain, and cruelty. Without requesting any further information, I went to introduce myself to Mr. W.

> Slowly, gently night unfurls its splendor;
> Grasp it, sense it...tremulous and tender...
> turn your thoughts away from cold, unfeeling light..
> And listen to the music of the night...
>
> -*The Music of the Night*

I found him sitting alone on the floor in the corner of the day room. His eyes were closed, his legs were crossed in a yogalike position, and he seemed immersed in a private meditative space. Up close and personal, it was quite noticeable that large chunks of flesh were missing from his forearms, upper arms, and inner thighs. I quietly introduced myself, apologized for interrupting him, and asked if we could meet and talk for awhile. Without saying a word, he slowly opened his eyes and, staring straight ahead as if in a trance, effortlessly rose up from his lotuslike position and, in one fluid motion, slowly began walking towards the office on the ward. He moved and carried himself in a most dignified and imperial-like manner. ...And I followed as he led the way.

When we arrived at the door of the office, he silently stepped to the side - actually, he glided or floated to the side- so that I could unlock and open the door for him. He entered, selected a chair, sat down, closed his eyes, and slowly folded his arms across his chest. And then, there was a long, deep, and dense silence. I had the experience that I was in the presence of royalty, had been granted an audience, and that the silence was not to be broken. After some time, there was an almost imperceptible nod of his head; it was now appropriate for me to speak. I reintroduced myself, mentioned that we could meet and talk, and invited him to tell us about himself. By way of responding, he remained silent and motionless for a very long time, occasionally stifling a yawn, and increasingly giving the impression that he was simply enduring the burden of my unwanted presence. I felt that I was draining him of his energy by simply being present with him. Eventually, he quietly said, "I'm tired. I have to rest now." The audience had ended. And there was another long and dense silence.

I broke the silence by mentioning that, indeed, he seemed very tired, and I asked what had been preventing him from getting his rest? He seemed mildly surprised and somewhat suspicious with my question. With his eyes still closed, he slowly responded, I just can't get any sleep. All day long, I have to protect my mother; every man who sees her wants to fuck her. I have to protect her virginity. Very solemnly he then declared, *My Mother is the Virgin Queen*; I've got to protect her, that's my job. After some silence, I asked him, How long have you had the job of protecting her? He replied matter-of-factly, Since I was placed on this earth. I asked, Have you been tired since you were placed on earth? No, he said. And he goes on to say, The Venetians come down every night and take me to Venus to nurse their babies 'til dawn, then they bring me back to earth. And I said, ...and then you have to be awake all day protecting your mother from the men who want to fuck her? He nodded. I continued, No wonder, you're so tired and need to rest. Sounding very drained and exhausted, he spoke once again of his protective vigil during the day, being taken to Venus at night, and that he is very tired and in need of rest.

> Close your eyes and surrender to your darkest dreams!
> Purge your thoughts of the life you knew before!
> Close your eyes, let your spirit start to soar!
> And you'll live as you've never lived before...
>
> -*The Music of the Night*

As I began saying that we could stop and meet again later in the week, Mr. W slowly unfolded his arms from across his chest, undid his halter, unbuttoned his shirt and let it hang loosely open, exposing his muscular chest. With his eyes still closed and his hands clasped in his lap, he sat quietly waiting. In this dense scene of silence, I wondered if we were engaged in a dance of seductive invitations. Was he responding to my invitation *to meet to talk* with his invitation to me to come to *his meat* and talk intimately by sucking from his breast? Did he somehow know the madness of my thirst to suck meaning from his life long sacrificial drama? The sound of my words invasively broke the silence as I found myself saying, No. If you and I decide to meet, I *won't* be sucking from you, or feeding off you; you *don't* have to nurse me. I think you've been telling us how tired you are of feeding everyone who comes to get you: the Venetians, the Venetian babies, and now me.

He opened his eyes and while staring at me with a great intensity and suspiciousness cautiously asked, Who are you? I again said who I was, that I was willing to meet and talk with him - if he was interested-, and, that maybe we could come to understand something more about that feeling of tiredness that had been haunting him for so long. I went on to say that it seemed that he carried a lot of responsibility for his mother, and that possibly through meeting and talking, we could figure out why he had been selected by the Venetians for the added and draining responsibility of keeping all the babies alive. I asked him what he thought. He studied me intensely for a long time. Slowly his eyes closed, and, after some time, he began making almost imperceptible sucking motions with his lips. I said that I understood that he was interested in the two of us meeting again. As he began buttoning his shirt and fashioning a halter, he said, When? I mentioned a time for the next morning. He stretched, yawned and said, I'm tired, I'm going to bed and getting some rest. And the session ended. I remember feeling-thinking-experiencing: Now that he's seen me, does he want to fuck me? I also wondered if his desire to see me had already resulted in the birth of another baby that he would have to nurse later that night?

We began meeting three times each week. For the first several weeks, our meetings were spent mostly in silence, except for every now and then he would repeat the story of his protective vigil by day and traveling to Venus at night. During the silences, he seemed to be quietly gathering his strength and getting the rest he needed.

THE THEATRE OF CRUELTY, PSYCHOANALYSIS AS A PERFORMANCE ART, AND SPEAKING WITH THE PHANTOMS OF THE SPIRIT REALM

> In the Theatre, the tendency for centuries has been to put the actor at a remote distance, on a platform, framed, decorated, lit, painted, in high shoes - so as to help persuade the ignorant that he is holy, that his art is sacred. Did this express reverence? Or was there behind it a fear that something would be exposed if the light were too bright, the meeting too near?
>
> -Peter Brook, *The Empty Space*

On psychoanalysis as a performance art: The phantom of the Paris opera house comes to Christine in the night, gently speaks her name, and takes her to the darkest and deepest regions of his inner world. The ghost of the Venetian opera house comes to Mr. W in the ebony black darkness of his night, gently speaks his name, and takes him to the darkest and deepest inner regions of Venus to nurse the babies. And in the dramatic performance of his private theatre, it seems that I am experienced as one of the Venetians coming to him in the day room, gently speaking his name, and taking him to the darkest and deepest inner regions of his-my inner world where I then transform into one of the Venetian babies waiting to be nursed. And quite unexpectedly, he later transforms into the baby sucking from me. What ghostly presence serves as the guide and guardian that leads us to the madness that gently speaks our names from within the dangerous reality of this stage?

In The Spirits of Life, Christopher Bollas (1992) speaks to the internal images of self and other as the spirits and ghosts of our past lives speaking, shaping, and interweaving their tissue-traces of historical meanings into the fabric of our everyday lives. Our internal representations of self and other are our spirits and ghosts, with *spirit* signifying the ghosts of others who have affected us as we travel through life, and *ghosts* signifying the essence of these past encounters. In their synthesis, they transcend our idiom and the structure of the object, but nonetheless owe their origin to each as they make their appearance on the stage and speak, in this instance, in their physical, concrete, and silent language of space and movement as the Virgin Queen Mother materializes and prepares to nurse me.

Artaud's *Theatre of Cruelty* transcends the realm of theatre per se and points to the broader question of the human subject's performance in poetic discourse. Theatre, Artaud says, must "call into question, organically, man, his ideas about reality, and his poetic place in reality" (quoted in Oswald, 1989, p. xiv). In the scene of silence of our first meeting, Mr. W's visual and verbal representations of *reality* and of *self* and *other* are understood as a poetic language in which movement is privileged over mimesis, space over speech, spectacle over meaning, and vision over voice. His mode of representation speaks an image-text by which he produces an essential presencing of his internal images of self and (m)other and something of the nature of their past encounters. In this instance, his image-text produces the ghostly images of *the Virgin Queen Mother nursing* –and- *Venetian baby sucking* in their essential presence. Further, it communicates something about the drama of his trauma with momma, as he experiences it to have been. And further, further, he plays the role of each character in the drama: father-man ever seeing, desiring, and fucking; mother-woman ever nursing, drained, and exhausted; and baby-boy ever birthed, hungry, and insatiable.

In this image-text, Mr. W visually shapes the relations between his self and (m)other in ways that at once reveal this division and invite me onto the stage, evocatively engaging me in an act of performance in which I be *baby nursing* in a role of complementarity to his being *mother preparing to nurse.* In wording that I would *not* be feeding off of him and that he would *not* have to nurse me, I reveal the place of my performance and the space of our mutual subjectivity, the complexity of which deepens and richens as we continue our conversation. In wording who I am not, that is, the baby sucking from him- which I could only do by, paradoxically, *being* and *experiencing* that which I say I am not- I do so *not* for the purpose of clarifying and improving his *reality testing* by making a statement of who I might believe I *actually* am; to do so would be little more than for me to seek and lay claim to a position of social dominance and authority. Rather, I say I would *not* be feeding off of him in the service of *reality tasting*; that is, I taste something of his world from the position and space of Venetian baby sucking so as to say, ... *NOT.* On this stage of extreme subjectivity where *reality* is redefined as an illusive imitation of an imitation, I shortly thereafter become *Queen Mother nursing* as he becomes *Venetian baby sucking* a little tasting from my reality.

On speaking with the phantom in the spirit realm: In *The Phantom of the Opera*, the ghost of the Paris opera house demands that Box Five be reserved for him for each and every performance; Box Five is the space reserved for the phantom. Although no one ever actually sees him, everyone anticipates his arrival, hears him enter the box, and feels his palpable presence (Leroux, 1910). And it seems that from the first time we meet, Mr. W and I are in the space reserved for the phantom of his opera: The ghostly presence of his Virgin Queen Mother is hidden in plain sight as she makes her palpable presence known in the way he dresses and floats into that space of preparing to nurse me. The ghostly presence of the hungry baby is also hidden in plain sight as revealed through my act of performance. Mr. W lives with his phantom of the Venetian opera house; the music of his night is expressed in the rhythms and rhymes that organize his life and which inevitably lead us to the sacred space where the phantom of his private theatre resides. In effect, Mr. W. takes us to Box Five, the sacred ground of the spirit realm in which space the mind-poet is always listening to the broader question of the subject's performance in poetic discourse. In so doing, the practitioner as mind-poet defies the act of Aristotelean closure of *being* or *meaning* so as to float and glide between the different subject positions of, for example, the Virgin Queen Mother or the Venetian baby, so as to speak from the subject position that materializes on the stage.

As Mr. W and I float and glide between the text and context, figure and ground, and self and other of his drama, his visual and verbal representations of self and other speak a poetic language, a more primal linguistic, that enables our passage through the gossamer-thin membrane separating the realities of everyday life from those of the spirit realm, which is understood as the specific sensory experiences of being inhabited by his spirits (history) and ghosts (its objects). Understood as another dimension of reality, the spirit realm is always present in the immediate moment, expressed through the associative-interpretive process, and waiting -just beyond our ghostly grasp- to be worded from the stage of this theatre where illusion is treated as reality. In the radical poetics of Artaud's theatre, these sensory experiences are communicated through the evocations and movements of the associative-interpretive process. During our first meeting, for example, Mr. W's visual and verbal representations of self and other speak contextually to his experience that I was draining him in the very act of my being physically present with him and asking him to speak. Indeed, I would have to have been blind to not see, feel, and experience how draining my presence was for him. In-no-cence, I had to open my Venetian blinds so as to see those aspects and hungers of my other (of *self*) as both Virgin Queen Mother and Venetian baby, thereby revealing my desire to receive his milk-filled words from which I could suck meaning.

As in the pre-Aristotelean theatre, the mind-poet performs as did Thespis, the Athenian from Icaria who introduced the first actor of the stage in the modern sense: He or she takes on multiple roles; becomes the character of each other in the play, for example, the phantom mother, father, or baby; and speaks from these different subject positions. The mind-poet performs in a way quite similar to how Mr. W floats and glides between the different subject positions of self and other in his portrayal of his family drama. Thus, the mind-poet occupies multiple subject positions at once, becoming nothing long enough to be someone or something else for the other as called upon to do so throughout the performance. Like dark matter having its gravitational effect on objects, invisible and mysterious forces pull the mind-poet to the specific subject position from which (s)he speaks in a language of materiality to that which lies just beyond one's ghostly grasp.

In speaking as the character of the other, the mind-poet gives his or her self over to the evocations of the music of the night. As the ghost of the theatre moves and creates its personal effects, impressions, and leaves its traces in the analyst's mental life, images, and sounds (Bollas, 1992), there is a doubling down of identity, voice, consciousness, role, discourse, and performance in the analytic narration. Speaking as the character of the other involves the mind-poet gradually freeing his or her self from the illusion and experience of an independently existing fixed-self, entering a Zen-like space of *no self* (*anatman*), and, in so doing, freeing his or her mind by being in a state of *no mind* (*mushin*) where he or she does not *think* but, rather, *knows*. In substituting his or her voice for that of the phantom other, the mind-poet wears a mask underneath which is found his or her self as narrator-in-disguise. In this state of *(k)no(w) mind*, he or she reaches -without reaching- deeply into the darkest inner-most regions of the self and the other (of self), flirting with a kind of death or state of non-being so as to think, feel, experience, and speak as might the ghosts and spirits of the subject's private theatre. In this way, the mind-poet steps onto the stage with another human being, interprets the other of self as if spoken by the self of other, for example, the narrator-in-disguise, and narrates the story as if it were the story of the other. In-no-cence, the mind-poet floats and glides to where he or she is needed in the performance to word the inexplicable, and in so doing participates in the masquerade –and, its cruel travesty— through a doubling of identity into a subject for *self* as mind-poet and a subject for *other*, thereby assisting in the subject escaping from the phantom's ghostly grasp.

ON ESCAPING THE PHANTOM'S GHOSTLY GRASP

> Softly, deftly music shall caress you...
> Hear it feel it, secretly possess you.
> Open up your mind,
> let your fantasies unwind, in the darknes
> which you know you cannot fight...
> the darkness of the music of the night...
>
> -*The Music of the Night*

In looking beneath the mask of the civilized, The *Theatre of Cruelty* reveals the dreams and myths of many if not all people. As the mind-poet looks at his or her face in the mirror and sees the phantom there inside, he or she might catch a glimpse of the more dangerous reality found beneath the mask of shared social realities and civilities. In so doing, the mind-poet might taste something of the phantom's sense of life and death, erotic obsessions and desires, and cannibalistic savageries and compassion. In the dangerous reality of this theatre, one's physical being replaces the verbal as the mind-poet *as human being* steps onto the stage in the place of a scripted character. ... One day after about three weeks, for example, as Mr. W was repeating his story of sacrificial drama and once again reiterating how very tired he was, I remember suddenly having the most intense and vivid of image-text experiences in which I was sucking and biting his nipples until they were bloodied and chewed into raw meat....

In the radical poetics of this metaphysical theatre, the analytic discourse is never too very far from the experiences of the human body, dissolves the borders between art and life, and resists the formulation of human experiences into a prepared text or pre-thought schema. As the borders between self and other dissolve, the mind-poet finds himself or herself immersed in the dramatic action of a world that is bloodthirsty and inhuman (*sanguinaire et inhumain*), engaged on an instinctive level with the performance. Indeed, cruelty "goes to the extremity of instinct and forces the actor to plunge right to the roots of his being so that he leaves the stage exhausted. A cruelty which acts as well upon the spectator and should not allow him to leave the theatre intact, but exhausted, involved, perhaps transformed!" (Artaud, 1974, p. 21).

As Mr. W. finishes his story with once again how tired he is and that he has to rest, I asked him for the first time, How come you have to rest?, What happens if you don't rest? After a lengthy silence, he replied, When I don't get rest, the concrete in the floors begins to melt from the heat of the furnaces in the basement, then they run up my legs. After a long silence, I gently ask, Who runs up your legs? ... *The rats*, he whispers, *they run up my legs and chew on my balls*. He goes on to describe how the chewing on his balls triggers a thick bone running from his testicles to a hydrogen bomb located in his navel. When that happens, it detonates the bomb destroying the US and Canada. It's happened many, many times before, he whispers.

In the collage of pictures in my mind, chunks of missing flesh from his arms and legs came rushing together with the pictures of me chewing his nipples and the rats chewing on his balls. And I be Brother Rat as I begin speaking with him about the necessity of getting rest for the sake of his survival and those around him, and how difficult it is to get rest with the hungry babies sucking and chewing on his nipples 'til they were bloodied and raw, *and* the rats chewing and sucking on his balls 'til *they* were bloodied and raw. So much had been torn and ripped from his flesh; so much had been taken from him as the little Venetian rug-rats sucked and chewed his life from him. He had to give everything of himself to keep others alive while feeling absolutely helpless to do anything about it except to endure...*and* try to get rest so that he could endure even more without exploding and destroying everyone and everything around him. I go on to say that his life consisted of having no life other than to forever be sacrificing his life so that others could live their lives; he could not desire anything for himself. With his eyes still closed, the deepest and darkest of sighs escaped from his ebony dark blackness as he slowly, silently nodded his head. His experiences of *being*, *non-being*, and *being-for-others* increasingly shaped the matrix of our being together, the melody of which produced the following verse in the music of our night.

> Floating, falling, sweet intoxication!
> Let the dream begin, let your darker side give in...
> to the power of the music that I write...
> the power of the music of the night...
>
> -*The Music of the Night*

The next time we met, Mr. W. seemed out of character. He was excited, animated, and spontaneous as he asked about my belt buckle: What's it made of? Where did you get it? How much was it? I asked him what he thought. He replied that it's probably made of a high grade silver metal alloy, that it's probably from the southern tip of Venus where the silver mines are, and with a gold-capped smile, he said that it probably cost me "an arm and a leg." He was absolutely incredulous that I could have such a buckle in my possession. Suddenly in mid-sentence, he stopped and asked, if he could he get a pass to leave the hospital for the upcoming weekend. I mentioned that by our previous agreement we still had time to hear what he had to say before we decided. The following two sessions were spent, for the most part, in a calmed silence with Mr. W. sitting with his eyes closed, his arms folded across his chest, and his seemingly getting rest while waiting for the session when we would make a decision about his pass.

> Let your mind start a journey through a strange new world!
> Leave all thoughts of the world you knew before.
> Let your soul take you where you long to be!
> Only then can you belong to me...
>
> -*The Music of the Night*

During the session in which we were to decide, Mr. W. speaks once again of leaving the hospital, still feeling quite tired (although not as tired as in the past), keeping the protective vigil over his mother, the Venetians still coming for him each night, the babies chewing on his nipples, the rats chewing on his balls, and of the detailed and intricate steps leading to the detonation of the hydrogen bomb. ...*But something's different now!*, he said. As he held out his hand, he informed me that he now has this special pair of pliers. Invisible though they seemed to me, they nonetheless were quite real as he held them in the palm of his hand. What makes them so special? I asked. In an instructive tone of voice, he said, These pliers are made of a special, high-grade silver metal alloy from the planet Venus; they are heat resistant, and they operate to deactivate H-bombs so they won't go off. With a burst of excitement, he claimed, They're all mine — see! He quickly put his hand to his mouth and swallowed the pair of pliers, after which he looked at me, took a deep breath, and said he could handle a pass now. *As he spoke, I had a picture-experience of the pliers having very long jaws, lined with strong little babylike teeth. Pit-bull-like, once they clamp down they never let go, a form of "pliers dentata," no doubt.* I agreed that it seemed like he could handle a pass.

As Mr. W. opened his mouth and swallowed his special pair of pliers, magic –that old nemesis of science- transcended the evil cruelties of his life as he perceived them to be and made its appearance on the stage of our little opera house in this inner city state hospital. Was Mr. W. escaping from his phantom's ghostly grasp and coming to life through an imitative form of magic? Artaud (1974) says about his *Theatre of Cruelty* that

> when the hidden God creates, he obeys a cruel need for creation imposed upon him, yet he cannot avoid creating, thus permitting an ever more condensed, ever more consumed nucleus of evil to enter the eye of the willed vortex of good. Theatre in the sense of constant creation, *a wholly magical act*, obeys this necessity. A play without this necessity, this blind zest for life,...would be useless and a failure as theatre. (p. 78, emphasis added)

Perhaps in this instance, the analytic process is more of a kindred spirit to the magical religious rites of ancient Baby-lonia where the Mouth Opening

Ceremony was held to breathe life into inanimate images (Bahrani, 2003), accompanied in this instance by the opening of my mouth in wonderment and amazement as I bore witness to the drama unfolding in the dream-like reality of this theatre.

Mr. W went on his pass and we resumed our meetings the following Monday morning and continued meeting for nearly four years on the stage of the inpatient unit and for another year in my office after he left. Over these five years, we reached further into the darkness of his ebony black night where we could hear the silent sounds and screams as the Venetian rug-rats chewed on him in his crib, his being unable to fend off their relentless chewing, and about which we could do nothing but endure, except to try to word his experiences. In so doing, words began filling the empty pages of his life. As his milk stopped flowing and dried up, the Venetians stopped coming to take him to nurse their babies. We were left with starving and dying babies all around us. In order to live, we had to feed off of them, rat bastards that we were. Nonetheless, we kept nibbling away at it, adding our mutually caressed words to the blank pages whenever we could.

Situated halfway between thought and gesture, the language of Artaud's theatre is similar to the language of poetry where thoughts, words, and sensory experiences are never completely separated. In this sense, the practitioner becomes a mind-poet who enters that space somewhere in-between feelings, sensory images, and words and speaks the ideographic story being told. The closer the mind-poet comes to speaking in verbal pictures or pictograms, the closer he or she comes to a more unmediated representation of the sensory-image of the thing or experience in question. As stated by Artaud, "Poets, unlike magicians, have knowledge of the void, of that abyss of horror from which the awakening consciousness has always been trying to escape into something. A world of parturition, not of something, but of nothing. The soul is nothing and knows nothing" (quoted in Hayman, 1977, 25).

As Mr. W and I repeatedly went to the edge of the abyss to speak with the phantoms of his theatre, the necessity of reliving his sacrificial drama diminished. And as we watched, listened, and worded these experiences, the primitive bloodthirsty baby beast within turned from the chewed-raw teat to enter a world of unbelievable loneliness, sadness, and darkness in the presence of which we, many times, could only sit in our silence. Just when everything seemed most uncertain, chaotic and fragmented, we somehow would find some words. Paradoxically, it was in this place and space that, in the words of Artaud (1974), that madman-philosopher, "cruelty connects things together, the different stages of creation are formed by it. Good is always an external façade but the inner façade is evil. Evil will eventually be reduced but *only at the final moment when all forms are on the point of returning to chaos*" (p. 79, emphasis added).

You alone can make my song take flight,
It's over now, the music of the night....
-The Phantom of the Opera

THE THEATRE OF CRUELTY AND THE QUESTION OF REALITY, REPRESENTATION, AND REPRESENTATION'S OTHER

> The poetic testimony reveals an other world inside this world, that other world is this world. ...Senses, without losing their powers, become servants of imagination and with them we can hear the astounding and see the invisible. Isn't this, by the way, the same that happens in dreams and the erotic encounter? Both in dreaming and in coupling we embrace phantoms....
>
> -Octavio Paz, *The Double Flame*

For the philosophers of ancient Greece, the essence of human nature was situated in rationality. The original essence of being was situated in the philosophy of consciousness that dominated in their art, literature, and science. As there was no concept of the unconscious in ancient Greece, the rational and sensual sides of human nature were understood as consciously locked in a continuous struggle, in which struggle psychological insights and knowledge were necessary to subordinate the disruptive passions of human nature to the reason and logic of rationality. In this cultural context, Aristotle's theatre was an art form that elucidated a character and typically solved a psychological conflict by the end of the play, the insights of which were to assist the spectator by providing an understanding of and mastery over the disruptive and turbulent passions underlying the basic dramas of everyday life.

In this genre of theatre, the performances of actors are understood as a form of direct imitation of reality or *mimesis*, meaning *a close copy of that which is* as it actually exists in a mind-independent and objectively knowable world. *Representation* is defined in terms of the actor's ability to imitate universal truths about people and the human psyche (Oswald, 1989). The dramatic representation in speech by the scripted character on stage is a mimetic copy of reality from which psychological insights derive for the benefit of the spectator. More specifically, the psychological insights that derive from the Aristotelean play assist the rational element (*logos*) in prevailing over the non-rational elements of lustful desire (*thumos*) and the heart's desire (*epithumia*) (Norman, 1983). In the Westernized cultures, the theatre developed in this tradition.

Artaud's theatre moves away from the classical understanding of *mimesis, reality*, and *representation* and moves closer to Freud's initial and intuitive grasp of the unconscious as *affectivity* or *life*. With his interpretive encounter with hysteria Freud marked the founding of psychoanalysis with the unconscious as its explicative principle. As its fundamental concept, the Freudian unconscious had no theoretical existence other than providing the only possible explanation for the discontinuities in the lived experiences of everyday life (Freud, 1895; 1900; 1905). With his concept of the unconscious, the original essence of being moved from the traditional center of consciousness to the more radical center of the unconscious. More than simply a negative determination of that which is not conscious, the Freudian unconscious rejected the traditional primacy of consciousness which became but the point of departure for the analytic inquiry (Henry, 1993). With his initial and intuitive understanding of the unconscious as *affectivity* or *life*, Freud stepped outside the Western philosophical tradition and described the crucial character of unconscious activity as falling outside of representability: *the unconscious* was *representation's other*.[2.]

Artaud's metaphysical theatre and Freud's initial grasp of the unconscious privilege the processes of life such as experience, body, and affectivity over an Aristotelean *representation of life* by the mind, intellect, and contemplation. In so doing, Artaud's theatre moves closer to the essence of human nature as situated in extreme inner experiences, the body, and affectivity, and moves closer to the original essence of being as situated in Freud's notion of the unconscious as *representation's other*. In the radical poetics of Artaud's theatre, a very different understanding of *reality, representation, and mimesis* underlies the performance. For Artaud, imagination is reality. Or put another way, reality is imagination represented in external form through the more primal linguistic of physical movement and gesture. This concrete and physical language of the stage gives expression to extreme subjective experiences through space and movement and, in so doing, transcends oppositions between body and soul, reality and representation, and voice and meaning in a movement of performance that lies closer to the phenomenal event (Oswald, 1989). Artaud's theatre does not strive to produce a direct copy of reality. His theatre is of another kind of reality that leads back into the world of dreams and primitive instincts where a world of the bloodthirsty and inhuman (*sanguinaire et inhumain*) is found (Artaud, 1958; 1968).

In Artaud's theory of theatre, the dramatic action on stage is not intended to provide insights about universal psychological truths in the service of reason conquering the disruptive passions of life. Rather, his theatre intends to generate awe, anxiety and terror in the audience for the purpose of causing an abandonment of reason. In so doing, a new set of truths emerge as the spectators connect with the more primitive forces of their being. "In true theatre, a play disturbs the senses' repose, frees the repressed unconscious, incites a kind of virtual revolution (which moreover can have its full effect only if it remains virtual) and imposes on the assembled collectivity an attitude that is both difficult and heroic" (Artaud, 1974, 16).

Artaud's theatre rests on a representational mode that developed quite apart from the post-Greek metaphysics and ideas of *mimesis, reality* and *representation*. His mode of representation appears to be quite similar to the rich philosophical conception of *representation* found in ancient Mesopotamia in which thoughts, images, and words are never completely separated; succinctly stated: the interaction of the verbal image and text constitutes *representation* (Bahrani , 2003).[3.] This form of representation combines the written, verbal, and visual to produce the conjuring presence of an image, the representation of which takes the place of *the real*. In the ancient Near East, ontology is grounded in notions of representation as much as it is in our postmodern philosophies.

In both pre- and postmodern philosophies, ontology and metaphor interweave to represent the person's state of being and reality; that is, *reality* is constructed by its *representation*: Thus, Mr. W's representation of his *Virgin Queen Mother* is not a substitute for the real object or experience. What he conceives of as *the real essence* of his phantom is present in his representational image of mother. His visual-verbal representation of himself as the Queen Mother through, for example, how he dresses, walks and continuously prepares for nursing the babies, constitutes, at once, his mode of representing and presencing her on the theatre's stage in the present moment of the past. In so doing, she floats and glides through the hallways of time, enters our private theatre, and makes her ghostly presence palpably known. His mode of representation corresponds with how he conceives of his (m)other and also something about the nature of his relationship with her, as he perceived it to be. It is this correspondence with his phenomenal past that constructs his experiences of both *reality* and *mimesis*. To the extent that his representations resemble the real as he perceives it to be –and, to have been—then to that extent do his representations constitute a mimetic representation of the reality to be understood in the unfolding performance.

CONCLUSION

Artaud's theatre presents another stage from which the mind of the poet might reach even further into the spirit realm to speak with the phantoms that reside in the private theatre of the other (of self). Stepping onto the stage of this more dangerous reality, however, involves stepping from behind the mask of logical discourse, immersing one's self in the associative-interpretive process, and entering the complexities of an extreme mutual subjectivity. Entry into the radical poetics of Artaud's theatre involves a reconsideration of our largely unquestioned assumptions underlying the concepts of *reality*, *representation*, and *mimesis*, and of our more traditional concepts of *the unconscious*. In this radical understanding of psychic theatre, psychoanalysis goes far beyond the more traditional notion of 'psychological insights' to reach into the metaphysical truths as revealed and concealed beneath the mask in one's private theatre.

As a performance art, the analytic discourse enters into the dramas of life and death as produced, directed, and choreographed by the subject and as communicated via the associative-interpretive process. In speaking as the character of the other, the mind-poet participates in the death of self so as to become nothing long enough to enter the dangerous reality beneath the mask where psychic theatre becomes a theatre of magic in which words have the power they have in dreams, language is a rhythmical incantation, and the essentially poetic nature of its discourse dances with the unconscious understood as representation's other. In so doing, the mind-poet might word the madness of self and other (of self) and contribute to the subject's escaping from his or her phantom's ghostly grasp.

An earlier version of this paper was first presented on June 16th, 2009 in Copenhagen, Denmark at the 16th annual conference of the International Symposium for the Psychological Treatments of the Schizophrenias and other Psychoses (ISPS). The organizing theme of this paper is *The Reach of the Mind.*

NOTES

1. The lyrics for the *Phantom of the Opera* were written by Charles Hart and Richard Stilgoe.
2. In *The Genealogy of Psychoanalysis (1993),* Michel Henry - a professor of philosophy at the Universite Paul Valery, Montpellier - calls into question the Freudian unconscious and its Lacanian reformulation. His central thesis develops from the radical distinction made between *life* and the *representation* of *life*. He asserts that it is impossible to represent life by the mind, intellect, and contemplation. As *being* is neither visible nor does it represent itself, representation is incapable of representing *life* or *reality*. No sooner, however, did Freud assert that the drive is "activity in its pure form and the principle of all activity" (quote in Henry, 1993, p. xvii) than he drew it back into the realm of representation by declaring that it acquires psychic reality only through the intermediary of its representative. Originally *representation's other*, the unconscious now contained representation. And in Henry's reading, the aberrant concept of a rational unconscious representation was born.
3. In *The Graven Image (2003),* Zainab Bahrani, an Edith Porada associate professor of art history and archaeology at Columbia university, notes that the study of representational practices through the analysis of semiotics and rhetoric, as well as the concept of mimesis, have become standard theoretical inroads for investigation in art history, literary criticism, cultural studies, and anthropology.

REFERENCES

Artaud, A. (1958). *The theater and its double.* (M.C. Richards. Trans.) New York: Grove Press.

(1968). *The Theatre of Cruelty.* In E. Bently. ed., *The theory of the modern stage* (pp. 66-81) New York: Penguin.

(1974). *Collected works of Antonin Artaud.* (V. Corti. Trans.) London: Calder & Boyars.

Bahrani, Z. (2003). The graven image: Representation in Babylonia and Assyria.

Philadelphia: University of Pennsylvania Press,

Bermel, A. (1977). *Artaud's Theatre of Cruelty.* New York: Taplinger.

Breuer, J. & Freud, S. (1895). Studies on hysteria. In J. Strachey. ed. and trans., *The standard edition of the complete psychological works of Sigmund Freud,* 24 vols. London: Hogarth Press, 1953-1974. *2*:1-307.

Bollas, C. (1992). *Being a character: Psychoanalysis and self experience.* London: Routledge.

Fischer-Lichte E. (1992). *The semiotics of theater.* (J. Gaines & D. L. Jones. trans.) Indianapolis, Indiana University Press.

Freud, S. (1900). The interpretation of dreams. *Standard ed.*, 4, 5.

(1905). Three essays on the theory of sexuality. *Standard ed, 7*: 123-244.

Hayman, R. (1977). *Artaud and after.* London: Oxford University Press.

Henry, (1993), *The genealogy of psychoanalysis.* Stanford, Calif.: Stanford University Press.

Jamieson, L. (2007). *Antonin Artaud: From theory to practice.* London: Greenwich Exchange.

Knapp, B.L. (1969). *Antonin Artaud: Man of vision.* New York: David Lewis.

Levan, M. & Caddick D. (1990). *The phantom of the opera.* [Canadian cast recording.] Toronto: Manta Sound Studios.

Leroux, G. (1910). *The phantom of the opera.* (L. Blair. trans.) New York: Bantam Books

McDougall, J. (1985). *Theaters of the mind: Illusion and truth on the psychoanalytic stage.* New York: Basic Books.

(1989). *Theaters of the body: A psychoanalytic approach to psychosomatic illness.* New York: Norton.

Norman, R. (1983). *The moral philosophers: An introduction to ethics.* Oxford: Oxford University Press.

Oswald, L. (1989). *Jean Ginet and the semiotics of performance.* Indianapolis: Indiana University Press.

Zinder, D.G. (1980*). The Surrealist connection, An approach to a surrealist aesthetic of theater.* Ann Arbor: University of Michigan Research Press.

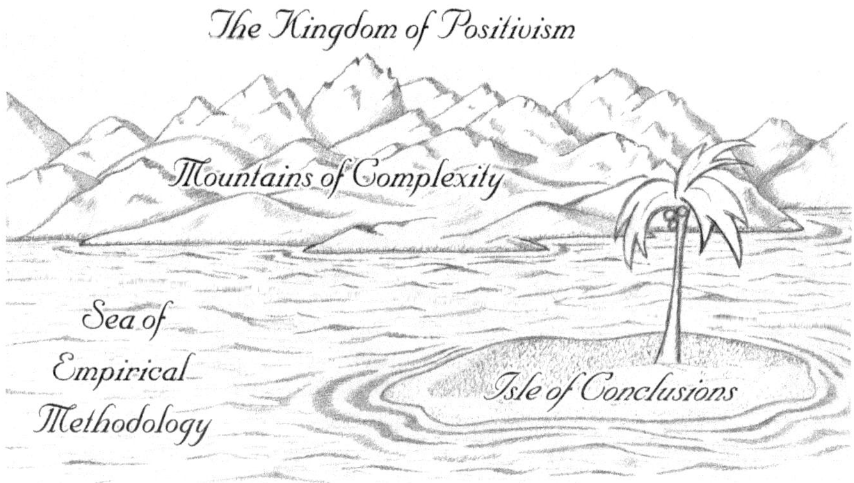

Eight

A Fractured Fairytale

The Story of Our Professional Lives in The Kingdom of Positivism

> Objectivism suggests more than a false expression of neutrality. In essence, it tacitly represents a denial of ethical values. Its commitment to rigorous techniques, mathematical expression and law-like regularities supports not only one form of scientific inquiry but social formations that are inherently repressive and elitist as well. Its elimination of "ideology" works in the service of the ideology of social engineers.
>
> \- Henry A. Giroux

A long time ago in a place far away, the little Kingdom of Positivism was settled on the western shores of the Sea of Empirical Methodology. Nestled in the foothills of Certainty, the kingdom's scientific vision of the world, people, and life held out the promise of safety, simplicity, and security in its citizens' lives from the time they emerged from the womb until they entered the tomb. The kingdom's royal family, The Family of Natural Sciences, lived on the Isle of Conclusions[2.] Located not too far from the mainland, it was possible to jump to the island on those days that the king and his group of ministers were gathered to make their far-reaching decisions for the greater good of the kingdom and its citizens.

King Technocracy 1st was known far and wide for his impartial rulings; his technocratic rationality was quite thorough, objective and efficient. He always relied on the wise counsel and advisements of his prime minister, Mr. Science, in determining the decisions that were in the best interests of his subjects. Of course, once he made his decisions, they were very hard to change: Prime Minister Science produced answers to some very complex questions at the .01 level of confidence, a very high level of confidence, indeed, which often led to some rather conclusionary conclusions coming from the Isle of Conclusions.

It was a very wonderful kingdom in which to live. Prime Minister Science and the rest of the royal family were like members of each citizen's family, sitting with them at the dinner table every night in their cottages and helping them make decisions about the stuff of their everyday lives. Their concerns invariably centered on the question, "How do we best live life on our journey from the womb to the tomb?" Prime Minister Science provided the best way to think about and answer such questions as: When is the best time to plant and harvest the crops? What kind of fertilizers should be used? Should the cottage be insulated? What subjects should the children take in school? Why isn't Milo paying attention in class? What and how much should the kids eat for lunch in the school cafeteria? And, What should they be when they grow up? The Prime Minister was like a spiritual minister to the family: He advised the family on their best choices and how to make the best decisions. And, he did that by dividing life into different phases with each having its phase-specific stages, conflicts, and issues.

Mr. Science knew, in advance, the most efficient pre-thought, pre-validated, and pre-approved solutions for the problems in living encountered by the family, the children, the young adults, the middle-aged, and the geriatrics, also known in the kingdom as "the old wrinkled ones." Mr. Science anticipated each phase of life and resolved its particular problems, even before the person actually lived the experiences or encountered the problems of the specific phase in question. It was very efficient in terms of time, cost and energy and the certainty provided was most comforting. Mr. Science, in collaboration with the royal family of sciences, could even provide efficient answers and solutions to the mysteries of life such as those surrounding death and dying: Funerals could be pre-paid, eulogies pre-written, and loved ones pre-grieved in identifiable sequential steps, no less. Indeed, he provided the citizens with answers to not only such questions as, "How should we think about things?" and "What should we do in certain situations?" but also, "What are the things that should matter in life?" Over the years, Prime Minister

Science had empirically established the normatively based ideal answer for many of the citizens' questions.

THE KINGDOM'S CULTURAL CONTEXT: A POSITIVISTIC IDEOLOGY

More than simply an epistemological doctrine, positivism was a potent form of ideology in the kingdom: It constructed its social reality in which there was only One True God, One True World, One True Logic, One True Essence, and One True Truth. Truth was revealed, of course, by Prime Minister Science; objectivity was the cornerstone for his methodology which constituted the only legitimate paradigm for knowledge production in the kingdom. It was really quite simple, and simply wonderful: Safety, simplicity and security flowed from the kingdom's positivistic ideological frame of reference. ... Oh, yes! There was something else.

Within the kingdom's socio-political universe, positivistic thought was committed to only one form of social formation: Those institutional structures that supported the kingdom's principles of hierarchy and control. Infused with the positivist's ideology, the kingdom's bureaucratic entities relied on positivistic beliefs and value systems to gather the citizens' consent for the social policies and practices developed on the Isle of Conclusions and communicated through the king's decrees. Consistent with its ideology, the kingdom's dominant values emphasized prediction and control in each of its socio-political spheres. King Technocracy 1st decreed, for example, that the goals of the royal family of sciences were to narrowly focus on objectivity, efficiency, and technique. Eventually, their goals and objectives led to the development of outcome-based objectives and measures in such diverse areas as education, the economy, manufacturing, and foreign trade.

The kingdom's scientific vision carried the implicit promise to the citizens that the cruelties of life did not have to enter the kingdom or their lives if they lived their lives within the parameters of the scientifically established normative ideal. Indeed, life could be relatively conflict-free. Of course, its positivistic ideology necessarily defined and restricted what was "acceptable" and "appropriate" discourse within the kingdom. Only certain ideas and social relationships were understood as natural, rational, self-evident, and universal which formed the underpinnings for the kingdom's positivistic notions of morality. Perversions and psychopathology, for example, were understood and defined by the number of standard deviations from the empirically established norm the relationship or idea in question was from that which was the natural, rational, self-evident, and universal. It was really quite simple. It was wonderful to live in a kingdom where Prime Minister Science and his trusted advisers from the royal family did all the thinking necessary for its people, whether citizens or professionals. With sufficient funding, progress would continue to forever expand the networks of safety, simplicity and security the citizens and professionals had come to know, expect and rely upon.

THE INDUSTRIAL AGE AND THE KINGDOM'S HEALTHCARE REVOLUTIONS

As in the larger kingdom, positivism in the analytic community was much more than simply an epistemological doctrine: It was a potent form of ideology that smothered the tug of conscience and blinded its adherents to the ideological nature of its own frame of reference (Giroux, 1997). From its early beginnings, the principles of rationality in the natural sciences were seen in the psychoanalytic community as vastly superior to the hermeneutic principles underlying the more speculative social sciences: A scientific vision of reality, people, and life formed the underlying assumptions of psychoanalytic knowledge and theories of practice. The psychoanalytic community shared many of the same beliefs, values, and attitudes as found in the larger kingdom such as, for example, the positivist's objective that sought the technical mastery of people through the scientific production and acquisition of knowledge. During the early years, the positivistic values of the analytic culture interfaced with those of the larger kingdom. As the years passed, however, they became inseparably intertwined.

The educational and political institutions in the analytic community supported principles of hierarchy and control and had done so since their early beginnings. Their conceptual foundations, rooted in biology, medicine, and the natural sciences, grounded the political and ideological hierarchies of *power* and *knowledge* in their institutions. And their educational institutions were the only authorized and legitimate sites of True Knowledge acquisition. Of course, madness was excluded from the psychologies of psychoanalysis just as the mad had been excluded from society by the rational ones who met on the Isle of Conclusions. King Technocracy 1st and the royal family thought it was a particularly enlightened decision to move the insane into psychiatric hospitals or asylums located far out in the country where they could be studied, treated and cured by the medical-scientific community.

Educated and trained as the kingdom's social scientists, psychoanalytic practitioners were very happy because they were invited to be major players in forming social policy on the Isle of Conclusions: They were social engineers in the sociopolitical movement to make the kingdom a better place in which to live, and to make the kingdom's citizen's happier and more productive in their villages.

Sometime during the latter days of the kingdom's industrial age – or, "Back in the olden days of the mid-1900's...", as the old wrinkled ones might say- healthcare was just a teeny-weeny sector of the kingdom's economy. It was back then that the first of several healthcare revolutions took place in the kingdom. The first revolution, named *The Era of Expansion* (Keisler, 2000), was a bitter, hard-fought, grass-roots revolution lasting from the late '40's through the mid-'60's. At the end of their political-legislative crusade, organized psychology and psychiatry emerged as full-fledged members in the family of healthcare professions. "We are independent healthcare professionals!," they joyously and proudly proclaimed. There were wild celebrations and dancing in the streets because now they could receive a government-issued license to diagnose the citizens of the kingdom, treat them with their talking therapy, and qualify for medical insurance reimbursement for their services. Of course, they also could be sued for malpractice if they happened to misdiagnose the pathological condition and apply the wrong treatment but they were not too concerned about that at the time.

Most of the kingdom's professionals were very, very happy. There were a few, however, that were somewhat concerned with declaring people with "problems in living" as having "diagnosable pathological conditions in need of treatment." "Don't worry," they were told by the older ones, "We don't really mean that people are sick; that's just a metaphor." And those who were concerned said, "Oh!" And, they became very, very happy because they realized that their professional organizations really didn't mean what they said: They were just talking metaphorically, even though their legal liability and exposure were quite real.

The kingdom's second healthcare revolution was kind of unexpected in the professional community. In contrast to the earlier grass-roots revolution, it started with the institutional representatives gathered on the Isle of Conclusions. Named *The Era of Cost Containment* (Keisler, 2000), it began in the mid-'60's and some say that it continues 'til this very day. A healthcare-industrial complex had gradually formed among various institutions in the kingdom and the talking therapy taking place in the kingdom's cottages was declared to be a "cottage industry" which meant, of course, that it was in need of industrialization. Although it wasn't fully realized at the time by those in the analytic community, the healthcare professions were moving from interfacing with the other institutions on the Isle of Conclusions to becoming inseparably intertwined with them. As a consequence, the healthcare professions slowly but inexorably became encircled by the various regulatory, legislative, governmental, and insurance entities.

The Era of Cost Containment witnessed the institutionalization of healthcare accreditation standards in education and the delivery of mental health services, national licensing examinations to assess minimal standards of practice competency, and utilization review committees to justify the medical necessity and appropriateness of the talking therapy. Once again, some professionals were growing concerned. It seemed to them that *the individual* was getting lost in the technocratic systems developing within and between the various institutions on the Isle of Conclusions: Their standards standardized the therapy, their regulations regulated whom they could see, and the decisions made by various institutions institutionalized their professional standards.

The Era of Cost Containment blended with the third and most recent of the kingdom's healthcare revolutions, *The Era of Assessment and Accountability* (Keisler, 2000). By this time, *interfacing* with the values of the larger culture had moved to becoming *inseparably intertwined* in the kingdom's Healthcare-Industrial-Complex, also known as the healthcare matrix. The kingdom's healthcare professions were in the final stages of being industrialized. More than just a trendy buzz-word, "being industrialized" meant something quite specific: The scientific management of the healthcare professional's education and practice now took place through the increased centralization of information, authority, and decision-making power in the kingdom's various bureaucratic entities, and through the uniformity of policies and procedures that defined and assured so-called "quality" in education and practice. As these principles of industrialization combined with the kingdom's long-standing tradition of utilitarian pragmatism, the educational industry "geared-up," so to speak, to mass-produce analytic practitioners for the mass-distribution and mass-consumption of time and cost-effective empirically based treatments (EBTs): Outcome-based education produced practitioners proficient in providing outcome-based therapy. It was really quite simple and straightforward as most things were in the kingdom.

By the latter part of the '90's, there was an inherent intolerance for the exercise of individual discretionary judgment in matters of education or practice. And the decree went forth from King Technocracy 1st into the farthest reaches of the kingdom,

> Henceforth, all healthcare professionals shall establish empirical data-bases justifying the effectiveness of their therapies. The design of and access to care in the healthcare delivery system will ultimately be determined by evidence-based strategies linking outcome and cost-effectiveness.

Of course, there were those concerned few in the analytic community who asked, "What do the methods and assumptions of a science of objectivity have to do with psychoanalysis as a science of subjectivity?" They didn't understand, of course, that in a positivist's framework, subjectivity is the internal *effect* that results from an external *objective cause* whether biological, social, or psychological. It really didn't matter, however, because nobody paid much attention to their concerns: It had been concluded on the Isle of Conclusions that it was for the greater good. "Don't worry," the Medical Minister of Psychoanalytic Sciences told them, "We're a natural science; we can empirically justify what we do. And besides, it's in the best interests of the public to empirically validate our services." And those who were concerned replied, "But we thought it was just a metaphor!" And very patiently, they were asked by the Medical Minister in his most ministerial of voices, "Can you spell *reification*?" And slowly, they came to learn what *reification of the metaphor* meant for their profession.

THE KINGDOM'S CHANGING SOCIAL FABRIC: INFORMATION TECHNOLOGY SYSTEMS AND CONFIDENTIALITY

At about the same time that the king's decree was issued directing healthcare professionals establish their empirical data-bases, other decrees were going forth into various sectors of the kingdom. Wrapped in the cloak of protecting the public, a maze of regulations and administrative rules were developed and implemented to provide for the increased security and safety of the citizens. As the Patriot Act of 2001, for example, was designed to increase the national security and protect the public in the larger culture, the Health Insurance Portability and Accountability Act of 1996 (HIPAA) was implemented to protect the public's privacy and confidentiality in the healthcare sector. Both the Patriot Act and HIPPA were approved on the Isle of Conclusions with the royal family's broad bi-partisan support. And yet, both acts were criticized by various independent citizens groups for giving greater rights of access to information to the kingdom's institutional representatives than to the individual citizen: Privacy in both the public and professional setting was becoming not so private.

While many healthcare professionals were concerned about the power usurped by the kingdom's governmental agencies and representatives through the Patriot Act, there was a thundering silence in the analytic community about the passage of HIPPA that, in effect, instituted a new HIPPA-cratic Oath for the kingdom's analytic practitioners. Indeed, most practitioners applauded the new HIPPA-cratic commitment to privacy. Focused on the most observable consequences of HIPPA, they saw signs reminding healthcare providers not to talk in elevators about patients, signs at Costco requiring customers to stand ten feet back from the pharmacy counter out of respect for the privacy of the person ahead, and signs for the receptionists and staff at clinics, nursing homes, and hospitals to be mindful of issues surrounding privacy and confidentiality. Otherwise, the chilling words, "HIPPAAAA Violationnnn!!!" might suddenly ring out over the loudspeaker. By and large, the increased awareness and respect for the individual's privacy was praised as a good thing in the analytic community. Beyond these everyday experiences, however, there was a significant indifference to HIPPA and the farther-reaching implications that sprang from the high-tech information systems that had developed and enveloped the kingdom's healthcare sector.

The underbelly of the HIPPA Act seemed to remain under the radar in the professional community: Whereas information could not be shared with a patient's family members without consent from the patient, all information could be readily shared among governmental and judicial entities without any such consent from the individual citizen. Specifically, HIPPA legitimized the sharing of records and information among the kingdom's institutional entities for purposes that included, but were not limited to: reporting sexual, physical and emotional abuse; health oversight activities; law enforcement needs and requirements; judicial and administrative proceedings; organ procurement programs; military and intelligence functions; worker compensation matters; healthcare research projects; marketing health-related products and services; and, providing data-bases for fund raising for health-related projects. Other than these and a few other exceptions, information gathered in a therapeutic situation was privileged and *strictly* confidential.

Re-assurances were given to the kingdom's citizens and professionals with the passage of the Affordable Healthcare Act of 2009: Electronic medical records and the sharing of information contained therein would remain privileged and *strictly* confidential. It was a little bit harder for both citizens and professionals to believe, however, when they learned that no one on the Isle of Conclusions had read the decree before its approval and implementation.

THE SHRINKING OF SPACES FOR PSYCHOANALYTIC EDUCATION AND PRACTICE: AN HISTORICAL PERSPECTIVE

Outcome-based education and therapy were the wave of the present in the kingdom. As were other healthcare professionals, psychoanalytic practitioners became known as vendors required to justify their professional existence by validating their talking therapy as a viable medical procedure in the insurance industry's product line of medical treatments. Identified by history and politics as healthcare professionals, the analytic educator and practitioner were caught in the redefinition of their professional standards: standards of practice and care, educational and training standards, and ethical standards and principles. Concepts like *medical necessity, ethics*, and *professional standards* in the mental health field were rapidly evolving in the context of physical healthcare. Of the two medical-scientific models dominant in the kingdom's healthcare matrix, the psychoanalytic model was in the process of being displaced by the bio-chemical imbalance model which was determined to be more time and cost-effective.

Most in the analytic community had somehow forgotten the political-legislative history that had brought about such drastic changes in the story of their professional lives. In 1989, King Technocracy 1st had decreed the '90's to be "The Decade of the Brain" and, in so doing, began funneling billions of dollars into brain-behavior research. Some in the analytic community thought that the evil pharmaceutical empire had infiltrated key positions of power on the Isle of Conclusions: The political machinations of the evil ones, they thought, had appropriated the royal family's decision-making power. The massive infusion of research funds and grant monies into the bio-chemical model brought surprise, shock, and alarm in the analytic community. By the mid-'90's, the alphabet soup of healthcare delivery systems flourished and came into its own. And the only reply from the Isle of Conclusions to the questions and protests from the analytic community was, "Can you spell HMO, PPO, and HAP?"

Some members of the analytic community mustered their most compelling and persuasive arguments and presented them to Prime Minister Science who, by this time, was also chair of the kingdom's Information Technology Systems. "You're not empathic!" they shouted in unison; "You don't care about people!," they screamed in frustration and, perhaps the most damning indictment of all, "The insurance companies and the pharmaceuticals have business profit motives!" Their arguments and accusations echoed throughout the kingdom until the major institutional players on the Isle of Conclusions took notice, paused, and replied, "Soooo?" And the analytic vendors replied, "Oh!" for they had come to realize that the insurance companies and pharmaceuticals were, indeed, businesses that functioned by business principles, were motivated by profits, and were major players on the Isle of Conclusions. It was really quite simple, as most things were in the kingdom.

Unfortunately, Mr. Science determined the psychoanalytical model to be the least effective form of medical treatment in the kingdom in terms of time, cost and predictive outcomes. When he related this to the kingdom's psychoanalytic professionals, they were very, *very* unhappy. They felt justifiably angry: Just because they were a medical specialty marching under the banner of the medical-scientific tradition, it seemed quite unfair that they were being held to the standards of medicine and science. At about the same time, the integration of mental health services into the healthcare delivery system was occurring very rapidly with systemic consequences appearing in the areas of education and practice. And so, organized psychoanalysis came up with some rather innovative ideas. First and foremost, psychoanalysis would move into the future by reemphasizing its conceptual foundations in biology, medicine, and the natural sciences. "We are a science!" they proclaimed, as they announced the wedding of psychoanalysis with the neurosciences.

The news spread like wild fire through the analytic community. Soon, slides of pretty multi-colored areas of the brain began appearing at various psychoanalytic conferences: Bright yellows and flaming reds, pretty blues and pale greens lit up different areas of the brain's darkened intellect in the darkened conference rooms across the kingdom. Practitioners rose excitedly from their chairs proclaiming, "Freud was right! His dream theory is valid!" The return to Freud's Scientific Project gave them hope. Some troubling questions, however, were quietly whispered in the shadows of the conference rooms: "How does conceptualizing the subject as a bio-neural organism in the multi-colored laboratory slides relate to conceptualizing the subject as a person in the analytic space?" "Isn't this dichotomous conceptualization of the person –and the scientific dissection of his or her brain- a remnant of a nineteenth-century worldview and science?," And of course, there was the, by now, familiar chorus of voices asking, "What does a science of objectivity have to do with a science of subjectivity?" And further, "What if in the analytic space, *subjectivity* is the primary framework of human experience, within which *objectivity* is a function of one's *subjectivity?*"

Nobody seemed to pay too much attention, however, amidst the excitement of yet another innovative idea: "We'll develop our own national healthcare accreditation standards so we can receive a government-issued license to practice psychoanalysis!" Sadly, it was much harder to celebrate wildly and dance in the streets as the old wrinkled ones had once done: There was an uneasy and growing awareness in the analytic community that they were participating in the process of industrializing themselves. They had become trapped in the time-worn argument of the encircled, "If we don't do it (to ourselves) then someone else will! We can at least do it in a more informed way." Ah! Such is the logic of the desperate. No one seemed to want to talk much about it, except those invested in maintaining and perpetuating the status quo. And, it was increasingly difficult for others to speak out because, as in most ideological kingdoms, there was a certain element of danger in doing so.

In the meantime, the changing needs of the marketplace required that integral aspects of graduate school education undergo major revisions in terms of its focus and emphasis. At the forefront of the kingdom's positivistic pedagogical paradigm was its preoccupation with the instrumental use of knowledge: "What tools do you have in your toolbox to fix depression, schizophrenia, or anorexia as specified in the DSM-IV (V, or VI)?" The graduate had to know the right tool to fix the right problem in the most cost and time-efficient way possible. Knowledge became prized for its predictive and control value; notions of meaning that could not be objectified and quantified were simply disregarded as irrelevant and of no pragmatic use. Outcome-based education was organized around normative conceptions of people and "successful therapy" was organized around theoretically anticipated and empirically validated outcomes. And, the neurosciences became part of the core bodies of knowledge(s) taught in accredited graduate school programs, the mastery of which was necessary for successfully passing the kingdom's national licensing exam.

Of course, there was no place for the Freudian unconscious in the kingdom's graduate schools. Indeed, the Freudian unconscious had been banished from the hallways of accredited analytic institutes since their inception. As a philosophy of life, the Freudian unconscious had not been permitted within their walls: IT – not to be confused with the IT of the Information Technology (IT) systems realm-was not measurable or teachable. Rumor had it that sometime back in '94 or '95 a Freudian unconscious had been spotted somewhere in the remote northern regions of the kingdom. The rumor was never substantiated, however, and there were no further reported sightings. Understood as *the life force*, the Freudian unconscious had been pretty much rationalized out of existence in the analytic community. IT had been diluted over the years and brought into the kingdom's Grand Technocratic Rationality: The positivistic culture privileged the *mind* and *intellect* over *bodily experiences* and *affectivity or life.*

In the service of demystifying psychoanalysis, the more traditional subject-object paradigm held much greater appeal in the community: The knowledge(s) generated from its paradigm were more rational, teachable, learnable, and testable on written exams. The assumptions of a universal, predictable, and empirically supported developmental psychology held a strong appeal in the community. The unconscious was re-conceptualized, for example, as a developing set of capacities that organized experiences in progressively more integrated and symbolic forms within the phase-specific logic of the particular sequential-stage. With a more rational view of the unconscious, the rational-empiricists excitedly declared, "We can empirically validate the unconscious and study the factors involved in a successful analytic outcome!" It was very sad, however, because nobody in the larger kingdom seemed too very interested, much less very excited.

THE LOSS OF INDIVIDUAL HISTORICAL CONSCIOUSNESS IN THE HISTORICAL DISCIPLINE OF PSYCHOANALYSIS

The decline in the value, interest and role of psychoanalysis in the kingdom was reluctantly addressed in the analytic community. The initial questions posed were deceptively simple: What happened to psychoanalysis in the kingdom? What accounts for its decline? The initial response was quite superficial and, in a not so veiled way, blaming of the citizens: "It's a fast-food society and people simply want a quick fix." People were not interested in investing the necessary time, money, and energy to be involved in psychoanalysis. Like a mantra, this understanding of the decline of psychoanalysis became the conventional wisdom, reflexively and frequently repeated in analytic circles. It seemed to be a simple, safe and secure explanation that brought great comfort to the analytic community.

Over time, however, this rather simplistic explanation made less and less sense, particularly as the analytic community began noticing that more and more of the citizenry were becoming deeply interested and involved in the eastern philosophies, forms of education, and therapeutic practices which often required considerable investments of time, energy and money: People did not seem to be searching for a quick fix. The conventional wisdom quickly faded as it was realized that the kingdom's citizens were spending approximately fifty-five cents of every healthcare dollar on alternative medicines and practices for which the services provided were not covered or reimbursed by medical insurance.

At about the same time that this realization was taking place, something was happening in the analytic community: A small group of psychoanalytic educators and practitioners were moving out of the kingdom's villages peacefully nestled in the foothills of Certainty and moving to the small villages near the tundra in the Mountains of Complexity where they formed the Colony of Critical Considerations, also known as the Colony. They were a group of loosely organized skeptical philosophers who were united in their dedication to critically thinking about the positivistic assumptions underlying psychoanalysis and the kingdom's natural order of things. They were a somewhat disagreeable group: They disagreed with the king's decree declaring that they were vendors; they disagreed with his educratic decree, "No Analytic Practitioner Left Behind;" and, they disagreed with his practice decree that "It Takes a Village to Regulate Psychoanalytic Practice."

Most immediately, their move to the Colony was prompted by the passage of a resolution by organized psychoanalysis urging the passage of licensing laws by those on the isle of conclusions in order to practice psychoanalysis. They posed what they thought was the obvious question: "Why was a license issued by the Isle of Conclusions necessary to practice the historical discipline of psychoanalysis?" "When did an individual's history and life story become a controlled substance?" And, there was another question of no less importance, "Is organized psychoanalysis an unwitting participant in the decline of psychoanalysis?"

Once settled in the Colony, they were concerned, first and foremost, with the troubling question, "What if there were no stories about peoples' lives that could be told in the analytic space outside of those that had been pre-approved on the Isle of Conclusions and pre-validated by its positivistic version of science?" And, they began thinking about what had happened to *psychoanalysis* and the *individual* in the kingdom's society that had brought about such a situation.

In thinking about the place of the *individual* in psychoanalysis, society and Mr. Science's systems of thinking, they came to the realization that positivistic knowledge is both *ahistorical* and *atemporal* in nature, the implications of which led them to a mind-numbing paradox that went something like this: If psychological laws, explanations, and meanings about the individual person could be discovered independently of that person and his or her historical and cultural context, then much of the thinking and theorizing in the analytic community had become historically neutral and unwittingly encouraged an uncritical reflection upon oneself. Underlying all the major assumptions of the culture of positivism was a common theme: The denial of human action grounded in individual historical insight (Giroux, 1997)). As an ideology, positivism denied the value of *individual* historical consciousness and offered social engineering and the applications of solutions from the Isle of Conclusions as a replacement.

From the Colony's perspective, the kingdom's promise of simplicity, safety and security was a grand illusion: The empirically based psychologies, formularies, and wisdoms of psychoanalysis had become ahistorical, universalizing, and impersonal knowledge(s) about the individual as if such knowledge existed independently of individual human beings and the historical context in which it was produced. A positivistic mode of rationality and history had operated in the kingdom, paradoxically, to undercut the value of history, to undermine, if not suppress, the importance of individual historical consciousness and insight in psychoanalytic education and practice, and to privilege a philosophy of consciousness over the Freudian unconscious as the essence of being.

Like a fractured fairy tale, the Colony came to realize that the historical discipline of psychoanalysis had unwittingly encouraged in their own candidates, students and the kingdom's citizens a distinctly anti-historical attitude and relationship to individual historical consciousness: The historical discipline of psychoanalysis had become anti-historical!!! Individual historical consciousness had become as irrelevant in the analytic community as it was in the kingdom's larger socio-political universe. In effect, Prime Minister Science and the royal family of sciences did the thinking for people, as citizens and professionals. And further, psychoanalytic education had become little more than an extension of the kingdom's ideology of social control, a form of social regulation that guided candidates toward outcome destinies that preserved the status quo: Conformity and compliance with the idealized Ought To Be was axiomatic in their outcome-based education and treatment.

Reflection on the formation of "what is" as opposed to "what should be" had been dismissed by the kingdom's positivistic culture. In other words, consciousness of historical forces and their relationship to everyday life had no place in the technocratic rationality of the kingdom's culture of positivism: The diminished value of *individual* historical awareness in the kingdom seemed tied to the decline of the historical discipline of psychoanalysis and had led to fewer and fewer spaces in the kingdom for psychoanalytic education and practice.

A SOCIO-CULTURAL PERSPECTIVE: ON THE DECLINE OF HISTORY AND THE HISTORICAL DISCIPLINE OF PSYCHOANALYSIS

The Colony asked the question, "How did it come about that both the discipline of history and the historical discipline of psychoanalysis diminished in their values and roles in the kingdom?" They began by considering that the historical discipline of psychoanalysis had much in common with the discipline of history: Each rested on the positivistic notions of history, truth, and causality, each was advanced as a natural science, and each was held out as having great promise for discovering the laws by which society and people functioned. In their division of labor, the discipline of history was to construct a science of society while the historical discipline of psychoanalysis was to construct a science of people. Combined, they could contribute to the creation of a wonderful kingdom. Their potential earned their welcome into the royal family of sciences on the Isle of Conclusions: Their respective discoveries would inform social policy and contribute to the betterment of society and people.

In the service of developing an historical perspective, the Colony began reading and studying the history of the discipline of history. Among other things, they learned that at the very time that Freud and Breuer (1895) were writing "The Studies on Hysteria" some historians were already seeing the death of European culture and the discipline of history as a science (Fischer, 1970). On reading further, it became obvious to the Colony's thinkers that a multi-leveled theme of historical positivism had dominated in psychoanalytic education, theory, and practice since the early beginnings. Psychoanalysis was deeply rooted in the positivists' notions of history in at least three major ways (Foucault, 1973): *history as reminiscence, history as scientific knowledge, and history as continuity.*

They considered that the positivistic notion of *history as reminiscence* assumes the individual's history is constituted by actual empirical events organized in a conceptual framework that presumes linear notions of time, place, logic, and causality. The factual representations in the positivist's view of history and truth were called into question and challenged: What is the influence of the practitioner's underlying assumptions regarding the nature of *time* in determining his or her understanding of the analytic discourse (Whitrow, 1989)? What is the role of perception, desires and other motivational states at the time of the experienced event? And, at the time of the person recalling his or her memories and events in the analytic moment? Does not history as a form of knowing have more to do with the perspective of the historian than with the so-called empirical events recorded (White, 1978)? And, Whose version of history is the truth?

They considered that *history as scientific knowledge* speaks historical knowledge as a scientific truth that recounts a one-dimensional past reality. As a scientific discipline, history studies the structures and patterns of events that develop over a prolonged period of time for the purpose of anticipating, if not controlling, future occurrences. If history as science were ever truly scientific, then the events of the twentieth century provided the perfect laboratory for its scientific lawfulness to be validated by the standards held in the natural science paradigm. As an empirical science, however, history became one of the casualties of the unpredictability and complexity of social phenomena (Oakeshott,1999; White, 1978). As a science, history failed to predict future outcomes, much less reach agreement on the empirical events of the past. The expected empirical regularities, predictive patterns, and universal laws failed to emerge from the data. Indeed, the ontological integrity of the data itself, historical knowledge, was severely compromised. The fact that people and society functioned according to rational and natural laws awaiting their scientific discovery rapidly dissolved by the events of the twentieth century.

Lastly, they considered that *history as continuity* was advanced in the kingdom as representing the empirical truth of past events and, as such, justified the unquestioned continuation of the institutionalized structures, assumptions, and ways of thinking of the past into the future. Whereas traditional historical scholarship reported on the biographies of kings and royal successions, the great wars and battles of the past, and the saints' holiness and devoted lives, the socio-political purposes of such scholarship became increasingly obvious to the Colony's members: To celebrate the achievements of the established order and, in so doing, justifying and perpetuating the power relations of the traditional institutional discourses (Hamerow, 1987). Historical tradition was used to justify and perpetuate the power relations in the present of that which had been in the past. In effect, historical consciousness was used to justify oppressive institutions and perpetuate the power systems of the ruling class in the service of suppressing and controlling the urban masses of the twentieth century.

It became obvious to the members of the Colony that there had been a gradual but steady erosion in the value of the positivist's view of *history, truth,* and *causality* which, in turn, led to the greatly diminished role of historical consciousness in the kingdom. The inability of history to live up to the burdens and proofs of the natural sciences coupled with the growing recognition of history as an institutionalized political perspective led to the development of an intensely anti-historical attitude in the kingdom's larger community of artists and social scientists (White, 1978). As it became more apparent to the citizenry that the carefully kept lessons of the past bore little relevancy to their current lived experiences, an anti-historical attitude brought liberation from the oppressive burdens of historical consciousness. The tyranny of historical consciousness led to the diminished value and role of history in the kingdom and to the ascendancy of King Technocracy, Prime Minister Science and the royal family of sciences.

Looking back in time, the unintended lessons of history became more fully appreciated by the members of the Colony, particularly as they applied to psychoanalytic education and practice. Specifically, the positivist mode of rationality underlying *history as reminiscences* was but one perspective among many, the positivist's notions of *historical knowledge* were simply *not* supported by the standards required for scientific lawfulness, and *history as tradition* had become the basis for continuing their own received assumptions, theories, and institutions without taking into account the ever-changing and complex reconfigurations of the kingdom's socio-cultural context. The mythology of history and psychoanalysis as natural sciences discovering the laws by which society and people functioned had cracked and shattered.

In the positivistic tradition, psychoanalysis had become an unreflective and uncritical discipline: It had failed to question its own cherished assumptions, beliefs, and ways of thinking. Furthermore, fostering the illusion that they could predict, control, and explain the complexities of people and social events had contributed to a dangerously false sense of safety, security, and simplicity by encouraging the substitution of historical knowledge for critical thinking and scientific predictions for individual judgments. Heated controversies and debates regarding the ontological integrity of the historical event, the lack of a scientific lawfulness in history, and, the rise of the king's technocratic rationality combined to lead the way from a general apathy regarding history to an open hostility in the kingdom towards the value and role of historical consciousness. Correspondingly, there was a dramatic decline in the value and role of both history and psychoanalysis in the kingdom: Their psychoanalytic institutions had become tired and cumbersome and their institutionalized concepts and paradigmatic assumptions belonged to an earlier time and place. They realized that those institutions having vested interests in perpetuating their own discourses tend to get stuck in time and are left behind.

As an impersonal institutional discourse, the king's technocratic rationality assesses, evaluates, and decides *as if* it is an *ahistorical* and *atemporal* process operating outside of a socio-political ideology. In such a discourse, any awareness of the history, purpose, and development of social institutions and professional organizations - and the systems, beliefs and values that produced them- is discouraged, if not actively suppressed. In effect, the kingdom's technocratic rationality diminished individual historical consciousness. It replaced human action grounded in historical insight with its empirical discourse in which Prime Minister Science revealed the facts, the truth and the meaning of life. Furthermore, he revealed the best decisions for citizens to make and the best practices for professionals to implement. Mr. Science did the thinking; citizens and professionals applied the findings. In such a technocratic system, the interests of the collective take precedence over the interests and judgments of the individual professional and citizen.

Over the years, the analytic community had come to take the king's technocratic systems for granted. The standards and regulations that governed so much of their professional lives had become part of the natural order of things in the learning and practice communities. Critical thinking had atrophied in the analytic community as individual judgment and decision-making were co-opted by an institutional discourse of conformity and compliance. Furthermore, a lack of critical thinking was fostered and encouraged as ethical decision-making and individual historical consciousness were separated from the everyday professional lives of educators and practitioners. The need and concern for individual theories of ideology, ethics, and political action became far-removed from professionals in the standardized, qualitized and homogenized analytic culture. And one day, they awoke to find themselves without the freedom to conceptualize, educate or practice outside of the healthcare matrix. With this realization, the residents of the Colony of Critical Considerations endorsed and advanced the proposition that in a free and democratic society, psychoanalytic or otherwise, human thought, experiences, and actions must be grounded in individual historical insights: A critical sense flows from an historical sense.

CONSTRUCTING AND PRESERVING NEW PSYCHOANALYTIC SPACES

There was a gradual return to history in the kingdom. Psychoanalytic spaces began re-appearing in the kingdom's villages and cottages. There was a new interest in thinking historically organized, however, around the view of history as a human construct that organizes and makes meaning of the past. The meanings of history are not in the events that constitute historical knowledge, but in the systems and historical context that make those events into historical facts, a perspective that acknowledged that people actively make and interpret meaning: Human constructs such as history and psychoanalysis have meaning-making functions organized around contextualizing meta-narratives such as the positivists' narrative of the scientific discovery of truth. This more contemporary and radical view shifted from the discovery narrative's emphasis on validation of the empirical event to how systems of discourse signify the meanings of the past for the collective, the group, or the individual. The implications for psychoanalytic theory, practice, ethics, and education were quite far-reaching and the formulation of a hermeneutic conception of psychoanalysis became one of the major efforts in the Colony in their rethinking of psychoanalytic thinking. And there was something more.

The construction of new psychoanalytic spaces in the kingdom was brought about, in large measure, by a radically different image of the analytic practitioner: He or she was a proactive participant-observer in the socio-political and legislative-professional systems that shaped his or her professional life on the Isle of Conclusions. As a group, these practitioners did not view themselves as a victim-class that simply conformed and complied with the kingdom's organizational policies, legislative actions, and administrative rules. They began joining the conversation that was redefining psychoanalytic education and practice, even if their participation was uninvited and unwelcomed. They were guided by a newly emerging ethic in which they had a moral and ethical obligation, first, to watch over their profession, second, to pre-serve and safeguard its essential and defining characteristics, and, third, to oppose and counter those industrializing and technocratic trends that compromise the integrity of spaces for psychoanalytic education and practice. The preservation and safeguarding of psychoanalytic spaces became the responsibility of each and every educator and practitioner in the kingdom.

Ultimately, the analytic community realized that the future of psychoanalytic education and practice rested on the freedom to question their received assumptions, theories, and institutions, and actively and strategically plan for the future. In so doing, they were able to renew their struggles against the institutionalized discourses that operated to prevent them from conceptualizing, educating and practicing outside of the kingdom's socio-political ideology and its healthcare matrix. And a dramatic shift in the nature of the relationship between the psychoanalytic community, the Isle of Conclusions and the citizenry took place. It became apparent in the community that their critical thinking and questioning was a fundamentally political act: The very act of questioning the *What Is* and the *Why* of the *What Is* in the kingdom disturbed its socio-political universe.

If the kingdom's psychoanalytic community spoke to the loss of individual historical consciousness did it not have to first go beyond its own common-sense positivistic assumptions and evaluate them in terms of their genesis, development, and political purposes? In so doing, however, would they not be entering the socio-political universe of their own cultural institutions, both educational and political? And, When a positivistic ideology exclusively determines that which constitutes psychoanalytic education, practice, and the standards thereof, are not significant questions of ethics, power, and conflicts- of-interest raised? In effect, does not such questioning ultimately lead to examining the relationship between psychoanalytic education and practice on the one hand and the Isle of Conclusions and its ideology of social control on the other?

There were no safe, simple, and secure solutions. And, nobody lived happily ever after. After all, this is a fractured fairy tale.

-The End-

---

1. An earlier version of this chapter was presented at the International Federation for Psychoanalytic Education's sixteenth annual interdisciplinary conference held in 2006 (Chicago). The theme of the conference was, *Psychoanalysis and the Stories of our Lives: Memory, Narration, and Discovery.*

2. The inspiration for this chapter was drawn from Norton Juster's (1961), *The Phantom Toll Booth.*

REFERENCES

Breuer, J. & Freud, S. (1895). Studies on hysteria. In J. Strachey. ed. and trans., *The standard edition of the complete psychological works of Sigmund Freud,* 24 vols. London: Hogarth Press, 1953-1974. 2:1-307.

Fischer, D. H., (1970). *Historian's fallacies: Toward a logic of historical thought.* New York: Harper and Row, Publishers.

Foucault, M. (1973). *The order of things: An archaeology of the human sciences.* New York: Vintage Press.

Giroux, H.A. (1997). *Pedagogy and the politics of hope: Theory, culture, and schooling.* Boulder, CO: Westview Press.

Hamerow, T.S. (1987). *Reflections on history and historians.* The University of Wisconsin Press.

Juster, N. (1961). *The phantom toll booth.* New York: Bullseye Books.

Keisler, C. A. (2000). *The Next Wave of Change for Psychology and Mental Health Services in the Health Care Revolution.* American Psychologist. Vol. 55. No. 5, 481-487.

Oakeshott, M. (1999). *On history and other essays.* Indianapolis: Liberty Fund, Inc..

White, H. (1978). *Tropics of discourse: Essays in cultural criticism.* Baltimore, MD: The Johns Hopkins University Press.

Whitrow, G.J. (1989). *Time in history: Views of time from prehistory to the present day.* New York: Oxford University Press.

Nine

Developing Competency in the Destruction of Psychoanalysis

An *Other* Approach

> When a form of thought seems to be growing old and nearing its end, we should question not its uncertain future but the long process of its maturation and coming to light to read there the omens of its destiny. A genealogy of psychoanalysis will instruct us about its fate more surely than its present successes or failures can. And when psychoanalysis, its therapy's usefulness ever more contested despite its popular audience, already wears the drab uniform of ideology, philosophy must explain the causes behind this decline by examining its theoretical corpus, initially presented as a total revolution in the manner of understanding man's most intimate being – his psyche-…
>
> \- Michel Henry

At the dawn of the twenty-first century, we come face to face with how little we know about that which we have been so certain for so long. It appears that the natural order of things in psychoanalysis is not as natural as we once had thought, nor is it in the order we so readily had assumed. As the emerging worldview of the twenty-first century weaves its epistemological design into the fabric of the analytic culture, there have been some rather abrupt and ruptured breaks with our more traditional ways of thinking about people, life and psychoanalysis. Disturbing, disordering, and dramatic as it might be, the discursive rationality of the analytic culture is changing.

During the modern era, psychoanalysis developed as an institutional system deeply rooted in the worldview of the early 1900's at which time the world was seen as fixed and stable, reality was unchanging and predictable, and adaptation to the status quo was the contextualizing value of both psychoanalytic education and treatment. In the emerging worldview of the twenty-first century, however, the world is seen as operating in a random fashion about which we can speak only in terms of probabilities, potentialities, and possibilities (Barratt, 1993). The fixed, stable and predictable world of modernity has transformed into a world that exists in a state of continuous flux, consists of a fabric of invisible relations, and in which world the events of everyday life are understood as irreducibly complex phenomena. Filled with uncertainty, paradox, and unfamiliarity, a quantum world is emerging in which dynamic patterns are continuously changing into one another in a perpetual dance of energy (Capra, 1982) and nothing is fixed and measurable (Zohar, 1994).

As a form of thought developed during the modern era, psychoanalysis is growing old and nearing its end. We find ourselves thinking about psychoanalytic thinking and, in so doing, rethinking the received wisdoms, values, and pieties of the institutionalized truth and ethic of psychoanalysis as epistemology, ethics, theory, practice, and education. Although philosophy is generally thought of as the antithesis of psychoanalysis, recent years have witnessed certain foundational questions - philosophical in nature - encircling the analytic community. Shaken out of our traditional ways of thinking, we find ourselves compelled to rethink such fundamental questions as: How do we know what we think we know? What is the nature of *human nature*, of *reality*, and of *time*, *process*, and *complexity* in the analytic engagement?

> The multiplicity of perspectives now entertained by psychoanalysis can generate a cornucopia of views on what we might call "clinical momentum." Attempts to give expression to complex experience challenge received understandings about what, in our ways of being with others and with ourselves, propels the forward motion of clinical engagement. The contemporary affinity for uncertainty, interest in complexity, and the appreciation of each treatment's unique flux, -moment by moment and through protracted time-, seize our attention (Program Brochure, 2007).[1.]

That which brings about changes in the analytic engagement is not as obvious as it once seemed to have been.

As we search to understand the specific nature and unique subtleties of the analytic experience, we find ourselves deeply implicated in matters of philosophy in the re-examination of our largely unquestioned assumptions regarding the nature of *time*, *process*, and *complexity* in the analytic engagement. In the medical model of psychoanalysis, for example, *time* is understood to be linear and sequential, flowing like a line independent of the events it supposedly contains and along which line events of the past occur *then* those of the present *then* those of the future. Indeed, all scientific processes of the modern era are assumed to occur along this invisible "line" of linear time (Slife, 1995; 1993). Such linear assumptions of *time* and *place* lay a deterministic foundation in psychoanalytic thinking in which past trauma psychically determines, of necessity, present symptoms. In the positivistic tradition, temporal succession and spatial proximity are axiomatic assumptions in arriving at causal explanations: What *happens* in the present and what *will happen* in the future results largely from what *has happened* in the past.

Philosophy converges with psychoanalysis in challenging our traditional assumptions regarding the nature of *time*, *process*, and *complexity* in the analytic engagement. As the assumptions of a linear and sequential time are brought into question, for example, the non-linear nature of *time*, *place*, *logic*, and *causality* are fore-grounded, revealing the incredible and irreducible complexity of the analytic process in which experiences of the past and future might co-exist, co-determine, and co-structure the present moment of the past in the ever-present now of the analytic engagement.

As the natural order of things changes in psychoanalysis, other questions of no less significance are raised such as, for example: As we call into question our received understandings about "what in our ways of being with others and ourselves propels the forward motion in the analytic engagement," are we not compelled to also challenge our received understandings of the practitioner's competency in bringing about –or in participating in the process that brings about- such changes? Is it not time to also call into question the question of competency in psychoanalytic education and practice, particularly given the diversity of contemporary psychoanalysis?

Our concept and measures of competency in psychoanalysis are deeply rooted in the worldview of the early 1900's. In the fixed, stable, and predictable world of the industrial age, the evaluation of competency in psychoanalysis centered on the candidate's mastery and application of received knowledge(s) premised on a nineteenth century worldview and science. Do these meanings and measures of competency continue as the unchallenged templates for evaluating the analyst's competency in the twenty-first century? And if so, does the analytic community remain stuck in time and, in so doing, unwittingly participate in the continuing decline of psychoanalysis as a viable form of thought in the twenty-first century?

This chapter speaks from the perspective of a skeptical phenomenalist to the question, "Who decides what counts as competency in psychoanalysis?" Its premise is that our understandings of *competency* and *psychoanalysis* are inextricably tied to the cultural and historical context in which they arise. Its thesis is that our industrialized and industrializing culture produces the image of the analyst, the version of psychoanalysis, and the concept and measures of competency most needed and sanctioned by the culture. Further, that our understanding of each is changing irreversibly as we transition from the industrial age of the modern era to the information age of the postmodern.

This chapter considers the genealogy of the concept and measures of competency from the perspective of, first, the institutional systems of psychoanalysis and the definition of competency developed during the modern era; second, the state's role and vested interest in determining what counts as competency in an industrialized and industrializing culture; and third, the significance of socio-political ideology in the interface between the political and educational institutions of the analytic culture and those of the larger culture.

Lastly, this chapter speaks in a voice of cultural otherness from our medical forms of psychoanalysis. It calls into question the assumptions that underlie our identity as healthcare professionals, and the socio-political, pedagogical and practice philosophies that flow from and sustain this identity as we venture into the twenty-first century. In the spirit of cultural *otherness,* an *other* approach to the question of competency is proposed, one that is more in keeping, I believe, with both a twenty-first century worldview and the diversity that characterizes contemporary psychoanalysis. Further, that we develop competency in challenging and questioning our received psychoanalytic wisdoms, knowledge(s) and truths as integral aspects of psychoanalytic education and practice, thereby engaging in the ongoing process of destruction -and renewal- of psychoanalysis.

WHO DECIDES WHAT COUNTS IN PSYCHOANALYSIS: INSTITUTIONAL SYSTEMS AND DEFINITIONS OF COMPETENCY

Birthed in the culture of positivism in the latter part of nineteenth century Germany, psychoanalysis was a child of the westernized cultures and psychoanalytic education was a product of its times. During the modern era, the world was seen as fixed in its essence, stable in its laws, and functioning according to universal and rational laws awaiting their discovery by science and its methodology. In its essential state, the world was mind-independent, predictable and knowable. It was a Cartesian-Newtonian world in which a Cartesian certainty of knowledge was made possible through the applications of a Newtonian-based science, method and form of explanation. Science was the paradigm of knowledge production during the modern era. It was the age of science and technology, objectivity and quantification, and measurement and metrics.

The modern era was grounded in a Cartesian self-consciousness, self-reflection and self-analysis. And science had become established as a mathematical, mechanical and empirical body of knowledge(s). The Cartesian ideals of rational universal knowledge combined with the Newtonian purity of scientific method to produce an epistemic context in which a masculine mode of detachment, rationality and clarity valued the purity of scientific discovery over the search for intuitive wisdom. The detached depersonalized quality of a rationalistic analysis of the world, life and people characterized the science, art and ethics of the time.

As a child of the westernized cultures, psychoanalysis adopted the scientific worldview, vision and reality most dominant in the culture at the time. As described in the last chapter -although just a fractured fairytale-, positivism was more than simply an epistemology, it was a powerful ideological frame of reference that constructed a social reality in which there was only one world, one logic, one essence, and one science. Science and its methodology provided the mind-independent, objective and rational means of discovering the nomothetic laws by which the world, society, and people functioned, the goal of which was the unification of all knowledge about the world, life and people.

As a form of thought, psychoanalysis was born into the pre-existing system of signification and signifying activities that had come to establish the natural order of things in the latter part of nineteenth century Germany. This system had been developing since the beginning of the Industrial Age in the early seventeenth century. It provided for the formation of "appropriate" institutional structures, prescribed the "appropriate" educational philosophy and relationship to knowledge(s), and defined the "appropriate" concept and measures of competency to be used in its industrialized and industrializing culture. A culture of positivism and its militant rationality provided the epistemic context for psychoanalysis as it developed as a form of thought during the modern era. And the medical-scientific traditions provided its legacy and legitimacy.

As the westernized cultures were transforming from land-based agrarian societies to urban-based industrialized societies, special institutions arose to meet their needs. Newtonian-based in their emphasis on structure and parts, the component parts of complex machinery and the assembly line of the factory served as the mental model for thinking about the structure and organization of institutions *and* people (Wheatley, 1994). The organizational charts of institutions depicted, at once, the efficient and predictable workings of their interlocking machine-like parts and their underlying philosophy: The whole is the sum of its parts. As a child of the westernized cultures, psychoanalysis adopted –or rather, was adopted into- the scientific and mechanical worldview, vision and reality prevalent at the time, a worldview that included the structure of its educational and political institutions. Psychoanalysis was seen as a natural science of the mind and those with a medical-scientific worldview tend to create systematic, rational, and scientific systems for education and training.

Founded in 1920, the Berlin Institute embodied the institutional structure, educational philosophy and model, and concept and measures of competency developed during the seventeenth, eighteenth, and nineteenth centuries. In the cultural context of the early 1900's, the Berlin Institute was a "good institution:" Vertically arranged and hierarchically organized, its structure mirrored the self-evident hierarchies believed to exist in the natural world, society and people as reflected, for example, in the hierarchical ordering of the training analyst, the analyst, and the candidate. Those higher up in the hierarchy possessed power and authority over those who were located in lower positions in the organizational chart. Clear lines of authority and chains of command delineated the functions and purposes of each machine-like component, element and part: Everybody knew his or her place, role, and responsibilities. Parenthetically, it is this Newtonian-based institutional structure that is crumbling as we transform from the industrial age of the modern era into the information age of the postmodern (Wheatley, 1994).

The culture of positivism grounded not only the vertically arranged and hierarchically organized Berlin Institute, it prescribed its linear educational philosophy (Kavanaugh, 1995). Within the walls of the institute, psychoanalytic education and training was conceptualized as a linear process in which the candidate moved in a linear and evolutionary way from a state of "not knowing" to a state of "knowing." Furthermore, it established a particular relationship to knowledge in which educational competency consisted of evaluating the candidate's mastery of knowledge(s) received through his or her coursework, supervision, and training analysis. Oftentimes, the training analysis was the central method of teaching and learning in psychoanalysis, whispers of discontent in the analytic community notwithstanding (Rose, 2000). And, practice competency consisted of evaluating the candidate's effectiveness in the applications of this knowledge, evidenced by the successful therapeutic outcome of control cases. The Berlin Institute was founded as if the unconscious did not exist in psychoanalysis (Safouan, 2000). Furthermore, the philosophy underlying its structure, educational philosophy and relationship to knowledge led to the establishment of a far-reaching precedent in psychoanalytic education and training.

In the winter of 1923-24, the training committee of the Berlin Institute –a really "big piece" in the institutional machine– imposed standards and regulations on the learning activities and experiences of its candidates. As the only legitimate center for psychoanalytic education and training, the institute was the Keeper of Theoretical Truth, imparting its Truth through the science and philosophy of teaching -or, pedagogy. As a derivation from the Greek *paidos*, meaning *boy*, and *agogos*, meaning *guide*, pedagogy literally translates as, *to guide the boy*. Uniform, objective and scientific methods in the evaluation and decision-making about the candidate's progression were applied to each phase of his or her education and training. The precedent was firmly established that it was the training committee's responsibility to guide the boy (or girl) through the various parts of his (or her) education and training. In so doing, the training committee became the *Who* that determined when the candidate demonstrated sufficient competency to progress from one "part" in the tri-"part-"ite model of education to the next; specifically, from his or her classroom didactics to the supervision of control cases to beginning the training analysis. In effect, the responsibility for determining competency shifted from the individual where it was situated in the earlier Vienna model to the institute in the Berlin model. With this shift, psychoanalysis became institutionalized (Safouan, 2000). And the infantilization of candidates became one of the ensuing problems in psychoanalytic education and training during the twentieth century (Kernberg, 2000).

More than simply an interesting aside, the tri-"part"-ite model of psychoanalytic education and training traces its genealogy to eighteenth century Prussia where conceptually fragmented components of knowledge such as science, language, literature, and mathematics fit together like the interlocking parts of a complex machine to produce the classical education of the modern era. Many contemporary educators understand Mary Shelley's *Frankenstein: The Modern Prometheus*, written in the early 1800's, as a commentary on the educational philosophy and model of the industrial age (Gato, 1992): Her time-less story tells how Frankenstein was assembled from the body parts taken from different bodies and how he was brought to life through science and the applications of its knowledge(s). If "parts are parts," then the question is asked, Is the formation of analytic identity simply a matter of assembling the tri-'parts' of analytical experiences and scientific knowledge(s) found in the institute?

With its actions, the training committee established the precedent in our educational institutions that a sovereign entity must develop the rules and evaluate matters of competency in each phase of the candidate's education and training. Otherwise, it was believed, he or she would be totally incapable of developing a responsible and reasonable mode of self-instituting analytic training. Thus in the best interests of protecting the public and psychoanalysis, psychoanalytic pedagogical philosophy embraced as one of its central tenets that an institutional rationality and oversight were needed -indeed, ethically required- to assure that the *good* and *right* take place in education and training.

Since the winter of 1923-24, the training committee's responsibilities have included the evaluation of the candidate's educational and practice competency in determining his or her progression through the institute. A positivistic relationship to knowledge enabled the construction of a theoretical reality that could be handed from one person to another: Knowledge could be passed from the most knowledgeable- the analyst and training analyst- down to the least knowledgeable- the candidate. A triumph of triangulation prevailed between the training analyst, the institute, and the candidate; the other-as-third became an integral aspect of institute education and training. And the beat goes on as we enter the twenty-first century.

In the summer of 2001, the Consortium - a group of, arguably, the major players in organized psychoanalysis - advanced the most recent institutional definition of psychoanalysis with the adoption of national healthcare accreditation standards for education and training. In so doing, they functionally defined a rather narrow, circular, and restrictive definition of psychoanalysis: What is psychoanalysis? Psychoanalysis is a healthcare profession, or a specialty thereof. What is psychoanalytic education? Psychoanalytic education is the successful completion of those analytical experiences taking place in an institute meeting healthcare and accreditation standards. And, Who is a psychoanalyst? A psychoanalyst is a mental health professional who successfully completes the educational and training requirements of an accredited institute. With the adoption of the Consortium's healthcare accreditation standards, the educational and political institutions in the United States become more deeply entrenched in conceptual foundations rooted in evolutionary biology, medicine and pathology, and the methods and assumptions of the natural sciences. And the triangulation between the training analyst, candidate and institute legitimized in the winter of 1923-24 interweaves with the equally complex triangulation of the training analyst, institute, and government legitimized in the summer of 2001.

A POSITIVISTIC RELATIONSHIP TO KNOWLEDGE AND MODERNISTIC NOTIONS OF COMPETENCY IN PSYCHOANALYSIS

As a product of the times, psychoanalytic education and its notions of competency were based on knowledge(s) that could be standardized and replicated, taught and learned, and measured and evaluated. The epistemological purification provided by a Newtonian based science paved the way for the discovery narrative that characterized psychoanalysis during the modern era. Science provided the mind-independent, objective and rational means of discovering the nomothetic laws by which the world, society, and people functioned. As the world and people functioned according to the same natural, universal and rational laws, psychoanalysis turned its rational and objectivizing gaze to man's *being* in its search for psychoanalytic bodies of knowledge(s) that would enable the scientific understanding, prediction and control of human behaviors.

Whereas science was the paradigm of knowledge production, the institute was the site of knowledge acquisition. Within the walls of the institute, the political and ideological hierarchies of *power* and *knowledge* were grounded in medicine, biology, and the natural sciences. Consistent with the empiricist's doctrine, the generation of psychoanalytic knowledge(s) rested on the assumption of a metaphysics of presence: "Something Real could be represented in thought, the Real was understood to be an external or universal subject existing 'out there,' and 'truth' was understood to be correspondence to it" (Flax, 1990, p. 34). For most of the modern era, psychoanalytic knowledge(s) were seen as scientific, objective, bounded, cumulative and context-free, far removed from the individual, political, and cultural traditions that structure meaning. As knowledge(s) were cumulative, theory could be continuously developed, refined, revised, and advanced as new discoveries were made. Bodies of knowledge(s) consisted of pre-thought thoughts, pre-packaged formularies, and pre-determined ways by which others ought to be. As such, they could be objectively recorded in the sacred text of Truth-Discovered, inscribed in standardized curriculum and taught as discovered rational knowledge about the historical and causal realities producing various symptom pictures (Kavanaugh, 2006; 1999).

As a form of thought of the modern era, psychoanalysis developed in ways consistent with the positivist's worldview and relationship to knowledge. As a research scientist of the modern era, the psychoanalytic practitioner collected without contaminating the scientific data in the analytic hour, developed sound formulations and testable hypotheses without figuring into the process of representation, and made the correct interpretation to bring about a theoretically anticipated outcome. In the positivist's ideological frame of reference: There was only one legitimate understanding of human nature, one self-evident and objectively knowable reality, one authorized science and methodology, one accepted form of logic and explanatory truth, one valid theory and technique, one transference and countertransference, one correct interpretation and outcome, and one legitimate institute from which to receive the one authorized body of knowledge(s) and set of analytical experiences in the formation of the analytic practitioner of the twentieth-century.

PSYCHOANALYSIS AS AN INSTITUTIONAL SYSTEM OF THE MODERN ERA: THE QUESTION OF COMPETENCY IN THE POSTMODERN

As our meanings and understandings of psychoanalysis change, does organized psychology and psychoanalysis continue into the postmodern era with the same concept and measures of competency received from the modern era? As an institutional system of the modern era, Barrat (1993) asserts that psychoanalysis, stands as a scientific framework for the discovery and learning of practices of effective therapeutic intervention, the efficacy of which is determined by empirically based outcome studies; is made up of a series of models of the mind which can be taught and learned as a law and ordering of discursive rules from which a lattice of psychotherapeutic interpretations may be generated, exchanged, or posited; and, rests on the learning of received knowledge(s), the rules of which are applied in the service of improving the individual's adaptation to a fixed and stable world. And with the actions of the Consortium in the summer of 2001, psychoanalysis is reducible to measurable sets of core competencies embodied in the education and training of the analytic practitioner as a mental healthcare professional.

Despite the celebration of diversity in contemporary psychoanalysis, a science and pathology-driven model of understanding people and life continues to provide the standards for education and training, produce the analytic practitioner of the twenty-first century as a healthcare professional, and prescribe the core competencies to be mastered and measured. The empirically derived "scientific fact" continues as the foundation for our received knowledge(s), the mastery and applications of which form the basis for demonstrating competency in psychoanalytic education and practice. The successful completion of psychoanalytic education and training now signifies that the graduate has demonstrated his or her mastery of the core competencies of a mental heath professional: The acquisition of a "culture of evidence" perspective about human behavior based on scientific inquiry and reasoning, replicable methods of observation and measurement, and interpretation of qualitative and quantitative evidence.

As we move into the postmodern era, there are certain ethical considerations that seem particularly significant and relevant, particularly given the pluralistic nature of the theories and assumptions of contemporary psychoanalysis. The bodies of knowledge(s) produced from an empirical discourse often become relevant to the degree that they constitute *description* and *explanation* of objectified data, conceived - a priori - as instances of possible universal laws and normative standards. As an institutional system of the modern era, psychoanalysis has come to stand for these nomothetic laws, concepts, and principles and their role in causing the symptoms of various pathological conditions. In so doing, psychoanalytic theory creates the illusion that these principles and laws hold for *each* of *many* individuals (Lemiell, 1987). Such universalizing and totalizing conceptions of people contain core ethical issues for the analytic practitioner and educator when the purposes of psychoanalysis are organized around normalizing and reparative objectives based on these empirically established normative standards. Specifically, bodies of psychoanalytic knowledge(s) intersect with power when, in the mind of the practitioner, empirically established normative standards move from describing *how things are* to representing truth-claims as to *how things ought to be* for the individual he or she is meeting with. And, these same bodies of knowledge(s) intersect with power and ethics when, as considered in chapter four, the analytic practitioner claims the moral justification, obligation, and authority to evaluate the other, to signify his or her meanings, purposes, and motives as pathological, and then to directly or indirectly influence, if not abridge, the individual's political, social, and personal freedoms and responsibilities.

If psychoanalysis is to be a viable form of thought in the twenty first century, then is it not time for a radical and ruptured break with the singularity of the positivist's paradigm having its roots in the seventeenth, eighteenth and nineteenth centuries? The empirically derived scientific fact remains as the foundation for our received knowledge(s) as we enter the twenty-first century, the mastery and applications of which continue to form the basis for demonstrating competency in psychoanalytic education and practice. For most of the twentieth century, the analytic culture has embraced a positivistic epistemology and has seemed blinded to the ideological nature of its socio-political frame of reference. Its scientific worldview encourages the learning of received wisdoms, theories and formularies. Unfortunately, it also discourages reflective thinking.

What happened to *the individual* in psychoanalysis during the modern era, the mechanistic age of science and objectification? Jonathan Lear (1990) asserts that the commitment to the individual is a tradition in the West and psychoanalysis is a manifestation of that commitment. Has psychoanalysis studied the individual in our individualistic society while leaving the uniqueness of the individual out of psychoanalysis? In agreement with Lear, psychoanalysis will flourish or wither depending on the value placed on the individual and his or her development in society. And also, depending on the value placed on the uniqueness of the individual in psychoanalysis itself; for example, "Does the culture of evidence perspective recently endorsed by organized psychoanalysis serve to further exclude *the individual* and the voice of his or her private *madness* from the discourse of psychoanalysis?"

The more that psychoanalytic knowledge(s) and wisdoms are reduced to the rules of empirical discourse, the more that the mystery, magic and muscle of the individual is reductively translated into the language of the scientist's symbols. And, the individual's psyche (soul) is empiricized.

WHO DECIDES WHAT COUNTS IN PSYCHOANALYSIS: THE ROLE AND INTERESTS OF THE STATE

As people moved from the farms to the factories at the turn of twentieth century, institutional systems developed for the mass production, mass distribution, and mass consumption of goods and services. As society became more industrialized in the United States, it came to rely on various governmental entities and industrializing principles to manage the quality, competition, and fairness in the production, distribution, and consumption of goods and services in such diverse and far ranging sectors as the economy, foreign trade, education, and business. If and when consumption in any sector of the society reached approximately sixteen percent of gross national product (GNP), that sector moved from being seen as a loosely organized cottage industry to an industry in need of regulation in the service of protecting the public. Under the social contract, the state has the authority, right and obligation to protect the public through the enactment of legislation, the development of industry-wide standards, and the licensure of service providers in the sector needing regulation. In these various ways, the state gives its assurance that minimal standards of quality are met in each of the respective phases of production, distribution, and consumption of the goods or services.

In the United States, the most highly industrialized, technocratic, and consumer-driven of societies, the costs of healthcare have reached sixteen percent of GNP and are rising. In response, the healthcare sector has been re-named The Behavioral Care Industry, an industry in need of regulation. And like-wise with the healthcare professional who has been renamed and is now known as a vendor or a provider in the healthcare industry. An industrialized culture industrializes its professions through governmental standards and regulations; its standards standardize, regulations regulate, and institutions institutionalize.

In many respects, the identity of the analytic educator and practitioner as a healthcare professional has become his or her strongest weakness: As a member of the healthcare professions, he or she is subject to the ongoing industrialization and commercialization of the healthcare professions taking place through the increased centralization of information, authority, and decision-making power in various educratic entities, an increased emphasis on a uniformity of policies and procedures in both education and practice, and the ongoing redefinition of professional standards by various educratic entities, national committees, and other healthcare interest groups (Kavanaugh, 1999). And there is something more about the healthcare reformation and its impact on the psychoanalytic community.

The psychoanalytic educator educates and the practitioner practices in the most recent of healthcare revolutions occurring since the late 1940's: The Era of Assessment and Accountability (Keisler, 2000). As described in chapter eight, this era is characterized by evidence-based strategies linking outcome and cost-effective research. The health care system's design and the practitioner's access to the system are contingent on time and cost-efficiency in providing predictable and measurable treatment outcomes. Practice competency is now concerned with such questions as, "How *effectively* do we do what we say we do?" and "Does the treatment we offer bring about the theoretically anticipated outcome in ways that are both *time* and *cost* effective?" Empirically based outcome studies organized around time and cost effectiveness provide the new standard of competency in both education and practice in the mental health professions.

Such industrializing efforts tacitly advance and endorse the principle of "economic credentialing" in which efforts are made to include only those who are competent in meeting certain levels of time and cost effectiveness in treatment which, in turn, leads to the recently increased emphasis on proficiency credentialing: Competency is increasingly organized around specializations in the mental health professions. Provider-specific credentials is just one of the new standards attesting to the practitioner's competency in his or her specific areas of ability. With this increased emphasis on specialization and credentialing, organized psychology and psychoanalysis follow in the footsteps of the medical model of specialization. In so doing, they contribute to the further conceptual fragmentation of people that, in turn, serves as both *the effect of* and *the cause for* further industrialization. And the beat goes on...

The market-driven focus on time and cost-effective outcome-based treatments has led to the increased emphasis on out-come-based education by various accreditation bodies. The industrialization of psychoanalytic education is reflected, for example, in the increased emphasis on more standardized programs of study, predetermined educational objectives and outcomes, and the mastery of predefined sets of core competencies centering on the student's or candidate's time- and cost-effective applications. In education, competency is concerned with the question, "Has the candidate or student actually learned what the training program says they are teaching them?" Educational competency continues to be demonstrated through the mastery of received knowledge(s) as measured by written and oral examinations, and practice competency continues to be demonstrated by achieving the theoretically anticipated outcomes with psychotherapy or control cases.

After receiving a government-issued license as evidence of one's competency to enter practice, evidences of continuing competencies -or, continuing professional development programs, as they are most recently referred to - are demonstrated by fulfilling mandatory continuing education requirements for license renewal. Wrapped in the cloak of protecting the public, the state increasingly requires evidences of competency in the education of the mental health professional or vendor (the production phase), evidences of continuing competencies in the delivery of their services (the distribution phase), and most recently, evidences of the efficacy of the services provided (the consumption phase). The standards of competency in each of these respective phases are based on measurable and predictable outcomes that are both time and cost effective.

The Affordable Care Act of 2009, the recently enacted national healthcare legislation in the United States, specifies the "best practices" for different diagnostic conditions. In so doing, the legislation functionally defines, in effect, the standards of practice for the healthcare professions. As a medical procedure, psychoanalysis is now appropriate for only certain diagnostic conditions: Is psychoanalysis the treatment of choice for madness? As a method of treatment, psychoanalysis is among the least time- and cost-effective of those medical procedures included in the pre-packaged healthcare product lines marketed by the insurance industry.

We currently bear witness to the semiotic reconstruction of a new professional identity for the psychoanalytic practitioner as a craftsperson, a provider on the factory floor of the healthcare industry.

WHO DECIDES WHAT COUNTS IN PSYCHOANALYSIS: SOCIO-POLITICAL IDEOLOGY AND THE INTERFACE BETWEEN ORGANIZED PSYCHOANALYSIS AND THE STATE

A socio-political ideology such as liberalism or conservatism contains its own distinctive worldview, forms of rationality and sets of core beliefs, values and attitudes. Each ideology represents a distinct conception of moral authority, apprehending reality, ordering experiences, and making moral judgments (Redding, 2005). Furthermore, each differs on its respective understanding of human nature, the effective remedies for social problems, and the extent to which individuals are responsible for their own life and life circumstances. The culture's dominant socio-political ideology has a profound influence in constructing what constitutes the natural order of things in society, including how its members come to understand and interpret themselves as citizens and professionals.

In their recent book, Wright and Cummings (2005) argue for a re-evaluation of the practices and policies of professional organizations in the mental health-care field. Self-described life-long liberals with distinguished careers as psychologists and leaders in the American Psychological Association (APA), they assert that the socio-political views guiding the research, advocacy, education, and practice of the mental health professions are most often guided by a liberal ideology and agenda. Further, they warn that psychology, psychiatry and social work have been captured by an *ultra*-liberal ideology, the agenda of which has trumped science at the highest levels of decision-making in the APA.

Richard Redding (2005), an associate professor of law at Villanova University and associate professor of psychology at Drexel University, elaborates further when he says,

> Although psychology celebrates diversity, which has come to be one of the profession's core values ...and strives to be inclusive by recognizing the value and legitimacy of diverse beliefs, the profession lacks socio-political diversity. Most psychologists are politically liberal, and conservatives are vastly underrepresented in the profession (p. 303).

The lack of ideological diversity in our leadership and governance bodies persists despite the ideals clearly espoused in the APA's ethical code urging psychologists to be sensitive to those cultural differences and biases that contribute to perpetuating a socio-political point of view that might exclude or oppress the perspectives of others, including those of colleagues. Operating in opposition to the profession's core ethical principles regarding diversity has had devastating consequences for the profession and practice of psychology.

> It biases research on social policy issues, damages psychology's credibility with policymakers and the public, impedes serving conservative clients, results in de facto discrimination against conservative students and scholars, and has a chilling effect on liberal education (Redding, 2005, p. 304).

The biased research on social policies at the forefront of the culture wars includes exploring the relationships between authoritarianism and conservatism, political psychology and restorative justice, and adolescent competence in making birth control and abortion decisions. Other areas include racism and affirmative action, welfare and school busing, individual v community rights and gay and lesbian parenting (Wright and Cummings, 2005). An ultra-liberal ideology and agenda has had a powerful voice in developing those policies that decide what counts for psychology and psychoanalysis in the United States during the latter part of the twentieth century and as we enter the twenty-first.

In the ultra-liberal worldview and tradition, the freedoms and responsibilities of both citizens and professionals are defined *exclusively* from within the social contract: The freedoms, rights, and responsibilities of each ultimately derives from the collective interests. Without the elevation of the collective's interests over the individual, it is believed, special interests take over, the social contract breaks down, and there is a generalized collapse of each sector of society into amoral chaos (Neville, 1989). Thus in the best interests of the citizenry, the state has the legal authority and moral responsibility to oversee all matters pertaining to citizens and professionals. From this perspective, the state's regulation of healthcare professionals, mental health or otherwise, is authorized by the social contract, defined by the interests of the collective, and embodied in the codification of law and ethics as recently embodied in the United States, for example, in the Affordable Care Act of 2009.

Liberalism is usually seen as representing progressive values, an emphasis on community, and as supporting government-sponsored programs designed for the larger good. As a socio-political ideology, conservatism is usually seen as representing traditional values, an emphasis on self-reliance, and a fierce opposition to government-sponsored programs. A conservative ideology, however, is vastly underrepresented in psychology's governance and policy-making, our ethical commitment to diversity notwithstanding. In general, it could be said that those of a conservative ideology probably would oppose the state's oversight in matters of competency in psychoanalysis while those of an ultra-liberal persuasion probably would expect, endorse, and support the state's oversight in deciding what counts in psychoanalysis through increased standards and regulations.

Developed in a medical-scientific tradition, the interests of organized psychoanalysis interface with those of the state and the political sciences: They share the same rationality that seeks the technical mastery of people through the scientific production, acquisition and application of knowledge(s) and their validation through outcome studies. In so doing, psychoanalysis and the political sciences interface with and sustain the state's ideology of social control: Both are interested in bringing about the person's conformity and compliance with the culture's dominant beliefs, values and attitudes. Their interests interface and overlap with the state's interest in maintaining social stability, predictability and control.

By history and politics, the institute – and, more recently, the institute in partnership with the state - is the *Who* that decides the *What* that counts in psychoanalysis. At what cost, however, to the public and to the future of psychoanalysis? The interweaving of ethics, power, and knowledge is found in the intersection where the state and institute meet to decide what counts before issuing the license to practice. How is the integrity of the profession impacted if a license to practice is granted to only those graduating from an institute meeting certain healthcare and accreditation standards? Is a license granted to those practitioners whose primary identity is *other than* a healthcare professional, whose perspective is *other than* a "culture of evidence" perspective, and whose conceptual foundations are *other than* biology, medicine and the natural sciences? Or to those versions of psychoanalysis that are inherently subversive by calling into question the structures of our social institutions and their formations, including those of the state and the institute and their prevailing socio-political ideologies – whatever they might happen to be?

As we enter the twenty-first century, we do so with a noteworthy lack of diversity in our intellectual and conceptual foundations, our pedagogical and practice philosophies, and, it would seem, in the socio-political ideology of our governance bodies. A series of difficult questions await the analytic community: Have the leadership and governance bodies of organized psychoanalysis been captured by an ultra-liberal worldview? If so, how has its ideology and agenda impacted our professional standards, theories and research? How have they influenced our notions of competency in education and practice? And, How does an ultra-liberal worldview influence our clinging to the institutionalized concepts and measures of competency that are growing old and nearing their end as we enter the information age of the twenty-first century?

As a form of thought of the modern era, psychoanalysis is growing old, is in a state of decline, and is nearing its end. The machine-like parts that construct its institutions and theories of people are wearing down and stopping. Our institutions remain rooted in a nineteenth century worldview, science and structure; our pedagogical philosophy, model and strategies remain virtually unchanged since 1922; and our standards of practice and care are organized around positivistic theories that gratuitously assume that people are the helpless passive victims of their life circumstances.

ON DEVELOPING COMPETENCY IN THE DESTRUCTION OF PSYCHOANALYSIS: MOVING INTO THE OTHERWISE OF THE 21ST CENTURY

> Psychoanalysis does not belong to the body of the sciences of man to which it is now attached…. It is, rather, the antithesis of those sciences. When objectivity ceaselessly extends its reign of death over the devastated universe, when life has no refuge but the Freudian unconscious, and when a living determination of life acts and hides under each of the pseudoscientific attributes with which that unconscious clothes itself, then we must say that psychoanalysis is the soul of a world with-

out soul, the spirit of a world without spirit.
-Francois Roustang

A new socio-cultural epoch is making its largely unexpected, if not unwelcomed, appearance in the culture: The information age of the postmodern. The westernized cultures are immersed in a turbulent transition from the industrial age of the modern era to the information age of the postmodern. The episteme of the modern era is fast becoming as obsolete and nonfunctional for the emerging postmodern as the episteme of the agricultural era was for the modern. More than just a thorough going critique of the assumptions of enlightenment and their foundation in notions of universal reason, the discourse of the postmodern introduces radically different ways of being, thinking and knowing about the world, people and life (Waugh, 1992). And validated or not by science, they are crossing the borders of the analytic culture.

Contemporary psychoanalysis is characterized by a rich diversity of psychologies that premise different understandings of human nature and the unconscious, posit different methods of knowing about people and life, and presume different purposes and outcomes for the analytic discourse. If our educational and political institutions continue into the twenty-first century with a nineteenth century worldview and concept of competency, do we not fail to match our understandings of competency with our more contemporary psychologies of psychoanalysis, many of which rest on different understandings of *time*, *process*, and *complexity* in the analytic engagement? In so doing, do we not perpetuate psychoanalysis as an institutional system of the modern era and participate in its continued decline? In the context of the postmodern, the question is raised: How do we think of the practitioner's competency in his or her ability to participate in the perpetual dance of energy in the analytic space in which nothing is fixed and measurable?

THE CONCEPT OF THE UNCONSCIOUS AND THE QUESTION OF PRACTICE COMPETENCY: AN *OTHER* APPROACH

The concept of the unconscious has been defining of psychoanalytic theory, practice, and education since the early beginnings. Our understanding of the unconscious forms and informs the basis of psychoanalytic practices. Without such a concept, the irrationalities, discontinuities, and madness of the human condition remain forever an enigma existing as phenomenon not having a self-defined meaning and purpose. Our measures of competency in psychoanalysis, however, do not match -and, never have in my opinion- with its defining concept which is, perhaps, more precisely thought of in contemporary psychoanalysis as the unconscious as conceptualized by the Freudians, the Jungians, the Kleinians, the Lacanians, the Kohutians, the Winnicotians, the relationists, the intersubjectivists, and those who speak from an existential, phenomenological, or other philosophically based paradigms - to name just a few.

If it is the individual therapist or unique relationship and not the mastery and application of received knowledge(s), techniques or procedures that propels the forward motion of the analytic engagement –assuming that "forward" is the direction that the discourse "ought" to move in-, are we not ethically compelled to match our understanding of psychoanalysis and concept of competency with the uniqueness of the practitioner and his or her theory of the unconscious - however it is understood to be? Given our conceptual diversity, the definition and measures of competency in psychoanalysis necessarily depend on the particular understanding of psychoanalysis and the unconscious in question, whether Freudian, Kleinian, Lacanian - or whichever: The concept of competency in psychoanalysis necessarily hinges on its defining concept of the unconscious, however it might be understood.

The core competencies of a mental healthcare professional do not match with that which constitutes competency in many of the diverse psychologies of contemporary psychoanalysis. For many, the assumptions of science and pathology underlying the healthcare model simply do not apply. By acting as if they do, however, the illusion is created that the demonstrations of competency as a mental healthcare professional is somehow related to -or is the equivalent of- competency in psychoanalysis. And representing this illusion of competency to the public seems rather disingenuous, at best.

The proposition that psychoanalysis as an institutional system is to the modern era as psychoanalysis as process is to the postmodern (Barratt, 1993) suggests a different way of thinking about competency in psychoanalysis in the twenty-first century. In what follows, the question of competency is considered from the synthesis and practice of psychoanalysis as, first and last, a venture into communication via the associative-interpretive process in the contextualizing metaphor of the psychic theatre of the mind. This understanding of psychoanalysis is centered in the realm of human experiences and is premised on Freud's initial and intuitive understanding of the unconscious as *life, affectivity*, or *the life force* (Henry, 1985).

A concept of competency that matches with this understanding of psychoanalysis is necessarily tied to the essential elements and purpose of its discourse. The first element has to do with communication, free association and the interpretive activity of the discourse, a *venture into communication via the associative-interpretive process.* And the second element has to do with the contextualizing metaphor from the performance arts, *the psychic theatre of the mind.* This synthesis of psychoanalysis is premised on the Freudian unconscious and, as a special mode of conversation, its purpose is for the wording of unconscious meaning, process and dynamic in ways that are meaningful to the other and furthers the associative process.

The Freudian unconscious has several fundamentally different meanings, the first of which is that the unconscious is "dependent upon the metaphysics of representation, expresses itself in the forms of presence and absence, the one never proceeding without the other. And, in this case, there is between the conscious and the unconscious a passage and a total reversibility. Whatever is unconscious can become conscious and vice versa" (Roustang, 1985, xiv). This first meaning is best exemplified, perhaps, in the personal meanings contained in the concrete representations of the small change (the coins) that made so much cents/sense to Mr. G after his father died as described in chapter five, or in the actions of Mr. P described in chapter two as he became "active with the radio" in the waiting room of my office, and in our subsequently speaking to something of the relationship between his actions and his "radioactive terrors" as a child.

The second meaning has reference to an ontology of life: "It asserts that the essence of the psyche resides in 'the radical immanence of its auto-affection' in a closed system within which psychic contents determine each other (Roustang, 1985, xv)." And in the eros of *being*, *knowing* and *presencing* in "the radical immanence of its auto-affection" is found something of the individual's personal ethic and truth, as revealed and concealed in the answers to the personal and intimate questions found at the end of chapter one: *Who am I? Where did I come from?* and *What stories do I have to tell?*

The Freudian unconscious is, at once, dependent upon a metaphysics of representation to express itself in and through various forms of presence and absence (a *representational unconscious*) and as an ontology of life concerned with "the radical immanence of its auto-affection," (*representation's other*) expressing itself in a closed system within which psychic contents determine each other in a matrix of non-linear time, place, logic, and causality. It is this understanding of the Freudian unconscious and its match with the concept of *competency* that did not fit -and still does not - with our received philosophical, scientific, or medical paradigms (Kavanaugh, 2006; Henry, 1985).

The concepts of *the unconscious* and *competency* are ultimately and inseparably tied to the mystical and intuitive forms of knowing and wording the *unthought known* or *representation's other* in ways that are, at once, meaningful for the other and furthers the associative-interpretive process. In so doing, there is an irreducible coming together of the unconscious of self as it speaks with that of the other, an inseparability of *bodymindthinkingspeakingfeeling* in which the unconscious processes of the two participants become one and, in the interpretive moment, the translations seem to speak themselves. In wording the inexplicable, the practitioner fulfills the mutually agreed upon and deceptively simple purpose for meeting: To understand and translate the language of the unconscious of the other (of self) in ways meaningful to the other. For example, the knowing of Mr. P's genie-ological narrative described in chapter three took place as the unconscious processes of two became one in the form of our coupling on the floor of the ward, his mixing the coffee and cream during our first office meeting, and his speaking with his head man on my shoulder speaking with him. And also, in the something more of the mystery, magic and muscle of the human spirit.

COMPETENCY AND ITS MEASURES

An understanding of competency that matches with this understanding of psychoanalysis, the individual, and the Freudian unconscious is suggested by Webster's (1999) college dictionary that defines *competence* as, "the implicit internalized knowledge of a language that a speaker possesses and that enables the speaker to produce and understand the language (270)." As the various ghosts of the theatre move and create their personal effects, impressions, and leave their traces in the analyst's mental life, images, and sounds (Bollas, 1992), the unconscious of the two participants become one in a spiritual mystical sense: Only the unconscious of one can understand the unconscious of other. In so doing, the practitioner comes to know and possess the knowledge that enables him or her to produce and understand the language of the unconscious as known and spoken in the discourse.

In this special mode of conversation, practice competency is inextricably linked to the complex process of listening, understanding, and responding to the language of the unconscious of the self (of other) and the other (of self), a language which is at once the primary source of knowledge and the primal linguistic of the discourse. This understanding of competency is closely tied to psychoanalysis as a performance art in which competency is captured and embodied in the interpretive moment: The very (f)act of being spoken by the practitioner performs the act being spoken and furthers the associative process.

From this perspective, the central question regarding competency is: "How well does the practitioner venture into communication via the associative-interpretive process in the play of the play of the psychic theatre?" Put another way: "How well can the practitioner step out onto the stage and speak the inexplicable in meaningful ways as the other (of *self*) speaks in his or her private theatre?" As considered in chapter two, the primary identity of the analytic practitioner is from the performance arts: He or she is a mind-poet speaking from within the bog-space of carnality, corporeality, and mystical causality and in which space the sacred and profane freely and fluidly co-mingle as psychic contents determine each other. As a mind-poet, he or she retells the story being told, from all sides at once in the context of the story's sensory-based experiences.

In this understanding of psychoanalysis, the associative-interpretive process transforms into a special mode of conversation that wonders about and questions every act of establishment in a way that is both scientific and emancipatory, freeing the *knowing* and *being* of the human subject (Bollas, 1999; Barratt, 1993; Kris, 1982). And, the concept of competency is inextricably tied to the ongoing venturing into communication via the associative-interpretive process in all of its textured and multiple meanings, levels, determinants, dimensions and layers on the one hand, and the equally complex process of listening, understanding, and responding in the interpretive moment on the other. In this synthesis, the understanding of *psychoanalysis* and *competency* turn on the unique personalities of each participant and how they come together to produce a unique discourse that pursues the personal meanings by which the person lives his or her life. As succinctly stated by Lear (1990), no drug can take the place of this pursuit.

If it is the individual therapist or the unique relationship that speaks to a *being*, *knowing*, and *presencing* of self with the other, then what are the meaningful measures of competency, if any, when the therapist's listening and speaking involves, at once, an intuitive and mysterious oscillation between subjective and objective states of mind, different orders of reality and mutual subjectivities, and different conscious-unconscious configurations, experiences and meanings occurring in the realms of both *representation* and *representation's other*?

As this synthesis of psychoanalysis is situated in the realm of human experiences, so too are its measures of competency. Specifically, competency is "measured" –for those given to measurement- through the sensory-based experiences of seeing, hearing and experiencing the resonations of self with the other (of self). Perhaps in this instance, competency in psychoanalysis is best thought of as obscenity or pornography is in the social community: "I can't define it in words, represent it through the scientist's symbols, or demonstrate it through outcome studies. I do know it, however, when I see it, hear it, and feel it."

As suggested in chapter five, this process understanding of the analytic discourse speaks to a way of *being*, *presencing*, and *knowing* that interweaves with an emotional, intellectual and ethical attitude that guides its ways of thinking and speaking and has as its *only* purpose the furthering of the associative-interpretive process. It is a rather mysterious process that is filled with conflict, dilemma, and the paradoxical, dances with the sacred and profane, and leads to unimagined and unpredictable outcomes that are limited only by "the possibility of possibilities."

As the participants in the discourse venture ever more deeply into the complexities of their mutual subjectivities, they enter that closed system wherein the sacred and profane comingle and psychic contents determine each other, the wording of which allows the knowing of the unknown known in a different way. In so doing, the practitioner participates in the perpetual dance of energy (Capra, 1982) of the analytic discourse in which nothing is fixed and measurable (Zohar, 1994). As narrated and dramatized in chapter seven, for example, Mr. W and I repeatedly went to the edge of the abyss to speak with the phantoms of his-my theatre, and, many times, we could only sit in our silence. And just when everything seemed most uncertain, chaotic and fragmented, we somehow would find some words but, as stated by Artaud (1974), "*only at the final moment when all forms are on the point of returning to chaos*" (p. 79, emphasis added).

This process understanding of psychoanalysis is positioned to continuously question its own received assumptions, knowledge(s), and socio-political ideologies. Its discourse is a discourse on discourse, which includes questioning the underlying assumptions and formations of its *own* discourse (Barratt, 1993). As process, it is a special mode of conversation that continuously turns in upon itself requiring that the practitioner be completely outside the process while, at the same time, remaining completely inside. And at the same time, being neither inside nor outside as there is no *inside* or *outside*. In contrast to an institutional system, this process view of the analytic discourse radically challenges the accepted and acceptable criteria of judgment, the entire tradition of "right-minded" or "appropriate" thinking, and does not posture as a modern science that is professionalized, standardized and technocratic (Barratt, 1993). And finally, in this synthesis and practice of psychoanalysis, the analytic discourse stands outside the linear and sequential assumptions of the natural sciences, exists in a non-linear matrix of *time*, *place*, *logic*, and *causality*, and runs counter to -indeed, defies- its own institutional systematization as it rests on the uniqueness of the two participants and the associative-interpretive process.

As to the question, "Who Decides What Counts in Psychoanalysis?" comes the reply: Outcome in psychoanalysis is highly ideothetic, the value of which is best judged by the participants in the process who are, ultimately, the *only* ones who can decide what counts.

SOME FURTHER THOUGHTS ON WHO DECIDES WHAT COUNTS IN PSYCHOANALYSIS: THE ANALYTIC EDUCATOR AND PRACTITIONER

If as Kirsner (2000) suggests, psychoanalysis is "a basically humanistic discipline that has conceived and touted itself as a positivist science while organising itself institutionally as a religion" (233), then is it not time to unabashedly acknowledge to ourselves and the larger community that we form our own community of practice, hold our own distinctive views of human nature of which the unconscious is central and defining -however it might be defined, and that we hold our own views of science and research methodology as found, for example, in the anthropic sciences (Eisler, 1965)?

As suggested by Bohart (1997), perhaps it is time to advance psychoanalysis as an incredibly complex, non-linear process, and that its discourse is not premised on assumptions that can be measured by traditional natural science criteria, however modified to appeal to business, governmental and educratic entities that think in medical model terms. As a humanistic discipline premised on a non-linear metaphysics and postmodern epistemology, the mechanistic assumptions of a natural science model do not apply. And in agreement with feminists and systems theorists, we hold a process perspective in which relational phenomena are fundamentally irreducible.

Irrespective of one's particular understanding of the unconscious, the more immediate question remains: Do we continue into the 21st century conceptually tied to our received notions and measures of competency that trace their genealogy to a nineteenth century mechanistic view of the world, people, and life? The reexamination of the question of competency in psychoanalysis involves the freedom to question the natural order of things in the learning and practice communities. And in so doing, to develop competency in the ongoing destruction *-and renewal-* of psychoanalysis by questioning and challenging our received assumptions, knowledge(s), and wisdoms in psychoanalytic epistemology, ethics, education, theory and practice.

---

1. An earlier version of this essay was presented at the 27th annual Spring Meetings of the American Psychological Association's Division of Psychoanalysis (39) in Toronto. The organizing theme of the meetings was: *On Clinical Momentum: Time, Process, and Complexity in Psychoanalytic Engagement.* This chapter elaborates on some of the thoughts and ideas presented as part of an invited panel that spoke to the question, *Competency in Psychoanalysis: State Regulation, Self Regulation, the Integrity of the Profession, and Who Decides What Counts for Psychoanalysis?*

REFERENCES

Artaud, A. (1974). *Collected works of Antonin Artaud.* V. Corti, trans. London: Calder & Boyars.

Barratt, B. (1993). *Psychoanalysis and the postmodern impulse.* Baltimore: The Johns Hopkins University Press.

Bohart, A. (1997). Guidelines for the provision of humanistic psychosocial services. *The Humanistic Psychologist, 24,* 64-107.

Bollas, C. (1999). *The mystery of things.* New York: Routledge.

(1992) *Being a character: Psychoanalysis and self experience.* London: Routledge.

Capra, F. (1982). *The turning point: Science, society and the rising culture.* New York: Simon and Schuster.

Eisler, K.R. (1965). *Medical orthodoxy and the future of psychoanalysis.* New York: International Universities Press.

Flax, J. (1990). *Thinking fragments: Psychoanalysis, feminism, and postmodernism in the contemporary west.* Los Angeles: University of California Press.

Freud, S. (1910), Observations on 'Wild' Psycho-Analysis. In Jones, E. (ed.) J. Riviere, trans. (1959).. *Sigmund Freud: Collected Papers.* The International Psychoanalytical Library. *8,* 297-304.

Gato, J. (1992). *Dumbing us down: The hidden curriculum of compulsory schooling.* Philadelphia: New Society Publishing.

Henry, M. (1985) *The genealogy of psychoanalysis.* D. Brick, trans., Stanford, CA: Stanford University Press.

Kavanaugh, P.B. (2006). On cutting the grass, psychoanalytic education, and the interweave of ideology, power, and knowledge. In Raubolt, R., (ed.) *Power games: Influence, persuasion, and indoctrination in psychotherapy training.* (119-156).

New York: Other Press, LLC.
(1999). *Thinking about psychoanalytic thinking: A question(ing) of identity, purpose and ethics*. President's Address: International Federation for Psychoanalytic Education, tenth annual interdisciplinary conference. San Francisco.
(1995). *Postmodernism, psychoanalysis, and philosophy: A world of difference for the future of psychoanalytic education*. International Federation for Psychoanalytic Education, sixth annual interdisciplinary conference. Toronto.

Keisler, C. (2000). The next wave of change for psychology and the mental health services in the healthcare revolution. *American Psychologist, 55*, 481-487.

Kernberg, O. (2000). A concerned critique of psychoanalytic education. International Journal of Psycho-analysis, *81*, 97-119.

Kris, A. (1982). *Free association: Method and process.* New Haven, CT: Yale University Press.

Kirsner, D. (2000). *Unfree associations: Inside psychoanalytic institutes.* London: Process Press.

Lear, J. (1990). *Love and its place in nature: A philosophical interpretation of Freudian psychoanalysis.* New Haven: Yale University Press.

Lemiel, J. T. (1987). *The psychology of personality: An epistemological inquiry.* New York: Columbia University Press.

Neville, R.C. (1989). Freedom, tolerance, and puritan commitment. 59-76. In *On Freedom.* L. S. Rouner (ed) Boston University Studies in Philosophy and Religion. vol. Ten, University of Notre Dame Press, Notre Dame, Indiana.

Nichols, W. R. (1999). *Random house Webster's college dictionary.* New York: Random House.

Redding, R. E. (2005). Sociopolitical diversity in psychology: The case for pluralism. In Wright, R. H. & Cummings, N. A. (eds.). *Destructive trends in mental health: The well-intentioned path to harm.* (303-324). New York: Routledge.

Rose, J. (2000). Introduction. In Safouan, M. (2000) *Jacques Lacan and the question of psychoanalytic training.* J. Rose, trans. New York: St. Martin's Press.

Roustang, F. (1985). A philosophy for psychoanalysis? In Henry, M.. D. Brick, trans. *The genealology of psychoanalysis.* (ix-xxviii). Stanford: Stanford University Press.

Safouan, M. (2000). *Jacques Lacan and the question of psychoanalytic training.* J. Rose, trans.. New York: St. Martin's Press, Inc.

Slife, B. and Williams, R. N. (1995) *What's behind the research: Discovering hidden assumptions in the behavioral sciences.* Thousand Oaks, CA.: Sage Publications.
(1993) *Time and psychological explanation.* New York: State University of New York Press.

Waugh, P. (1992) *Postmodernism: A reader.* New York: E.A. Mold.

Wheatley, M.J. (1994) *Leadership and the new science.* San Francisco: Berrett-Koehler, Inc..

Wright, R. H. & Cummings, N. A.. (2005). (eds) *Destructive trends in mental health: The well-intentioned path to harm.* New York: Routledge.

Zohar, D. (1994) *The quantum society.* New York: W. Morrow, Inc.

Ten

How Will Bodies of Knowledge(s) Speak the Psychoanalytic Practitioner in the 21st Century?

On Madness, Shamans and the Psychoanalytic Arts

> Psychoanalysis and ethnology occupy a privileged position in our knowledge – not because they have established the foundations of their positivity better than any other human science, and at last accomplished the old attempt to be truly scientific; but rather because, on the confines of all the branches of knowledge investigating man, they form an undoubted and inexhaustible treasure-hoard of experiences and concepts, and above all a perpetual principle of dissatisfaction, of calling into question, of criticism and contestation of what may seem, in other respects, to be established.
>
> -Michel Foucault, *The Order of Things*

If psychoanalysis is what organized psychology and psychoanalysis profess it to be then psychoanalysis in the United States is a medical-scientific way of thinking rooted in positivistic assumptions that come together to form a nineteenth-century worldview. These essential assumptions are philosophical in nature: naturalism, linear time, determinism, atomism, nomothetic laws and explanations, and an amorality in science. Collectively, they premise the medical model's epistemological and intellectual foundations in which the biology of mind is foundational: The *mind* is a function of the physiological processes of the brain; the physiological substructures of the organism constitute the true foundations of conscious and unconscious mental life.

For the greater part of the past century, organized psychology and psychoanalysis has held science as an epistemic ideal in which the empirical validation of psychoanalytic constructs is essential to validate psychoanalysis as a science of mind. As we enter the twenty-first century, the psychoanalytic community continues to pursue the status and respectability of a causal-empirical science in its ongoing search for a new and biologically sound meta-theory in which the findings of psychoanalysis and neurophysiology intersect. Derived from a nineteenth century metaphysics, the medical model produces and reproduces its paradigmatic ways of thinking, perceiving and knowing through its pedagogical and political institutions. A nineteenth-century metaphysics continues to cast its shadow over the identity, purpose, and ethics of the analytic practitioner as we enter the twenty-first century.

The medical model of psychoanalysis refers to a distinct and paradigmatic way of thinking, knowing and perceiving, is premised on medical-scientific conceptual foundations from which derive our professional standards, and represents the identity, purpose, and ethics of the analytic practitioner as *exclusively* those of a healthcare professional who has graduated from an institute meeting healthcare accreditation standards. As a paradigmatic way of thinking, the medical model contains the shared images, assumptions and practices that have formed the foundations for our learning and practice communities during the past century. As noted by Kuhn (1970), such paradigmatic ways of thinking, "govern in the first instance, not a subject matter but a group of practitioners" (p. 80). The continued and unquestioned allegiance to such bio-medical traditions, beliefs, and values – and the institutionalized power relations in the analytic community – perpetuates the nineteenth-century worldview underlying our mainstream psychologies, techniques of practice, educational philosophy, and ethical standards and principles.

For quite some time, different ways of thinking about the world, people and life have been crossing the borders of the analytic community from other disciplines. Our understanding of psychoanalysis is changing as the concepts and meaning of *causality*, *identity*, *the subject*, and *truth* are changing. The empiricist's doctrine and thesis have been drawn into question: Correspondence between a value-free science and objectivity on the one hand and reason and a unitary truth on the other is becoming an interesting historical fiction. The alphabetized structures of thinking that have housed and signified our conceptions of people for most of the past century are in various stages of deconstruction: The A B C's of knowledge production are changing.

This chapter has the two-fold purpose of, first, considering the medical model of psychoanalysis as an institutional system of thinking that developed in the epistemic context of the modern era, the underlying assumptions of which produced the bodies of knowledge(s) that spoke the analytic practitioner of the twentieth century as a healthcare professional, research scientist, and social engineer. And second, suggesting that contemporary psychoanalysis is moving away from a medical-scientific view of madness with its foundations rooted in evolutionary biology, westernized medicine and the natural sciences to a literary, spiritual and mystical view of madness with its conceptual foundations situated in philosophy, the humanities and the arts. This paradigmatic shift produces bodies of knowledge(s) that, in my opinion, speak the analytic practitioner as the contemporary shaman of the twenty-first century: The One Who Remembers as a poet-shaman who sees the world through a magical –as opposed to a scientific- visionary experience and whose bodies of knowledge(s) and learning philosophy match more closely with the Freudian unconscious.

THE MEDICAL MODEL OF PSYCHOANALYSIS AS A MODERNISTIC SYSTEM OF THINKING

Psychoanalysis is inseparable from the cultural and historical context of the times. As a modernistic system of thinking, psychoanalysis was birthed in the culture of positivism prevalent during the latter part of nineteenth century Germany. Its epistemic context constituted the natural order of things at the time.

The Epistemic Context of the Modern Era: Descartes, Locke, and their successors brought into question the Greek and medieval philosophic tradition of rational intuitionism. A ruptured and radical break from the Greek classical tradition took place with the Newtonian synthesis of the empirical inductive method as represented by Bacon and the rational deductive method as represented by Descartes, a synthesis that provided the methodology upon which natural science was based during the modern era (Capra, 1982). An Aristotelean rational intuitionism resting on intellectual insight was displaced by a Cartesian rational objectivism resting on science and the scientific method. A Cartesian certainty of knowledge about the world and people was possible only through the applications of a Newtonian based science, method, and explanation. In so doing, the scientific method gradually displaced the authoritative sources of knowledge of the agricultural age: the church, divine revelation and dogma.

In the Cartesian worldview, thinking is the essence of human nature and *Identity* and *Being* are found in thought and the rational mind as succinctly expressed in the Cartesian cogito: *I think, therefore I am.* The Cartesian subject was constructed as fully conscious, autonomous, coherent, self-conscious, self-knowable and as speaking without being spoken (Sarup, 1993). The subject of modernity was constituted as a *rational subject* with the sensory experiences of the body subordinated to rational thought. The dualistic solution of an interaction between the mind and body privileged the mind over the body, the conceptual over the physical, and cognition, thinking, and objectivity over passion, intuition, and subjectivity.

In the Cartesian-Newtonian world of the seventeenth, eighteenth and nineteenth centuries, a self-evident and dichotomous metaphysics was foundational in thinking and speaking about the world and people. Dichotomous distinctions between the sacred and profane, the mind and body, and the outer objective and inner subjective were developed in a system of binary logic, beliefs and values. Descartes distinguished the outer physical world from the inner world of the mental and claimed to prove that the physical has a separate existence from the mental (Clarke, 1997). And with the reification of sensory impressions came the deification of science as the ultimate signifier of meaning and knower of truth.

The scientific method and experiment became the paradigm of knowledge production during the modern era. Science and its methodology provided the objective, rational, and value-free means of discovering the nomothetic laws by which the world and people functioned. Not only was a unification of all knowledge regarding the universe possible, it was the goal of science: Science would discover the universal laws, unifying concepts, and unitary Truth of the world, society and people. A Cartesian-Newtonian way of thinking provided the ontological and epistemological assumptions, premise, core values, and context for the development of the scientific bodies of knowledge(s) of the modern era

Psychoanalysis in a Culture of Positivism: The historical discipline of psychoanalysis was founded in the culture of positivism prevalent in the latter part of nineteenth-century Germany. With their publication of the "Studies on Hysteria" (1895), Freud and Breuer introduced a revolutionary way of thinking about the significance of past events and their role in providing clues to the understanding of present symptoms: A psychological way of understanding cause and effect relationships in mental life was discovered. Anna O's cathartic treatment revealed that the symptoms of hysterical patients are founded upon scenes in their past lives. Far from being arbitrary and capricious, hysterical symptoms had both rhyme and reason and meaning and purpose: "Hysterics suffer from reminiscences." And these reminiscences were understood from the perspective of an historical positivism.

In the nineteenth century, many considered the discipline of history as one of the natural sciences, a view of history that provided psychoanalysis with the promise of a scientific solution to the problems of symptoms and mental disorders. In the positivist's view, past events exist as empirical objects with their historical and causal realities contained in linear time. History viewed as a natural science provides the historian with impartial and objective recordings of factual events as they actually occurred in the past. In the positivist's view of history, the objects of the historian's inquiry are precisely that, objects, out there in a real and single past. Historical controversy among historians in no way compromises the ontological integrity of the event in question (Gay, 1989).

Functioning as a scientist-historian, the analytic practitioner inquires into a real, knowable, and singular past through the historical approach, discovering empirical events as found objects in the hallways of time-past and then bearing witness to their having occurred. The practitioner functions as an historian of the individual's history, deciphering his or her personal record of past events and, then, speaking as if from outside the story being told with his or her language referring to empirically real objects or events that occurred at specific points in time-past.

In this cultural and historical context, stories and storytelling were hardly scientific as Freud suggested –and struggled with- in the "Studies on Hysteria" (1895).

> It still strikes me myself as strange that the case histories I write should read like short stories (*Novellen*) and that, as one might say, they lack the serious stamp of science. I must console myself with the reflection that the nature of the subject is evidently responsible for this rather than any preference of my own. (160).

Imaginative writers, as Freud wrote in 1910, "produce intellectual and aesthetic pleasure," while scientists like psychoanalysts must undertake "the most complete renunciation of the pleasure-principle of which our mental activity is capable" (S.E., *11*, 165). The poet does "the same as the child at play;" the poet daydreams while the psychoanalyst performs the difficult task of confronting "reality" (S.E., 9, 144) (cited in Kendrick, 1996, 98). As a dispassionate scientist, the psychoanalyst discerns, depicts, and confronts "reality" as it is: singular, mind-independent and objectively knowable.

Freud went to great lengths from the "Studies on Hysteria" (1895) onward to distinguish his method from anything literary. Stories about people and madness more appropriately belonged to the literary realm while scientific case studies about patients and their psychotic symptoms belonged to the psychoanalytic realm where the scientific principles of treatment and cure could be discovered. Indeed, the physician's ignorance of these scientific principles and his or her non-compliance with carrying out certain of its technical regulations –along with a lack of tact and consideration in discussing sexual matters- constituted "wild analysis" and represented "a danger to patients and to the cause of psychoanalysis" (Freud, S.E., *11*, 303).

ASSUMPTIONS UNDERLYING THE MEDICAL MODEL OF PSYCHOANALYSIS

Linear Time and Determinism: In "The Studies on Hysteria," Freud and Breuer (1895) theorize that the traumatizing events in Anna O's past life are located at specific points along a continuum of linear time and space. These past events, in turn, determine the symptoms developing later in her life. Freud's historical approach rests on the underlying assumptions of a linear and sequenced time in which time flows like a line independent of the events it supposedly contains. Time advances uniformly and sequentially forward as an invisible medium for all events in which events of the past occur, *then* those of the present, *then* those of the future: Those events that precede in time are related to those that follow in a causal, deterministic, and evolutionary manner. All scientific processes of the modern era –including the notion of history as science- must occur along this invisible "line" of linear time (Slife, 1995; 1993).

Mediated by a medical ideology, Anna O's hysterical blindness, rigid paralysis, speech and eating disorders, and "conditions of absence" are understood as symptoms (symptomatology) caused by the repression of certain archaic traumatizing events from her past life (etiology) which interfere with her adaptations to current reality (psychopathology). In Freud's pathogenic memory model, Anna O's symptoms are conceptualized as disguised representations of traumatic archaic events and are understood as corresponding to actual people and empirical events in her past life. Her symptoms are contingent on and produced by these events; they have meaning and purpose that derive from an earlier time and place. Treatment and cure take place through the recovery of these memories and the accurate reconstruction of the archaic events of her personal history.

Notions of a linear and sequenced time are pivotal assumptions underlying Freud's historical approach to the understanding of hysterical symptoms: Temporal succession and spatial proximity are axiomatic assumptions in arriving at causal explanations in mental life. Linearized assumptions of *time, place, logic* and *causality* laid a deterministic foundation in psychoanalytic thinking in which past trauma psychically determines, of necessity, present symptoms. This spatio-temporal framework makes it possible to also infer past events retrospectively from present symptoms, thereby enabling accurate and precise genetic reconstructions of what must have happened to have resulted in the individual's current configuration of symptoms.

Conceptions of a linear and sequenced time are axiomatic in a nineteenth-century worldview and understanding of mental causation. They provide the foundational assumptions for the medical model's organizing conceptual framework of symptomatology, etiology, and psychopathology. And the medical model of psychoanalysis continues to rather naively assume that the individual's history is empirical in that what *happens* and what *will happen* results largely from what *has happened* in the person's early relationships and childhood surround.

In the positivist's tradition, such dogmatic unities as the past preceding the present and cause preceding effect have been foundational in our conceptions of mind, causality, and science since the publication of "The Studies on Hysteria" (1895). Linearized assumptions of time, place, logic and causality are premised on Newtonian conceptions of space and time which are understood as separate and physically independent, autonomous entities. Our modernistic theories of *mind* and *causation* developed and are understood within this spatial and temporal context. Rooted in a Newtonian framework, such causal theories commit psychoanalytic thinking to a Cartesian view of *mind* in which actions are understood as the consequence of interactions between the outer objective states of the physical (reality) and the inner subjective states of the mental (fantasies) (Child, 1998). Until relatively recently, these presuppositions and their implications have remained largely unquestioned and unexamined in the analytic community.

Evolution, Naturalism, and Atomistic Thinking: Freud was profoundly influenced by the assumptions, ways of thinking, and the historical approach of Charles Darwin. Indeed, so pronounced was Darwin's influence on Freud's thinking that Ernest Jones, in the earliest authorized biography of Freud, acclaimed Freud to be "The Darwin of the Mind" (Jones, 1953). Freud adapted the historical method and assumptions of evolutionary biology to psychoanalysis: The historical approach became the primary mode of inquiry and evolutionary biology served as the model for personality development in psychoanalytic thinking. Evolutionary doctrine grounded psychoanalysis in scientific biological foundations.

Darwin utilized an historical approach to find a scientific solution to the problem of species. His researches in biology extended the validity of the historical approach as a scientific method of inquiry from the inorganic world of geology to the organic world of biology (Ritvo, 1990). Through his "Studies on Hysteria" (1895), Freud extended the scientific validity of Darwin's historical approach further along the continuum from the organic into the realm of, supposedly, the highest forms of organic life: people and mental life. In so doing, he justified the scientific study and investigation of mental phenomenon and provided further support for the philosophy of Naturalism.

Naturalism assumes a unified theory of nature, life, and science in which natural phenomena are governed by rational, predictive and natural laws according to the intricate, predetermined, and pre-ordained designs of nature. A grand and unifying rationality underlies these intricate and complex designs of nature: The laws of nature constitute the natural order of things, deviations from which constitute the perversions thereof. Nature is a rational and intelligent workman with its creations possessing those powers and attributes permitting generation, growth, and evolutionary progression (Robinson, 1989). Furthermore, the different branches of science are unified by a single overarching theory in which, for example, biology follows the laws of physics, chemistry, and the other natural sciences.

An evolutionary model suggested a way of thinking by which psychoanalytic theory could understand the development of people and mental life as sequential, orderly, natural, and law-governed. In biology, ontogeny recapitulates phylogeny in that organisms functionally resembling each other reflect similar phylogenic origins. In psychoanalytic thinking, the history and development of the individual constitutes a more or less complete recapitulation of the developmental history of the species. The historical development of the species is mirrored in the individual's developmental history (Ritvo, 1990): The development of the individual's mental life follows the same rational laws as the physical world.

American psychoanalysis, in particular, has been wedded to notions of sequential stage theories and developmental paradigms in which a progressive and hierarchical development of mental functions is determined by the development and hierarchical arrangement of the central nervous system. Mental functions are dependent on a somatic substrate in the central nervous system with the causal factors of symptoms and mental disorders understood from the conceptual framework of evolutionary biology. Phase-specific disruptions in infancy or childhood, for example, have adverse effects on the development of particular systems of motives, character traits, object relations, and ego or self-structures.

With conceptual foundations rooted in evolutionary biology, the psychoanalytic construct of *mind* is inseparably linked to a somatic substrate: The mind is a function of the brain. A dichotomous Cartesian construction of *mind* and *body* with its emphasis on the interaction between the two separate entities premises much of our current psychoanalytic thinking and research. This construction is expressed, for example, in the dualistic conception of *the person as agent* in clinical practice and *the person as organism* in scientific research. Person *as agent* engages in those activities that involve conscious choice; person *as organism* exists by means of physiological processes (Gedo, 1999). In his discussion advancing psychoanalysis as a science, Rubinstein (1997) provides further clarification: "In clinical practice we see man unequivocally as a person. However, *to justify our hypotheses about unconscious mental events*, we must turn our attention to the organism this person is also" (emphasis added; cited in Gedo, 1999, 19).

A Cartesian construction of *the person* places conceptual primacy with organismic realities such as observable physiological processes and advances the notion that *mind* is to *conscious choice* as *body* is to *unconscious process*. The rationality of the mind (conscious choice) is privileged over the sensory-based experiences of the body (unconscious process). This dualistic construction of *the person* translates the abstraction of *the unconscious* into a concept standing for certain factual and observable physiological processes, a conception of *the unconscious* structured by the scientific notions, imagery of people, and ways of thinking from a very different and earlier time and era. For psychoanalysis to be recognized as a natural science, however, there is a compelling necessity for such a dualistic construction of *the person*: Person *as organism* provides the objective conditions necessary for the scientific validation of psychoanalytic constructs.

In the medical-scientific tradition, empirical research rests on the assumption that everything the person experiences can be reductively analyzed into component elements and the interrelationships between those elements, with the result that mental processes are reduced in complexity and simplified into predictable, measurable, and law-like behaviors (Russell, 1985). Logical atomism walks hand in hand with logical positivism: Both assume that *the person* is the sum total of his or her atomistic experiences, an assumption underlying the belief that science can hold the human being in its objectivizing gaze. The psychology implicit in such causal theories, however, is thoroughly Cartesian, as is their epistemology (Hyman, 1992). In its quest for causal empirical knowledge, the concept of *the unconscious* is reduced to physiological processes and the soul can be empiricized.

Ontogeny recapitulates phylogeny and phylogeny informs psychoanalytic thinking as to how the individual ought to develop. Implicit in the empirical construction of normatively-based developmental standards is the idea that deviations from these standards constitute empirical evidences of psychopathology as discovered, translated and inscribed in our diagnostic and statistical manuals. In effect, "differences among people" are understood as "evidences of pathology," the severity of which is measured by the number of standard deviations from the norm.

Such universalizing and totalizing conceptions of people contain core ethical issues for the analytic practitioner and educator when the purpose and ethics of the analytic discourse are organized around the idealized, empirically established normative standards of the healthcare model. Specifically, knowledge(s) based on these statistical norms intersect with the discourses of ethics and power when, in the mind of the practitioner, these normative standards move from *how things are* to representing truth-claims as to *how things ought to be* in terms of the person's development. In such instances, the analytic discourse is organized around the person's conformity with the idealized normative of the *Ought-To-Be* and psychoanalysis becomes a discourse of conformity and compliance.

Nomothetic Laws and the Amorality of Science: As a branch of the biological sciences, psychoanalysis modeled itself on the methods and assumptions of the natural sciences for the greater part of the past century. The assumptions of historical and causal realities in the positivistic tradition made it possible for the practitioner to trace back to earlier or more primitive stages of development the origins of symptoms as Darwin had traced back the origins of organisms functionally resembling each other to the same primitive structures (Ritvo, 160). And, the assumptions of *historical* and *causal* realities made it possible for psychoanalysis to develop as a nomothetic discipline.

As a derivation from the Greek *nomos,* or *lawful,* and *thetikos,* or *knowledge,* the term nomothetic translates as "lawful knowledge," "lawful thesis," or "dogma" (Lemiell, 1987). As a scientist-historian, the analytic practitioner searches for the repeatable structures and lawful relationships existing between internal mental events and the external social realities that determine or cause those internal events. Knowledge of and about these causal realities is possible only if the knowledge discovered in the hallways of time-past is objective and scientific. In the quest for knowledge, historical truth must be separated from narrative truth, fact separated from fiction, as the practitioner is obligated to scientifically validate the causal connections between current symptoms and the earlier events of childhood. Ultimately, he or she must validate the links between the mental functions of *the person* to the neural substrate of *the organism*. In so doing, "lawful knowledge" is discovered, creating the illusion that the nomothetic principle(s) and law(s) hold for each of many individuals (Lemiell, 1987).

Consistent with the empiricist's thesis and doctrine, psychoanalytic theory, process, and interpretation must transcend the practitioner's subjectivity. Each should attain an objective scientific standard *as if* science and its methodology are unmediated by values, presumptions, and ideological context. Indeed, *as if* scientific knowledge, itself, is mind-independent and value neutral: Science is *amoral.* Put another way: Nomothetic principles and laws governing mental life simply exist "out there" in a mind-independent, objective and knowable world awaiting their scientific discovery, as do the laws of nature and society. In this way, the modernistic myth is perpetuated that research, science and the empirical knowledge(s) generated in the social sciences exist outside of historical, cultural, and socio-economic influences.

A LITERARY, SPIRITUAL AND MYSTICAL SENSE OF MADNESS:

> In a philosophy of life, the fundamental determinations of existence are foregrounded: body, action affectivity. Such a philosophy takes into consideration the very soil in which thought grows. Indeed, in Schopenhauer, there emerges a new thematic of corporeality, instinct, sexuality, love, shame, cruelty and even those particular yet crucial problems posed, or rather played out, on this level –"dramas," Politzer would have said – such as the way lovers choose each other.
>
> -Michel Henry-

The passage of the construct of madness as a religious phenomenon to the more recent phase of madness as an objective medical essence does not represent an evolutionary progression of understanding moving from the more primitive and superstitious to the more advanced and scientific. Indeed, Foucault (2009) suggests that the modern experience of madness as an objective medical essence "has already been transformed in some respects by a new, literary experience of madness, obvious in late romantic works (Nerval) and in part of the avant-garde of the twentieth century (Roussel, Artaud)" *(Khalfa, xvi).* The literary and spiritual experience of madness noted by Foucault seems to be ushering in a literary construct of madness that enables a more inclusive relationship and dialogue between madness, literature, and psychoanalysis. And in this intersection, culture and psychoanalysis are inseparable.

Literature is the inherent frame of reference by which psychoanalysis names its findings and itself (Felman, 1993). The culture's mythical stories and bodies of literature brought psychoanalysis into existence by naming and giving narrative meaning to many of our most human of experiences. Literature was busy articulating the dimensions of the unconscious long before Freud made a science of it. In speaking of twenty year old Gwendolen Harleth in Eliot's *Daniel Deronda* (1876), Kendrick notes (1996), for example, that George Eliot, Britain's most intellectual novelist of the time, weaves "the mad and the sane absolutely together, to write a character whose mental discourse exactly resembles the reader's, except for occasional lapses that make her as mad as any hatter" (112). Eliot invited her reader to see Gwendolen's ailment as a familiar condition, which could be understood not by setting it apart as madness but by acknowledging its kinship to the reader's own mind.

> The narrative method by which she achieved this feat counts as one of the triumphs of 19th century English fiction. At once subtle and grand, it moves smoothly from the mind's darkest places out into the light, comprehending the internal and the external with a single, sweeping glance. Later novelists –from Joseph Conrad and E. M. Forster to Henry James, James Joyce, D.H. Lawrence, and Virginia Woolf – profited first of all from Eliot's bequest, whatever use they made or refused to make of Freud's. In a sense, they did not need Freud, because, as he himself correctly said, literary artists had already plumbed the mind's depths long before him. (Kendrick, 1996, 117)

By the 1850's, middle class British readers were ready for a madman's monologue without the storyteller and audience standing aloof, rationally observing the madness, "sustained by a logical, linear style of writing that asserted the triumph of reason even when it narrated irrationality" (Kendrick, 1996, 106). In literature, madness was moving away from the rationalistic standard in which those who were mad blindly followed blind passions and were incapable of self-knowledge –to- madness as an aspect of the human condition in which empathy with "crazy" characters was possible as the reader could see him or herself in the madness: The line between madness and sanity was less sharply drawn as readers could see the method to the character's madness. While literature and psychoanalysis are, indeed, different from each other, they are "also 'enfolded within' each other, as it were, at the same time outside and inside each other, we might say that they compromise, each in its turn, the interiority of the other" (Felman, 1993, 9).

The more contemporary narrative of madness as a literary, spiritual, and mystical phenomenon suggests a very different way of thinking about psychoanalysis as theory and discourse, and the theory of its discourse with madness. Indeed, the retellings of the various life-stories in the earlier chapters of this book resituate the analytic endeavor in a literary frame of reference while elaborating its epistemology, theory, and practice in the realms of philosophy, the humanities and the arts. And listening, understanding and responding to a person's unique life-story suggests an understanding of psychology as being *other than* a causal empirical science or a form of social learning theory.

THE PSYCHOANALYTIC PRACTITIONER AS THE SHAMAN OF THE 21ST CENTURY: THE ROMANTIC PSYCHOLOGIES OF PSYCHOANALYSIS

At first glance, it might appear that contemporary psychoanalysis is in a state of disarray as the consequence of the irreconcilable philosophical differences between the different ways of thinking that characterize the field. After all, the more contemporary psychologies of psychoanalysis premise different understandings as to the basic nature of people, posit different methods of knowing about people, and assume different purposes for the analytic discourse. On closer look, however, these different psychologies all converge around an overarching concern that spans their individual differences: The human "life world" and the lived experiences of everyday life (Schneider, 1998). They emphasize three main elements that distinguish them from the sterility of psychoanalysis as a causal empirical science: The interrelated wholeness of experience, access to such wholeness in the analytic discourse, and the qualitative or descriptive accounts of such processes.

These more contemporary psychologies speak from the perspective of an artistic and intellectual movement having its origins in the late eighteenth century: The romantic perspective which arose in opposition to enlightened rationality with its emphasis on a reductive, linear and causal knowledge.

> For the romantic, the world was much too broad and interconnected to be 'dissected' in such ways. According to the romantic, a return to the lived world and childlike openness was needed. Correlatively, there needed to be a return to the tacit state of experience prior to intellectualization. Although this tacit state was considered primitive by many Enlightenment onlookers, it was neither primitive nor backward to thoughtful romantics but deep, reverential, and comprehensive.
>
> (Schneider, 1998, 278)

Grouped together, these more contemporary psychologies of psychoanalysis form what could be called *The Romantic Psychologies of Psychoanalysis*, the emphasis of which is on the depth and variety of human experiences. They represent what psychoanalysis is in the process of becoming: A conceptually rich and multi-versal community of scholars wherein there is a deep appreciation and respect for the infinite variety of differences among people. And, they speak the analytic discourse as complex, holistic, and multi-textured.

> Although distinct themes can be gleaned from the life-world, they are always contextualized by related themes in a continuing evolving gestalt. One does not speak of linear causes from this standpoint, but of atmospheres, salient themes, and structures. (Schneider, 1998, 280)

For the romantic psychologies, the analytic discourse is of a fundamentally different epistemological and ontological order than is a social, medical, or empirical discourse. The romantic psychologies and the neurosciences, for example, study processes and phenomenon of the human condition but from very different perspectives and for very different purposes.

The emphasis of the romantic psychologies on the interrelated wholeness of experience reflects the emerging worldview of the twenty-first century in which everything in the world is inseparably interconnected. This worldview rests on the thinking of theoretical physics, the mysticism of the Eastern and Asian philosophies, and a systems theory that speaks to the spirituality of the *something more* of the person: his or her mind, psyche or soul. Underlying the illusion of a literal concreteness and separateness in our everyday lives of space, time and the objects contained therein is a realm of frequencies and interconnected potentialities. The physical entities that seem separate and discrete as conceived in the classical reality of Newtonian physics are actually linked or unified in an implicit or underlying fashion. In the manifest realm of space and time, objects and events *appear* separate and discrete; in the world of subatomic physics, however, there is no space *and* no time. In the subatomic world of the frequency realm, all things and events are spacelessly, timelessly, and intrinsically one and undivided (Wilber, 1985). In the blended space between classical and quantum thinking is found the lived experiences of the life-world.

In Chinese thought, this inseparable interconnectedness is reflected in the *Principle of Relationship* (Zheng He Lu) and constitutes the essence of dialectical thinking: Nothing is isolated and independent; everything is connected. This holistic mode of thought rests on the assumption that everything exists in the mystical integration of *yin* and *yang*, entities that are opposed to each other and, at the same time, are also connected in time and space as a whole in space-time (Peng & Nisbett, 1999). The romantic psychologies of psychoanalysis seek to understand this interrelated wholeness of the subject's experiences and are more allied with the magical –as opposed to the scientific- visionary experience: They do not aspire to scientific status nor do they posit underlying biological referents for their constructs. They neither seek nor claim validation from the atomistic thinking of a medical-scientific ideology.

The romantic psychologies are concerned with the individual's personal meanings, understandings, and knowledge(s) of the world. Their discourse pertains to the individual's point of view, knowledge(s), or thesis. As an historical mode of inquiry, the romantic psychologies of psychoanalysis rest on the assumption that every individual's personality consists partly or entirely of traits or experiences *not* found in the personality of every or, perhaps, even any other person: Each person is unique. A unified theory of nature, life, and science is *not* assumed by the romantic psychologies of psychoanalysis: They are not pursuing a search for general or universal laws. Indeed, empirical evidence generated by individual differences research has absolutely no legitimate interpretation whatsoever at the level of the individual. Instead, the analytic discourse encourages the description and understanding of the personal meaning(s) of phenomena as defined, consciously or otherwise, by the individual. And, the romantic psychologies also raise the question of the practitioner's identity as being *other than* a healthcare professional in the medical-scientific tradition in the twenty-first century.

As considered earlier in chapter 4, the question of identity, purpose, and ethics are the questions of self-definition in everyday life as an analytic practitioner, the questioning of which is an unavoidable aspect. The romantic psychologies of contemporary psychoanalysis speak from a different worldview, establish different intellectual foundations for psychoanalysis, and suggest the identity of the analytic practitioner as *other than* a healthcare professional in the medical-scientific tradition. The romantic psychologies reintroduce the identity of the analytic practitioner as a poet-shaman: A mind-poet and philosopher-historian in the shamanic traditions.

As the poet-shaman of contemporary times, the analytic practitioner is understood as *The One Who Remembers* the events of yesterday and today out of a deep and sacred respect for the ways of others, helps people make sense of their experiences and the lives they are living, and provides a sense of continuity with their experiences and traditions of yesterday as they are relived in the present moment. As a poet-shaman, he or she is a participant-observer in the analytic process, is guided by an ethic of free association, and, in the interpretive moment, words the inexplicable in meaningful ways for the purpose of, at once, enabling the person's escape from his or her spirit's ghostly grasp and furthering of the associative-interpretive process. The poet-shaman organizes, structures, and speaks to the relationship between the person's phenomenal past and his or her speaking *of it*, speaking *with it*, speaking *from it*, and speaking *in it*... all at the same time: Madness is included in the psychology and discourse of psychoanalysis.

Situated in the romantic psychologies, the analytic discourse is concerned with the person's theory of personal knowledge (epistemology) and his or her construction of reality (ontology). These questions are philosophical in nature, pertain to the person's interpretive design of the world, and implicitly speak the purpose of the analytic discourse as understanding the various meanings and motivational causalities in the person's story and interpretive design of the world (Kavanaugh, 1995). It is the individual who has the privileged relationship to truth; it is the privilege of the action of the analysis to attempt to understand his or her truth. The conceptual premise and understandings of this discourse are found in the realm of human experiences. Furthermore, it is not necessary for the person to participate in quasi-public self-declarations of psychopathology as a pre-requisite for participating in this unique psychological discourse.

THE FREUDIAN UNCONSCIOUS, THE MAGICAL VISIONARY EXPERIENCE, AND THE ANALYTIC DISCOURSE

> ... Life or affectivity knows itself only insofar as it experiences itself, insofar as it affirms itself through the exercise of its force. ... That life is source and origin inasmuch as it is self-immanence and unbroken subjectivity, has as a result not the broadening of our knowledge and the extension of the domain of science, but on the contrary the recognition of the derivative and unreal nature of all that is produced within the register of representation.
>
> -Francois Roustang-

The genealogy of the Freudian unconscious traces its roots back to the shaman's mystical conceptualization of the underworld and practice of primitive medicine (Ellenberger, *1970).* Freud's initial and intuitive grasp of the unconscious as *life* or *representation's other* places psychoanalysis outside of the scientist's classical worldview and moves it into the world beyond into mysticism which understands affectivity as the life force: *Affectivity* is at the heart of the mystical traditions, beliefs, and values. Freud's intuitive grasp of the unconscious as *life* interweaves with the mystic's notion of the *life force* to speak to the experiences of aliveness, connectedness, and belongingness in the lived experiences of our everyday lives.

As *representation's other*, the Freudian unconscious is an ontology of life that emphasizes the process nature of our lived experiences in which unrepresentability, invisibility, and formlessness are core characteristics. It is this meaning of the unconscious that refers to a philosophy of life in which the unconscious is the original essence of being and "secretly refers to *being's* fundamental structures, which it exposes in its own way (Roustang, 1993, xiv)." In a Freudian philosophy of life, *the unconscious* is the essence of life: It is the interpretation of *being* as *life* as opposed to the conscious *representation of life.*

As a shamanic discourse, psychoanalysis is deeply rooted in spirituality, science, and the lived experiences of everyday life: It is grounded in the poetical, metaphorical language of the shaman's spirituality and the technical language of the life systems sciences such as cultural anthropology and deep ecology. It is a spiritual discourse inextricably tied to a radical subjectivity in which the person's reality is whatever his or her senses reveal it to be (Eaker, 1975). From this perspective, psychoanalysis is understood as a science of subjectivity, is concerned with archaic forms of mental functioning, and understands love as a basic force in the analytic discourse (Lear, 1990).

Magic -that old nemesis of science- has its own visionary experience, perception, and reality. The mind-poet's ways of *being, knowing and presencing* in the analytic space are contextualized by the magical –as opposed to the scientific-visionary experience. In this visionary experience, the poetic-artistic perception takes precedence over so-called objective reality, the magic of which is found in uniting the elements of sensory experiences in ways usually not seen and expressing this alternative reality in ways usually not expressed as exemplified, for example, in chapter three as Mr. P's reality is expressed in the sensory form of the coffee and cream and is acknowledged and responded to in another sensory form as his experiences of *self* and *other*. In so doing, the seemingly disparate elements of objective consciousness are united in the space in-between.

In the magical visionary experience, there are multiple levels of order, meaning, and reality. The poetic perception acknowledges the interrelationships between these multiple levels. The shamanic voice narrates from somewhere in the space in between and, in so doing, speaks to the interrelated wholeness of the subject's experience. The poet-shaman alters his or her state of consciousness –at will- to enter the sacred space of the spirit realm wherein *affectivity* has its own mode of knowledge and *knowing* occurs through the immersion of self in the sensory-based perceptions and experiences of the other.

This is the highest level of spirit where the soul becomes being in a non-dual state of radical intuition and the unconscious of self listens, understands and responds to the unconscious of the *other* (of self) without the intermediary of representation. Indeed, one of the key tenets of mysticism is that subject and object become *one* in the act of knowing. The primary source of *knowledge* in the spirit realm is the Freudian unconscious; the primary way of *knowing* is through the perceptual-sensory experiences of the associative-interpretive process walking hand in hand with the aesthetic process of the magical visionary experience.

Freud's understanding of *life* as self-immanence and unbroken subjectivity speaks to a form of knowledge very different than that spoken by empirical science. Indeed, the shaman's shadows are to the mysteries of the soul, death, and the sacred narratives of human existence as the scientist's symbols are to normative conceptions of people, the DSM-V, and E(mpirically) B(ased) T(treatment)s. As *life*, the Freudian unconscious does not produce knowledge of reality -and never will- if *knowledge* is understood as objectively and scientifically spoken via the scientist's symbols (Henry, 1985). The illusory nature of our shadowed realities and the unreal nature of all that is produced within the register of representation speak to the futility of psychoanalysis seeking its truth and validation from the assumptions, methods, and explanations of a logical-positivistic science. As a science of radical subjectivity, psychoanalysis is unproven and unprovable by the assumptions, methods and explanations of a rationalistic science (Lear, 1999). From the standards of a medical-scientific framework, however, a shamanic discourse is, of course, a sham discourse: It's "wild analysis."

THE FREUDIAN UNCONSCIOUS AND THE QUESTION OF PSYCHOANALYTIC EDUCATION AND TRAINING

Freud's initial and intuitive grasp of the unconscious as *affectivity* or *life* caught a glimpse of a very different view of the world and reality, and of people and life. His interpretive encounter with hysteria marked an *epistemological event* requiring a rethinking of traditional understandings of cause-effect relationships in his theory of the unconscious; a *self-analytical event* requiring the examination of his desires and their role in analytic practice; a *literary event* requiring new ways of thinking and writing about people in a narrative story format; and, an *ethical event* in which the psyche and symptoms spoke a very different relationship between medicine, pathology, and that which constitutes the Good (Rajchman, 1991). His interpretive encounter with hysteria failed, however, to mark an *educational event* that matched an educational philosophy, set of practices, and modes of knowledge with his most radical and revolutionary concept: *the unconscious*. Freud never did conceive of another type of knowledge other than that provided by the subject-object relation that, by definition, passes through representation.

A philosophy of consciousness underlies the traditional subject-object paradigm of Western metaphysics: Consciousness and rationality, paradoxically, are privileged over the Freudian unconscious in our educational and political institutions. And apparently, will continue to be into the twenty-first century following the Consortium's adoption of healthcare accreditation standards in the summer of 2001, as considered in chapter nine: Psychoanalytic education and training –and its underlying philosophy- continues in the traditions of the Berlin model of 1922. In so doing, the Consortium's actions reduces the complex issues of diversity and education in contemporary psychoanalysis to a unified and unitary master narrative that minimizes their differences in assumptions, theories, notions of the unconscious, and objectives. The mystery, magic and muscle of the Freudian unconscious continues, nonetheless, to gently rise outside the walls of our educational institutions.

Understood as *life* or *the life force*, the conceptual singularity of the unconscious places psychoanalysis outside of the classical worldview and the scientist's symbols. The Freudian unconscious is, at once, dependent upon a metaphysics of representation to express itself in and through various forms of presence and absence (a *representational unconscious*) and, as an ontology of life, is concerned with "the radical immanence of its auto-affection," (*representation's other*) expressing itself in a closed system within which psychic contents determine each other (Roustang, 1993, xv). It is this latter understanding of the Freudian unconscious that did not fit -and still does not - with our received philosophical, scientific, or medical paradigms (Henry, 1985). As *representation's other*, the Freudian unconscious cannot be represented by the scientist's symbols, explained by the positivist's rationality, or taught in the analytic experiences of our educational institutions.

How we understand and interpret ourselves as psychoanalytic practitioners is contained in the traditional stories that have defined who we are, where we come from, and how we imagine ourselves into being. As the narrative changes, how will bodies of knowledge(s) speak the analytic practitioner of the twenty-first century? The diversity of theory and practice that characterizes contemporary psychoanalysis anticipates, I believe, a pluralism of educational and training programs in North America. In the European community, the faculty-centered Institute in the Berlin tradition is but one of the training models available. Sandler (1990), who has reviewed the diversity of training programs in the European community (1982), says that while there is no one ideal model for psychoanalytic training in North America, the merits of the Berlin institute and the student-centered model in the Vienna tradition are both models that need to be debated and explored openly.

An innovative vision for the future of psychoanalytic education and training in North America is suggested by the European community's diversity of educational models: A continuum of educational possibilities that allows for, encourages and preserves the diverse and interdisciplinary quality of contemporary psychoanalysis. Specifically, as suggested by Hyman (1990), the Institute model is one model situated at one end of a continuum of training possibilities and at the other end is found those educational opportunities in which there is no organizational structure whatsoever. This continuum of educational possibilities has the threefold advantage of recognizing the diversity of thinking in contemporary psychoanalysis, matching the forms of education with the particular theory of psychoanalysis under study, and acknowledging in a meaningful way the individualized nature of the person's educational experiences.

As the contemporary shaman of the twenty-first century, might the analytic practitioner turn to shamanic principles of learning for the purpose of cultivating his or her awareness of the alternative realities existing at any given moment in the analytic discourse? As the genealogy of the Freudian unconscious traces its roots to the shaman's ancient tradition's, might the philosophy and principles of shamanic learning write a new chapter in the story of how we imagine ourselves into being, and in which story our modes of knowledge(s) match more closely with our understanding of the Freudian unconscious?

A SHAMANIC MODEL OF LEARNING IN (THE SPIRIT OF) THE VIENNA TRADITION

A shamanic program of study in psychoanalysis is organized around the transmission of those knowledge(s) and skills that, at once, contribute to the formation of the practitioner as a poet-shaman and match with the Freudian unconscious. The educational philosophy and principles of a shamanic model of learning is organized around Bernfeld's (1962) view that psychoanalytic education must be student-centered in the Vienna tradition and is situated at the less-structured end of Hyman's (1990) continuum of educational models. Examples of educational models found along this less-structured continuum of possibilities are found in the Michigan model (Hyman, 1990), the Free Association model (Thompson, 2000), and the Society of Psychoanalysts (Safouan, 2000), a model that rests on certain minimalist principles.

Perhaps, the most radical aspect of a shamanic program of study is the underlying view of the student as the responsible author of his or her own professional life: Each student is seen as self-directed, self-motivated, and more or less self-selecting into a largely self-designed program for the study of psychoanalysis. Its narrative of education and training values and encourages individual responsibility and critical thinking as foundational and integral aspects of the learning process. The student makes the decision, for example, as to whom he or she might meet with for supervision, learn about different theories and practices of psychoanalysis, and who he or she might meet with for his or her personal analysis - as opposed to his or her training or educational analysis. Thus, anyone interested in psychoanalysis could, on his or her own initiative, seek psychoanalytic supervision, didactic experiences, and a personal analysis with someone who seems to know a bit more and is deserving of his or her trust.

In contradistinction to the longstanding ambiguity and confusion regarding the ending of psychoanalysis in the Berlin model, the student in the Vienna model ultimately decides when the analysis is ended and when certification of self as a poet-shaman is warranted, the time-worn and thread-bare arguments of "protecting the public" notwithstanding. The authority to authorize him or herself as a poet-shaman is inextricably tied to the question of the end of analysis and can be answered, in the final analysis, only by the student. The authority to translate unconscious experience, process, and dynamic derives from his or her experiences of analysis (Safouan, 2000); the desire to translate unconscious experience, process, and dynamic is intrinsic to the individual student and his or her ways of *being*. Much can be learned in the praxis of the analytic discourse, very little can be taught, however, as human experience, psychoanalytic or otherwise, is not didactic.

In the shamanic tradition, psychoanalytic learning takes place through the apprenticeship to an older practitioner, someone deserving of respect and from whom the student believes he or she might learn: The mentoring relationship is essential, collaborative and based on mutual respect. It is the medium through which psychoanalytic wisdoms, values, attitudes and beliefs are transmitted, similar in nature to the relationship between Wang Fo and Ling as they travel the Kingdom of Han in chapter five. In this conception and philosophy of learning, identity is not assumed, sought, or received. As suggested in chapter four, one's identity must be continuously questioned, the skeptical questioning of which, paradoxically, becomes a major aspect of one's identity as a poet-shaman.

The Vienna model provides each poet-shaman-in-the process-of-becoming with the opportunity to learn in a highly individualistic manner in terms of the timing and pacing of his or her analytic experiences, selecting with whom he or she might enter into analysis or supervision, and selecting the format most relevant and meaningful for his or her learning: seminars, study groups, or individual tutorials. An ongoing process of self-evaluation takes place in the mentoring context and is integral to its process, the purpose of which is the development of a way of *being*, *knowing* and *presencing* that cultivates the eyes of fire that see through the ordinariness of everyday life and perceive the wonders and terrors that lie beyond. In so doing, the student may be able to more fully participate in a discourse that, at once, includes the voice of his or her own private madness and allows for that of the other.

A SHAMANIC PHILOSOPHY OF LIFE AND LEARNING: STU-CHERING, THE SPIRIT REALM, AND THE FREUDIAN UNCONSCIOUS

For the poet-shaman, the world is a fundamentally interconnected and interdependent network of phenomenon that engenders a profound sense of connectedness, context, and belonging. In the shamanic tradition, all aspects of psychoanalytic learning are organized around this worldview in the service of cultivating a mystical state of consciousness and, in so doing, enabling his or her entry into the spirit realm where there is an all-pervading unity in which "this" and "that" are no longer separate entities. It is here in the space of the shaman's radical intuition that the unconscious of self listens, understands and responds to the unconscious of the other (of self) without the intermediary of representation: The unconscious of two become one.

The highest level of spirit is in this mystical oneness where the soul becomes *Being* in a non-dual state of radical intuition (Wilber, 1985): *Affectivity* or *representation's other* has its own mode of knowledge known only through this immersion of self in the sensory-based perceptions and experiences of the other (of self). The poet-shaman learns to alter his or her state of consciousness at will to enter this sacred space of the spirit realm where only subtle and minimal subject-object distinctions exist. In the learning process, the student and teacher become one in the act of knowing, as perhaps best represented by the linguistic and blended reversal of *the student* and *the teacher* into the construct of *the stu-cher*, signifying that the learning process itself enters and takes place in the spirit realm. Psychoanalytic learning in the shamanic tradition is a process of *stu-chering* in the classroom didactics, the supervisory process, and the discourse of one's analysis (Kavanaugh, 1995).

Entry into the spirit realm involves the *stu-chering* process gradually freeing itself from the illusion of an independently existing fixed-self, and entering a Zen-like space of *no self* (*anatman*) and, in so doing, freeing one's mind by being in a state of *no mind* (*mushin*) so that one does not *think* but, rather, *knows*. In the stead of the Cartesian cogito, *I think therefore I am*, is the premise of shamanic learning: *I am where I do not think*: Passion, intuition and subjectivity interweave with each other in the formation of the dynamical and unpredictable systems in which psychoanalytic knowing takes place in the spirit realm.

The spirit realm is the highest of all possible domains of being: The Being beyond all beings, the domain of no other domain where the soul preserves its radically transcendental nature. In this universe of the sacred, the spirit realm is the Set of all possible sets, the Condition of all conditions, and the Nature of all natures: The spirit realm is the *something more* of being human. As described by Wilber (2001), the spirit world is not a realm set apart from all other realms; it is the Ground or Being of *all* realms. The spirit realm is, at once, the context of all text and the ground of all figure and, at the same time, it is both the text and the figure. Within the processes of the spirit realm, the stu-cher reflects and is skeptical while, paradoxically, being neither reflective nor skeptical: He or she is in neither and both states of mind at the same time.

Psychoanalytic learning in the shamanic tradition involves nothing less than learning to *presence* one's self in the un-teachable and silent knowledge(s) of the Freudian unconscious. Specifically, for the stu-cher to *presence* him or herself in the invisible and incomprehensible universe that ordinary perception does not perceive: the universe of the sacred. In effect, he or she engages in a gradual transformative process of his or her usual ways of *knowing*, *being*, and *presencing* in the world. In its radicality, a shamanic program of study involves nothing less than the transformation of the stu-cher's experiences of reality. In so doing, he or she cultivates the ability to enter an altered state of consciousness –at will- so as to access, interact with, and use ordinarily hidden realities within him or herself to acquire sacred knowledge(s) and power in the service of helping the other. Towards this end, all learning is organized around harnessing energy fields not usually accessed, the purpose of which is to heighten one's states of awareness so as to see the invisible and speak the inexplicable.

Lastly, shamanic learning takes place within the grand paradox of life, and particularly so for those attempting to word-bridge the space between the realm of *representation* and *affectivity.* Succinctly stated: All of shamanic learning is organized around entering the spirit realm, the purpose of which is to speak the inexplicable and word that which cannot be represented in language. The radical phenomenality of the unconscious speaks, however, to the essentially unreal nature of all that is produced within the register of representation. The unconscious has need of representation through various systems of signification *not*, however, in order for *life* to exist but, paradoxically, for the person to experience *self* as existing in *life* (Henry, 1985). Although representation creates an unreal and illusory world, it is, at the same time, inseparable and indispensable to the person's experiences of *reality* and *life*. Thus, it is vital and necessary that all learning in the shamanic tradition be conceptualized. And, it is equally vital and necessary to know, at the same time, the unreal and illusory nature of the conceptualization itself.

PSYCHOANALYTIC BODIES OF KNOWLEDGE(S) SPEAKING THE MIND-POET: THE PROFANE AND THE SACRED

What are the bodies of knowledge(s) that might transmit something about the mystery, magic and muscle of the shaman's poesy of care and, as suggested by Whitaker (2002), might lead the individual to do much better than when meeting with a healthcare professional with medical-doctor anti-psychotic medications? Psychoanalytic learning in the shamanic tradition is organized around the sacred narratives of human existence, is premised on the sensory perceptual experiences of one's analytical experiences, and involves the study of the psychoanalytic arts: the Arts of Critical Thinking, the Arts of Communication, and the Arts of Continuity (Kavanaugh, 1998). These bodies of knowledge(s) contribute to speaking the analytic practitioner as the contemporary shaman of the twenty-first century: A mind-poet who, as suggested in chapter two, sees and speaks the individual's poem and poetry from all sides and everywhere, at once.

In the shamanic tradition, psychoanalytic learning has a two-fold emphasis. The first pertains to attaining knowledge(s) of the cultural meanings, mythologies, and metaphors of everyday life (the profane) (Rigoni, 2002). In this first area of emphasis, a shamanic program of study is interested in and organized around the study of the Arts of Communication such as, for example, literature, prose, poetry, music, mythical stories and storytelling, and semiotics; the Arts of Critical Thinking such as pre-modern, modern and post-modern forms of philosophy, their respective philosophical issues and modes of inquiry; and, the Arts of Continuity such as the culture's history, mythology, religion, science, theatre, film, dance, folklore, and those traditions that link our phenomenal past with an anticipated future.

The second area of emphasis pertains to the development of one's states of heightened awareness (the sacred) (Rigoni, 2002), without the distracting intervention of the spoken language of the profane. The learning experiences of the sacred involve the ecstatic in which the poet-shaman-in-the-process-of-becoming engages in the process experiences of dreams, visions, and trances, particularly as experienced in his or her analysis or supervisory experiences, either of which might provide the opportunity to see and experience how the sacred intersects and interweaves with the profane in endless, profound, and myriad ways.

In the shamanic tradition, psychoanalytic learning is not organized around learning bits of information *about* some aspect of life such as death, adolescence, or madness. Everything is understood in relationship to the student and teacher in the context of the world of the visible and invisible, ... except, of course, when it is not. Information is never separated from its context, purpose, and relationship to the whole process: Learning is a stu-chering process, continuously interweaving the profane with the sacred, text with context, and figure with ground. Furthermore, a shamanic program of study continuously weaves and interweaves its learning experiences with the three interrelated elements of the Freudian revolution in which psychoanalysis is understood as a science of subjectivity, is concerned with archaic forms of mental functioning, and understands love as a basic force in its discourse (Lear, 1990).

In this way, the poet-shaman-in-the-process-of-becoming is concerned with, becomes aware of, and attends to the networks of unconscious meanings in every aspect of life and learning. An attitude and way of being is cultivated in which the Freudian unconscious, understood as *life,* is seen as influencing and interweaving with all of conscious thought, as having an elegance of rhyme and reason and meaning and purpose, and as revealing its radical phenomenality through the fluid flow of the associative-interpretive process. In once seeing the sacred, the profane is no longer the same. And in this way, the iron-spiked fence that separates the sacred and profane –and the sane from the insane- gradually deconstructs and dissolves itself.

Finally, information does not matter as much as the experience of the relational process it sets in motion between *self* and *other* and the *visible* and *invisible* in the formation of the student's identity, purpose and ethic as a poet-shaman. In this way, he or she might gradually learn of the power within him or herself through his or her heightened awareness in *perceiving*, *knowing*, and *being* in the social system of which he or she is inseparable and, in which system, he or she eventually will practice the arts of psychoanalysis.

PSYCHOANALYSIS AS A SCIENCE OF SUBJECTIVITY: PSYCHOANALYTIC STORYTELLING AND THE RELATIVITY OF REALITY

The stories of our lives are the sacred narratives of our existence: They tell us where we come from and who we are, the wording of which is a powerful experience. It is the means by which we might come to know our interpretive design of the world and the ancient truths contained therein. And in its telling to another, the story's life and power is unleashed. As considered in chapter one, the subjective *I* is at the center of the individual's existence, generates his or her unique reality, and is the ultimate referent in telling his or her story. The subjective *I* is ever present in organizing and communicating his or her life-story: The quest of the subject walks hand in hand with the question of subjectivity.

As a science of subjectivity, psychoanalysis is the science of *I*, is deeply rooted in the Freudian unconscious, and –from this perspective- invites the poet-shaman into the intimate story told: The poet-shaman ventures into the individual's story via the associative-interpretive process in the contextualizing metaphor of the psychic theatre of the mind. A shamanic program of study organized around this particular synthesis and practice of psychoanalysis is designed to match with its major conceptual elements: *Venturing into the person's communications via the associative-interpretive process* necessarily places an emphasis on the study of the Arts of Communication and Critical Thinking; and, *in the contextualizing metaphor of the psychic theatre of the mind* emphasis is placed on the Arts of Continuity. It is not, however, an *either…or* emphasis or focus: Psychoanalytic learning takes place in the ongoing and continuous interweaving of these bodies of knowledge(s) and their relationship to the something more of the person's life-story.

The magical visionary experience is most appreciative that the world we see is only our view of the world, the reality we know is whatever our senses reveal it to be, and the link with psychoanalysis is found in the nature and role of perception in shaping, if not creating, the universe around us. The appreciation of *the relativity of reality* among people is foundational in the poet-shaman's ability to listen, understand and respond to the stories told in the analytic space. In contrast to ordinary communication in everyday life, "Psychoanalytic communication accepts the relativity of reality and the ultimate correspondence between man's sense of reality for the world and his sense of responsibility for himself" (Weisman, 1965, viii). Each person's story communicates his or her unique configuration of subjective and objective reality and his or her ideothetic ways of polarizing existence: Every individual selects that which constitutes "the facts" of his or her life-world, organizes these "facts" in ways that are meaningful to him or her, and understands and interprets these "facts" in ways that, at once, confirm and conform with certain pre-existing images of self and other.

Developing an appreciation for the relativity of reality necessarily involves the study of the Arts of Communication and Critical Thinking, the continuous interweave of which is central to learning both *about* and *from* the multiple and, often times, contradictory realities revealed in the storytelling process. Thus, the theoretical and applied aspects of perception occupy a central place in a learning philosophy and experience organized around psychoanalysis as a science of subjectivity.

The uniqueness of *being* and *reality* in the analytic discourse pertains to each participant in a discourse that cannot be anticipated or replicated. The poet-shaman's appreciation of the relativity of reality underlies his or her development of a core existential attitude that appreciates and respects the unique and fundamentally different versions of reality and the multiple meanings each version holds for each person in an analytic conversation. In the shamanic tradition, the learning process is re-situated in the perceptual sensory experiences of the associative-interpretive process as opposed to the learning and application of the formularies and institutionalized intellectualizations of the various institutional systems of psychoanalysis of modernistic times.

The quest of psychoanalysis is found in the participants' collaborative effort to understand the subject's construction of reality and his or her interpretive design of the world as it unfolds on the stage of the analytic space. And further, to symbolize in words the as of yet un-symbolized; to elaborate in words concealed dimensions of experiences not yet known, revealed, or recognized; and, to explain certain discontinuities in the person's experiences from his or her world of action and consequence and meaning and purpose.

THE INTRINSIC MADNESS OF THE ASSOCIATIVE-INTRPRETIVE PROCESS: ARCHAIC EXPERIENCES AND THE CONTEXT OF LOVE

In the telling of his or her story, the individual's various experiences and constructions of reality come to contextualize the analytic space, encircle both participants, and provide the associative context for their ensuing discourse. In so doing, the discourse returns again and again to the organizing and structuralizing power of emotions and desires and the archaic organizing unconscious scripts of the participants' private and personal madness. As both participants enter the complexities and realities of their mutual subjectivities, they come to speak from within the wellsprings of madness of self and other. In so doing, the subjective experiences of the subject - the *I*, the *Je* – interweave with his or her archaic memory-event-experiences to co-structure and co-determine the reliving of something about his or her world -as he or she perceives it to have been - in the present moment of the past. The material phenomenality for the basic referents in this reality and the stories told is found in the reality constructed by the individual.

One of the more radical and far-reaching implications that derive from this quantum, mystical, and spiritual worldview is that the romantic psychologies of contemporary psychoanalysis dance with the ultimate in paradox and self-reference. In this unique psychological discourse, the practitioner speaks, listens, and interacts, ultimately, with him or herself cast in the image of the other. As a derivation from the Latin *solus* and *ipse*, solipsism translates as "I myself alone." And a particular form of solipsism can be stated for the associative space and context: "I cannot know that anything exists other than the *experiences* of myself, my mental states past and present, and my *experiences* of a material world" (Kennick, 1970). In effect, the world is each individual's *representation* of the world, including the experience that there *is* a world. In the analytic space, objective reality is understood as the person's subjective experience, aspects of which are experienced as objective. This skeptical form of solipsism is epistemological in character as it poses the question, "How do we ever know for sure what we know?" And, "What is it exactly that we do know?" The questions of ethics and epistemology are inextricably linked to the solipsistic nature of the analytic space and moment.

In this solipsistic space, I *as listener* interact with my experience of self *as speaker* in the form of the other (of self); *affectivity* knows and recognizes itself in the other (of self) in the realm of the spirit where all things and events are spacelessly, timelessly, and intrinsically one and undivided. In this space where *self* interacts with the *other-of-self*, the soul apprehends Being while still maintaining an irreducible boundary between *self* and *other*: In the primal linguistic of one's bodily experiences, there is always and only spirit. In this intimate space of shared bodily experiences, psychoanalytic knowledge is known as the unconscious of *self* comes to know and speak with the unconscious of the *other* (of self). In so doing, our analytic experiences match more closely with our understanding of the Freudian unconscious as process, as *life*, and as *representation's other*.

The poet-shaman ventures into the individual's communications via the associative-interpretive process for the purpose of understanding and translating into words, as best as he or she might, the rhythms and rhymes and meanings and purposes of whatever reality unfolds on the stage of the theatre. The primary source of knowledge in the analytic space is the unconscious; the primary way of knowing is through the associative-interpretive process, the heart of psychoanalysis. In his philosophical reflection on the paradox of the analytic process, Bollas (1999) says that the associative method of inquiry runs contrary to everything we are taught is the logical, rational and "scientific" way to acquire knowledge. Yet, he says, it is only through using such an apparently illogical and subversive method that the person's psychic truth can be articulated: More than simply a methodology, the associative-interpretive process speaks to a revolution in the mind's access to its unthought forms of knowledge.

In its radicality, the hyphen in the associative-interpretive process signifies, at once, the dissolution of the traditional subject-object division of western metaphysics and entry into the solipsistic nature of the analytic space. As the invitation to enter the mystical space of the spirit realm is mutually accepted, two human beings come together in the splendors and terrors of their shared humanity and speak with the essence of the psyche (the soul) in the "the radical immanence of its auto-affection" where psychic images and experiences determine each other and the *other* as speaker becomes inseparable from the experiences of *self* as listener. In this space, there is an inseparable interconnectedness between the observer and the observed; the poet-shaman is always an integral aspect of that which is observed (Becvar and Becvar, 1996). In this solipsistic space, the listener must be *with the words*, and *in the words*, and *be the words*, yet, at the same time, go beyond the literal signification of the words. The listener is in the dimension of a literal signification of words and, at the same time, in a dimension beyond words and speakers.

In this contextual field, the analytic discourse unfolds in a timeless and space-less sphere of conflict, dilemma, and the paradoxical wherein both participants exist as literally separate and discrete entities as in classical physics, yet, *at the same time*, as inseparably inter-connected as-a-whole in space-time as in quantum thinking. In effect, the poet-shaman experiences the internal other as external to, separate from, and different than self, not unlike phenomena one might experience in a dream where the dreamer is both the one pursued by the monster *and* the pursuing monster. The practitioner listens, understands, and responds through a blending of literal meaning with contextual meaning and speaks from somewhere in the space in between. In so doing, he or she makes a leap, a discovery, and a creative solution that is *something more* than what could be represented in any other way. Perhaps, it is in the *inter-pret* that one speaks to the *something more* of the psyche (the soul), the inexplicable *something more* of the mystery, magic, and muscle of the person to which linear words, formulaic logic, and inductive or deductive reasoning cannot go.

Psychoanalytic knowledge comes from an immersion into the person's story via the associative-interpretive process. Psychoanalytic knowing occurs by entering the silent knowledge(s) of its sensory-based images and experiences, coming to know them as they are relived in the present moment, and wording the mutually shared bodily experiences that unfold in the analytic space. The knowing of psychoanalytic knowledge occurs as the poet-shaman enters the other's story, images and sounds while permitting them to enter him or herself. As considered in chapter two, he or she walks around in them, smells them, tastes them, knows them, inhabits them, breathes them, and becomes them so as to speak from within the other (of self): He or she comes to know the story by heart in order to speak it from the heart. In the *presencing* of self in the intimate space of the spirit realm comes the *knowing* of the other (of self).

In this process understanding of psychoanalysis, love is expressed through the practitioner's willingness to listen, understand and respond to the person's experiences of reality without attempting to correct or normalize them or organizing the discourse around a theoretically anticipated outcome. Love is expressed by respecting and accepting that the reality of the other is an integral aspect of his or her story as revealed and dramatized through the associative-interpretive process (Bollas, 1999; Barratt, 1993; Kris, 1982). The interpretive activity of analysis is an act of love in unifying what previously had seemed disconnected and unrelated. It "raises them up to a new unity and allows the person to move forward in ways that would not have been possible before the interpretation" (Lear, 1990, 12).

A PHILOSOPHY OF DIFFERENCES, SEMIOTICS, AND THE RELATIVITY OF REALITY: *THE STUDY OF THE ARTS OF COMMUNICATION AND CRITICAL THINKING*

There is a world of differences between and within different cultures and people: The world is a World of Differences. Indeed, the only world that can ever exist and be known *is* this World of Differences: A world of interpretations of the world. Human reality as a construction and product of signifying activities speaks to a worldview premised on the philosophy of differences of Nietszche and Heidegger wherein there is an appreciation of the infinite interpretability of reality among people. A philosophy of differences contextualizes a world of differences for psychoanalysis as learning and discourse in the twenty-first century.

From this perspective, differences among people in their construction of reality are considered to be "the stuff of life" as opposed to "distortions of reality" or "evidences of psychopathology." In this worldview, there is no perception independent of one's perception, there are no *facts* except as construed within the mind of each person, and truth as to the question of *essence* is found in the values of the subject (Vattimo, 1988): Reality and the nature of reality are found in the eye of the beholder. It is the appreciation of this World of Differences that spans the differences between people and, paradoxically, unites them in a World of Sameness.

The linguistic turn in philosophy about a century ago reflected a ruptured break with modernistic philosophers, the problems and questions that preoccupied them, and seeking universal truths in their philosophic inquiry (Clarke, 1997). In this conceptual revolution in philosophy, language itself became the privileged object of thought and a problem arose with those bodies of knowledge(s) premised on classical epistemology: Our modes of understanding the world, others and self depend on language, itself understood as an organized system of signs and mode of representation (Dickens and Fontana, 1994).

Saussure in Europe and Charles Sanders Peirce in the United States introduced the discipline of semiotics. As a philosophy, semiotics is concerned with the study and analysis of language, systems of signification, and the structures of thought and experiences: It is concerned with the nature of *representation* and provides a perspective by which we might conceive of human reality as a construction, as a product of signifying activities that are both culturally specific and generally unconscious. (Sarup, 1993). As a mode of knowledge, semiotics understands the world as a system of interconnections and interrelations.

As a philosopher-historian, the poet-shaman is concerned with the nature of representation, the philosophy of language, the culture's systems of signification, and the individual's history and life-story. The subject of contemporary times is understood as an *historical subject* spoken by language, history, and the specific discourses of the culture: He or she is constituted by its interrelations and interconnection and is understood as being *something more* than the sum of his or her identifiable "parts." People and the external world are understood as shaped, if not constructed and constituted, by language, texts, codes, and images. From this perspective, the analytic discourse is understood to be a semiotic discourse, understood as one might understand a poetic text. Like poetry, the analytic process is, one of the most complex forms of human discourse in which *all thinking* is, at once, literally real and radically metaphoric.

Philosophic inquiry provides the basic, necessary and vital kind of freedom to place into question that which is considered to be the foundational essence of the traditional "What Is" (ontology) and the logic of the "Why" of the "What Is" (epistemology) (Rajschman, 1985). The freedom and willingness to question the natural order of things is central to the analytic discourse and, thus, to its program of study. The study of the Arts of Critical Thinking is for the purpose of developing the critical capacity to question what is assumed to be natural, self-evident and common sense in, for example, our cultural and social formations, our notions of reality and knowledge(s), and our moral pieties and identities as analytic practitioners.

As a philosophy of language and mode of knowledge, semiotics raises such questions as: What is the poet-shaman's relationship to language? Is language object-based and simply *reflects* reality as it exists out there in the real world as assumed by classical epistemology? Or, Does language *create* and *structure* reality as suggested by philosophy's linguistic turn? Or, Does the dichotomous structuring of this question in an *either ...or* form dissolve into a different question: Does language speak reality, the world, and people as we speak language?

A shamanic learning process might inquire into our bodies of knowledge(s) as historically produced and contingent perspectives and might study the history of various psychoanalytic concepts, notions of pathology, and the standardized curriculum in our educational institutions. Consideration could be given to how the *other* is constructed in the institutional systems of thinking of the modern era: the student, the analysand, the psychotic, the body, and the unconscious. Will there be but *one* body speaking in the more contemporary World of Differences? Is the body not signified differently in different cultures and differently in different discourses of the same culture? and Is *the body* signified differently by each person in the same culture?

Consideration could also be given to various historical constructions of the body and to the role that gender differences has played in the production, evaluation, and teaching of these bodies of knowledge(s) and their subsequent influences in the analytic discourse (Irigaray, 1985, Cixous, 1993, 1986; Grosz, 1995). What is the constellation of economic, political, legal, and social interests that these bodies of knowledge(s) support in the analytic community? What institutional structures and pedagogical paradigms do such knowledge(s) justify and perpetuate? In the analytic culture, our bodies of knowledge(s) are historically contingent on economic, political, and social forces, a contingency that links the discourses of knowledge production *and* acquisition with the discourses of power and ethics.

STORYTELLING AND LEARNING IN THE SHAMANIC TRADITIONS: THE ARTS OF COMMUNICATION AND CRITICAL THINKING

In the ancient oral traditions, storytelling is the medium through which knowledge is transmitted: The telling and retelling of stories provide the means of educating the next generation in the instrumentalities of the culture: Its traditions, values, beliefs and sanctioned ways of knowing and doing things. As story telling is the medium of exchange in the analytic discourse, so too is storytelling integral to its learning process. Learning in a shamanic program of study takes place through psychoanalytic storytellers for whom words are magical, invisible and powerful: They imagine the world of which they speak and make it stir with life. As considered in chapter one, the psychoanalytic storyteller must *passionately* believe in what he or she says in telling the story: Passion is the life-blood of the learning process as it is in the associative-interpretive process. The infusion of passion in the learning process can profoundly alter the student 's state of consciousness, allow a different view of reality to emerge, and permit entry into that space where he or she might find his or her storytelling voice that, as suggested by Cixous "trembles, reddens, and bleeds" (1993, 32).

The organizing stories told within the analytic profession can be studied to learn something about our history and legacy as analytic practitioners: Who are we? Where did we come from? And, How have we imagined ourselves into being? The organizing stories of ourselves as professionals are contained in such stories. The stories told by Freud of Anna O, Dora, little Hans, the Ratman, and the Wolfman could very well be told, studied and thought about *not*, however, to receive, master and apply Freud's knowledge(s) and truth. Rather, for the purpose of seeing, hearing, and experiencing his truth from, for example, the worldview of his times, the perspective(s) of the different psychologies of the modern era, or from the different perspectives of contemporary psychoanalysis. In a shamanic philosophy of learning, the student seeks what the masters sought, not the truths they found.

A shamanic learning philosophy encourages a "learning style of no style" in the development of one's "storytelling style of no style," the highest form and most meaningful of storytelling styles, as suggested in chapter one. The development of one's storytelling style, takes place through the student's analytical experiences which includes presenting and discussing one's own process material: The essence of psychoanalytic learning is found in the interpretive encounter with the multiple perspectives of the other (of self). In this way, a shamanic learning process matches more closely with, at once, the Freudian unconscious as a process of unbroken subjectivity, the process nature of life and its experiences, and the process nature of the analytic discourse.

HISTORY, MYTHICAL STORIES, AND THE PERFORMANCE ARTS: THE ARTS OF CONTINUITY

A shamanic program of study is designed and organized around its particular understanding or synthesis of psychoanalysis. In this instance, psychoanalysis is understood as a venture into communication via the associative interpretive process in a contextualizing metaphor from the performance arts, the psychic theatre of mind. *Venturing into the person's communications via the associative-interpretive process* places emphasis on the study of the Arts of Communication and Critical Thinking. The second element, *in the contextualizing metaphor of the psychic theatre of the mind*, places emphasis on the Arts of Continuity: The study of the culture's history, mythology, religion, science, theatre, film, dance, folklore, and those traditions that link our phenomenal past with an anticipated future. In a shamanic program of study organized around this particular synthesis of psychoanalysis, *history*, *mythical stories*, and *the theatre* are of particular interest.

History: In a shamanic program of study, psychoanalysis continues as a historical discipline: The basic project of the analytic discourse consists in wording the tissue-traces of historical meaning as it survives in the person's present life (Strenger, 1998, 1991). The romantic psychologies reintroduce history as an *interpretive* discipline in contrast to history as an autonomous, self-authenticating, scientific discipline. The poet-shaman speaks collaboratively with the individual as the experiences of his or her past blend inseparably into the reality of the present moment (of the past).

In this unique psychological discourse, a history is constructed not, however, in the sense of discovering facts about what must have happened, but a history in the sense of shaping a meaning: A history that is continuously written and rewritten in the text and context of the analytic discourse. Remembering in words rather than repeating in actions speaks to making aspects of the unacknowledged present into an historical experienced event (May, 1990). And with this historification, the potential for new and different thoughts and actions becomes possible.

The poet-shaman's phenomenalistic premise and perspective reflects the idea that the reality of everyday life - as is Beauty, Goodness, and Truth - is ultimately found in the eye of the beholder. In his or her quantum, mystical and spiritual world, *reality* is a living and breathing always changing dynamic construction of signifying activities. In Chinese thought, existence is not static but dynamic and changeable: The Principle of Change (Bian Yi Lu) holds that reality is a process and that "the concepts that reflect reality are also active, changeable, and subjective rather than being objective, fixed, and identifiable entities" ((Peng & Nisbitt,

1999, 743). An individual's meaning and reality is communicated through the systems of signification by which each person makes sense of his or her current and past experiences. Our constructs and systems of signification organize the facts of our experiences in everyday life. From this perspective, the analytic discourse is a semiotic discourse, understood as one would understand a poetic text. And in this context, the discourses of history and fiction figure prominently in making sense of our everyday lives: History and fiction are inherently and inseparably interwoven in our dynamic constructions of reality.

The poet-shaman's historical mode of understanding appreciates the imaginative construction and reconstruction of the person's past and present reality. Long neglected conceptions of time have come to the forefront in the romantic psychologies of psychoanalysis in which, for example, the experiences of the phenomenal past are understood as co-existing, co-structuring, and co-determining the person's construction, experience, and meaning of current reality (Le Poidevin, 1997; Slife, 1997). The reality and centrality of the past as we recall it to have been continuously unfolds in the present moment of the past as we construct and give meaning to the world around us. In effect, our personal history is *always* contained in our perceptions and dynamic constructions of our present reality: We cannot stand outside of our own history and speak from a value-free context.

This historical mode of understanding recognizes the continuous interweave of the lived experiences of the phenomenal past with the individual's present wishes, desires and longings *and* incorporates his or her purposes and future goals. Psychic determinism is, perhaps, best conceptualized by the poet-shaman as a non-linear determinism responsive to a complex dynamic interplay of contextual and teleological forces in the mind that represent a complete, yet ever changing, dynamical system at any given point in space-time. He or she might understand psychic determinism as the consequence of multiple contextual/experiential forces emanating from the internal representations of *self* and *other*.

Mythical Stories: The Shaman's Story and Psychoanalysis. Mythical stories are organizing of the culture and of our lives, as citizens and professionals. Mythical stories are basic to human thinking. They are the sacred narratives explaining how the world and humankind came to be in their present form. They transmit beliefs and emotions, ways of thinking and being, and ways of knowing and doing. They transmit the sanctioned and legitimate ways of perceiving, thinking and knowing about the world people and life. And, they provide ways by which we might understand and interpret human experiences. The study of mythical stories permits entry into different ways of thinking and being and into different psychologies and realities. The shaman's story, for example, seems to have molded our perceptions of psychoanalysis as our perceptions of psychoanalysis have molded our perceptions of mythical stories. Ellenberger (1970) speaks to the remarkable similarities between the shaman's primitive beliefs and practices of medicine and Freud's early psychoanalytic theories of mental life and treatment. The shaman's story and relationship to psychoanalysis goes something like the following.

According to an ancient concept shared in many cultures, the preservation of the person's soul is a prerequisite for living a normal and healthy life. During sleep the soul temporarily leaves the body and wanders into, visits with, or performs the actions taking place in the person's dream. The soul is given expression in the sensory images, forms, and context of the dream: The story of the dream contains the spirit of the soul. Disease occurs when the soul loses its way in its wanderings, is injured or separated from the body if suddenly awakened or frightened, or is stolen by evil ghosts or sorcerers from the underworld.

As the community's medicine man and spiritual leader, the shaman enters the mysterious underworld of the evil ghost-like spirits in search of the lost soul. The shaman's ability to alter his or her state of consciousness enables him or her to see beyond the ordinariness of everyday life (the profane) into the sacred aspects of reality. And further, he or she functions as a mediator between the worlds of the dead and the living. In so doing, he or she bargains, negotiates, or fights with the evil spirits that refuse to release the lost soul. Healing consists in finding and restoring the person's lost soul to his or her deprived body (Ellenberger, 1970). And such mythology constitutes the psychology of ancient times.

In classical psychoanalysis, sleeping, dreams, and altered states of consciousness also occupy a central theoretical position. Dreams constitute the royal road to the unconscious, the invisible reality where mysterious and ghost-like forces reside. The analyst enters this psychic world of primary process and wish-driven fantasy in search of the missing thought, the alienated experience, or the repressed event. And, the associative method provides access to this strange state of consciousness and being. Like the Shaman, the analyst mediates between the irrational instinctual wishes of the unconscious and the person's more rational conscious thoughts by rationally explaining the contradictions or discontinuities in the person's logic or experience, negotiating with these forces through intellectual persuasion, or "fighting with the evil spirits who refuse to release the lost soul" through strategic confrontations and interpretation of transference resistances.

Eventually, through hard-won insight, the light of the rational narrative enters the nether regions of the dark side and the lost memory, event, or experience is recovered and liberation from the grips of the evil ghost-like forces occurs. Rational understanding and secondary process thinking prevail over the fantasy-driven evil forces of the primary process. Healing consists of finding and restoring the repressed, estranged, or alienated aspect of self to the person's body of rational knowledge. And such psychology constitutes the mythology of our more recent times.

The Performance Arts: The Theatre. As our lives are lived, experienced, and recounted in the narrative form of a story, so too the unconscious understood as *life* is conceptualized as remembering, preserving, and organizing the stories of our lives in a narrative, holographic and dramatized form. As a contextualizing metaphor for the analytic process, the theatre provides the stage onto which the person's construction of reality and his or her archaic experiences might be spoken in the more primal linguistic of *bodymindthinkingspeakingfeeling*, as dramatized, for example, in Mr. J's radio active transmissions of his childhood memories in chapter two, Ms. A searching for the memory-experience-events stored in her shoeboxes in chapter six, or Mr. W granting me an audience and, later, preparing to nurse me in chapter seven. Drama is the stuff of life, the lived-experiences of which is the stuff of psychoanalysis.

> Life, or existence, is action, interaction, speaking: it is inherently dramatic, from the Greek root *dran*, to act. Lives of persons can be stories of past events, remembered and narrated, or they can be *dramatized*, ... As a literary form, genre, and structure, drama *enacts* life, representing it not once removed as in narration, but directly in the here-and-now, through various dramatis personae acting, emoting, speaking and gesturing in dramatic *scenes.* (Lothane, 2009, 135)

Furthermore, as suggested by Artaud (in Oswald, 1989, xiv), the drama that unfolds on the stage of the analytic space transcends the realm of theatre per se and, paradoxically, points to the broader question of the individual's performance in poetic discourse, calling into question, organically, his or her ideas about and experiences of reality, and his or her poetic place in that reality.

In the theatre of mind, the poet-shaman steps out onto the stage, enters the stories of madness that, often times, are spoken somewhere in the space in-between the dramatized feelings, sensory images, and word-pictures. And, he or she translates the ideographic story into words. The closer the poet-shaman comes to speaking in verbal pictures or pictograms, the closer he or she comes to a more unmediated representation of the sensory-image of the thing or experience in question. In so doing, the analytic discourse enters a space where logic cannot go to engage and speak with the inexplicable: Freud's initial and intuitive grasp of the unconscious as *representation's other*.

The complexities of this dramatic encounter with the private madness of self and other occur in the context of love, the experiences and expressions of which take place through the poet-shaman's coming to know and give voice to something of that reality and madness of the other (of self) through the interpretive activity of the discourse. As the context for the analytic process, the theatre provides the framework in which,

> Love is the great container: it frames the dramatic-psychoanalytic encounter and allows for living and confronting that drama and analyzing the conscious and unconscious elements of acting and acting out as aspects of reality and transference." (Lothane, 2009, 141-142)

The synergism of analytic attitude and interpretive activity takes place in the context of the theatre in which *reality* is inseparable from our systems of signification, semiotics is inseparable from ontology, and the poet-shaman's purpose is to translate into words the reality that unfolds in the performance. And from this perspective, anything else is "wild analysis."

REFERENCES

Barratt, B. (1993). *Psychoanalysis and the postmodern impulse.* Baltimore: The Johns Hopkins University Press.

Becvar, D. S. and Becvar R.J. (1996). *Family therapy: A systemic integration.* 4th ed. Boston: Allyn and Bacon.

Bernfeld, S. (1962). On psychoanalytic training. *Psychoanalytic Quarterly*, 31, 453-482.

Bevan, W, (1991). Contemporary psychology: A tour inside the onion. *The American Psychologist.* 46 (5), 475-483.

Bollas, C. (1999). *The mystery of things.* New York: Routledge.

Capra, F. (1982). *The turning point: Science, society and the rising culture.* Simon & Schuster, N.Y.

Cixous, H., (1993). *Three steps on the ladder of writing.* (trans.) Cornell, S. & Sellers, S., Columbia University Press.

(1986). & Clement, C. *The newly born woman.* B. Wing (trans.), Theory and his tory of Literature, vol. 24. Minneapolis: University of Minnesota Press.

Child, W. (1996). *Causality, interpretation and the mind.* Oxford Philosophical Monographs. Oxford: Clarendon Press.

Clarke, D.S. (1997). *Philosophy's second revolution: Early and recent analytic philosophy.* Open Court, Chicago.

Cohen, A. & Dascal, M. (1989). *The institution of philosophy: A discipline in crisis?* New York: Open Court Publishing.

Dickens, D.R. & Fontanna A., (1994). (eds.) *Postmodernism and social inquiry.* New York: Guilford Press.

Eacker, J. N. (1975). *Problems of philosophy and psychology.* Chicago: Nelson-Hall.

Ellenberger, H.F. (1970). *The discovery of the unconscious: The history and evolution of dynamic psychiatry.* New York: Basic Books, Inc.

Eco, U. (1984). *Semiotics and the philosophy of language.* Bloomington: Indiana University Press.

Felman, S. (1993). *Literature and psychoanalysis; The question of reading: Otherwise.* (ed.) Baltimore, MD: Johns Hopkins University Press.

Fisch, M. (1978). Pierce's general theory of signs. In T. Sebeok, (ed.) *Sight, sound, and sense.* Bloomington: Indiana University Press.

Foucault, M. (2009). *History of madness.* Jean Khalfa (ed. and trans) New York, Routledge.

Freud, S. (1953-1974). *The standard edition of the complete psychological works of Sigmund Freud.* (24 vols.) J. Strachey (Ed. and Trans.). London: Hogarth Press.

Gay, P. (1989). *The Freud reader.* (ed.) New York: W. W. Norton & Co..

Gedo, J. (1999). *The evolution of psychoanalysis: Contemporary theory and practice.* New York: Other Press.

Gottdiener, M. (1994). Semiotics and postmodernism. In D.R. Dickens, & A. Fontanna (eds.) *Postmodernism and social inquiry.* (pp.155-181). New York: Guilford Press.

Grosz, E. (1995). *Space, time, and perversion.* New York: Routledge.

Henry, M. (1985). *The genealogy of psychoanalysis.* D. Brick, (trans.), Stanford, CA: Stanford University Press.

Hyman, J. (1992). The causal theory of perception. *Philosophical Quarterly*, 42: 277-296.

Hyman, M. (1990). Institute training and its alternatives. In *Tradition and innovation in psychoanalytic education.* (pp. 77-85). M. Meisels and E.R. Shapiro (eds.). Hillsdale, New Jersey: E., Lawrence Erlbaum Assocs.

Hunter, G. (1998). Forgotten cemetery blocks development. *The Detroit News*, Nov. 1

Irigaray, L. (1993). *je, tu, nous: Towards a culture of difference.* Martin, A. (trans). New York: Routledge.

(1991) *Philosophy in the feminine.* New York: Routledge.

(1985) *This sex which is not one.* C. Porter, (trans.)

(1977) Ce sexe qui n'enest pas un, Cornell University Press

Jones, E. (1953-57). *The life and work of Sigmund Freud.* 3 vols., New York,: Basic Books.

Kavanaugh, P. B. (1999). *Thinking about psychoanalytic thinking: A questioning of identity, purpose, and ethics.* President's Address: International Federation for Psychoanalytic Education. tenth annual interdisciplinary conference. Sir Francis Drake, San Francisco, CA.

(1998). *How will bodies of knowledge(s) speak the psychoanalyst in the 21st century? Some thoughts on the art(s) of psychoanalytic education.* President's Address: International Federation for Psychoanalytic Education. ninth annual interdisciplinary conference. New York: Fordham University.

(1995). *Postmodernism, psychoanalysis and philosophy: A world of difference for the future of psychoanalytic education.* International Federation for Psychoanalytic Education. sixth annual interdisciplinary conference. Toronto, Canada.

Kendrick, W. (1996). Writing the unconscious. In L. Adams and J. Szaluta, (eds.) *Psychoanalysis and the humanities*: Current Issues in Psychoanalytic Practice. Monographs of the Society for Psychoanalytic Training, No. *6*. New York, Brunner/Mazel.

Kennick, W. E. (1970). On solipsism. In C. Hanly and M. Lazerowitz (eds.) *Psychoanalysis and philosophy*. New York: International Universities Press.

Khalfa, J. (2009). Introduction. In Foucault, M., *History of madness.* J. Khalfa (ed. and trans.). New York: Routledge.

Kris, A.O. (1982). *Free association: Method and process.* New Haven: Yale University Press.

Kristeva, J. (1989). *Language: The unknown.* A. M. Menke (trans.) New York: Columbia University Press.

Kuhn, T. (1970). *The structure of scientific revolutions.* 2nd ed. Chicago: University of

Chicago Press.
Lear, J. (1999). *Open minded: Working out the logic of the soul.* Cambridge, MA, Harvard University Press.
(1990). *Love and its place in nature: A philosophical interpretation of Freudian psychoanalysis.* New Haven: Yale University Press.
Lemiell, J. T. (1987). *The psychology of personality: An epistemological inquiry.* New York: Columbia University Press.
Le Poidevin, R. and MacBeath, M. (ed.) (1997). *The philosophy of time.* Oxford Readings in Philosophy, Oxford: Oxford University Press.
Lothane, Z. (2009). Dramatology in life, disorder, and psychoanalytic therapy: A further contribution to interpersonal psychoanalysis. *International Forum of Psychoanalysis.* vol. 18, *3*, 135-148.
Marcus, G. & Fischer, M. (1986). *Anthropology as cultural critique: An experimental moment in the human sciences.* Chicago: University of Chicago Press.
May, R. (1990). The idea of history in psychoanalysis: Freud and the "Wolfman." *Psychoanalytic Psychology.* 7 (2),163-183.
Meisels, M. & Shapiro, E.R. (1990). *Tradition and innovation in psychoanalytic education.* New Jersey: Erbaum Assocs., Inc.
Nietzsche, F. (1967). *The will to power.* (1901). W. Kaufmann and R. Hollingsdale (trans.). New York: Random House.
Oswald, L. (1989). *Jean Ginet and the semiotics of performance.* Indianapolis: Indiana University Press.
Peng, K. and Nisbett, R.E. (1999). Culture, dialectics, and reasoning about contradiction. *American Psychologist,* 54 (*9*), 741-754.
Rajchman, J. (1991). *Truth and eros: Foucault, Lacan, and the question of ethics.* New York: Routledge, Chapman, and Hall, Inc.
(1985.*) Michel Foucault: The freedom of philosophy.* New York: Columbia University Press.
Rigoni, D. (2002). *Teaching what can't be taught: The shaman's strategy.* Lanham, MD. Scarecrow Press.
Ritvo, L. R. (1990). *Darwin's influence on Freud: A tale of two sciences.* New Haven: Yale University Press.
Robinson, D. N. (1989). *Aristotle's psychology.* New York: Columbia University Press.
(1982). *Toward a science of human nature.* New York: Columbia University Press.
Roustang, F. (1985). A philosophy for psychoanalysis? In M. Henry. D. Brick (trans.) *The genealology of psychoanalysis.* (ix-xxviii). Stanford: Stanford University Press.
Rubinstein, B. (1997). *Psychoanalysis and the philosophy of science.* Psychological Issues, Monograph 62/63, ed. R. Holt. Madison, CT: International Universities Press.
Russell, B. (1985). *The philosophy of logical atomism.* Chicago: Open Court.
Safouan, M. (2000). *Jacques Lacan and the question of psychoanalytic training.* J. Rose, (trans..) New York: St. Martin's Press, Inc.
Sandler, A. (1990). Comments on varieties of psychoanalytic training in Europe. In *Tradition and innovation in psychoanalytic education.* (pp. 45-58). M. Meisels and E.R. Shapiro (eds.). Hillsdale, New Jersey: E., Lawrence Erlbaum Assocs.

(1982).The selection and function of the training analyst in Europe. *International Review of Psychoanalysis. 9*(38), 357-385.

Sarup, M. (1993). *An introductory guide to post-structuralism and postmodernism* (2nd ed.) , Athens: University of Georgia Press.

Schneider, K.J. (1998). Toward a science of the heart: Romanticism and the revival of psychology. *American Psychologist. 53*(*3*), 277-289.

Slife, B. (1997). *Challenging our cherished theoretical and therapeutic assumptions.* Paper presented at the Michigan Society for Psychoanalytic Psychology's Fall Workshop: *What Have We Been Thinking?!!? Discovering Hidden Assumptions in Theory, Research, and Practice.* Oakland University, Michigan.

Slife, B. and Williams, R. N. (1995). *What's behind the research: Discovering hidden assumptions in the behavioral sciences.* Thousand Oaks, CA.: Sage Publications.

(1993). *Time and psychological explanation.* New York: State University of New York Press.

Spence, D. (1987). *The Freudian metaphor: Toward paradigm change in psychoanalysis.* New York: W.W. Norton & Co..

Strenger, C. (1998*). Individuality, the impossible project: Psychoanalysis and self-creation.* International Universities Press, Inc. Madison, CT.

(1991). *Between hermeneutics and science: An essay on the epistemology of psychoanalysis.* Psychological Issues, Monograph 59. Madison, CT.: International Universities Press,

Thompson, M. G. (2000). Free association: A technical principle or a model for psychoanalytic education? *Psychologist-Psychoanalyst: Official publication of division 39 of the American Psychological Association.* Vol. XX, Spring 2000, no. *2*, 7-10.

Vattimo, G. (1988). *The end of modernity.* J. Snyder(trans.). Baltimore, Johns Hopkins University Press.

Weisman, A.D. (1965). *The existential core of psychoanalysis: Reality sense and responsibility.* London: J.&A. Churchill, Ltd.

Whitaker, R. (2002). *Mad in America: Bad science, bad medicine, and the enduring mistreatment of the mentally ill.* Cambridge, MA.: Perseus.

Wilber, K. (2001). *Quantum questions: Mystical writings of the world's greatest physicists.* (ed.) Boston: Shambhala Press.

(1985). Physics, mysticism and the new holographic paradigm: A critical appraisal. In K. Wilber (ed.). *The holographic paradigm and other paradoxes: Exploring the leading edge of science.* Boston: Shambhala Press.

www.ingramcontent.com/pod-product-compliance
Lightning Source LLC
Chambersburg PA
CBHW071246230926
51849CB00001B/245
9789042034877